Why Surgeons Struggle with
Work-Hour Reforms

Why Surgeons Struggle with Work-Hour Reforms

JAMES E. COVERDILL
AND JOHN D. MELLINGER

VANDERBILT UNIVERSITY PRESS
Nashville, Tennessee

Library of Congress Cataloging-in-Publication Data

Names: Coverdill, James E., author. | Mellinger, John D., 1958– author.
Title: Why surgeons struggle with work-hour reforms / James E. Coverdill
    and John D. Mellinger.
Description: Nashville : Vanderbilt University Press, 2020. | Includes
    bibliographical references and index.
Identifiers: LCCN 2020034115 (print) | LCCN 2020034116 (ebook) | ISBN
    9780826501059 (paperback) | ISBN 9780826501066 (hardcover) | ISBN
    9780826501073 (epub) | ISBN 9780826501080 (pdf)
Subjects: MESH: General Surgery—organization & administration | Surgeons |
    Workload | Policy Making | United States
Classification: LCC RD110 (print) | LCC RD110 (ebook) | NLM WO 21 | DDC
    617.0068—dc23

LC record available at https://lccn.loc.gov/2020034115
LC ebook record available at https://lccn.loc.gov/2020034116

To Patrick, my amazing ten-year-old son, and Nathalie, my equally amazing but slightly older wife, for love, laughter, and epic Nerf-gun battles (from Jim)

To Elaine, whose love and support has brought richness to my life, and to Heather, Jordan, Caleb, and Courtney, who have amplified that yet more (from John)

Contents

Acknowledgments   ix

INTRODUCTION. Explaining the Struggle:
Culture, Social Organization, and Work-Hour Reforms   1

1. Fatigue as Impairment or Practical and Educational Necessity?   27

2. Patient Handoffs: Can't Colleagues Assume Care Capably?   50

3. Stay-or-Go Decisions by Residents: Why Not Leave When
a Shift is Over or Hour Limits Are Reached?   74

4. Professionalism, Old and New: Time and Morality in
Surgical Training and Practice   100

5. Less for You, More for Me? Changing Workloads for
Attendings and Advanced Practice Providers   123

6. Revisions Imposed and Rescinded: The Sixteen-Hour Shift
Limit for Interns   150

CONCLUSION. Policy to Practice: Muddling through
Work-Hour Reforms   172

References   191
Index   203

Acknowledgments

One of the great joys of conducting social research is the opportunity to routinely encounter profound expressions of generosity. To conduct our research, we needed to enlist the help of many people, from those who staff the offices of the many institutional review boards from which we needed approvals to those who kindly offered to complete surveys, participate in interviews, or be observed as part of the field observation component of the project. All told, 1,421 surgeons completed a survey for us, 258 offered an interview, and countless medical students, residents, attendings, nurses, and hospital staff accommodated and engaged Coverdill during his field observations in a general surgery residency program. What was especially remarkable about the generosity that we encountered is the context: virtually everyone we asked to participate in a survey or interview was already giving so much of their time and talents to others as they learned, practiced, and taught the craft of surgery. People, in short, made time, often texting about availability during a lull between cases or a slow time during a night shift. To all who gave of themselves in this way, and who must remain unnamed per the conventions of social research, we were, and remain, grateful.

We also benefitted from tangible support in the form of release time and support funds. The Franklin College of Arts and Sciences at the University of Georgia offered a few course releases, which made the early portion of the field observations possible, and support for research expenses. Likewise, the project was generously supported by funds from the J. Roland Folse Endowed Chair in Surgery at Southern Illinois University School of Medicine.

We also wish to thank a large network of surgeons who became collaborators due to their interest in, and support for, our research. We thank Gina L. Adrales, Adnan Alseidi, Kimberly D. Anderson, James. G. Bittner IV, Bruce W. Bonnell, David C. Borgstrom, Alfredo M. Carbonell, Joseph B. Cofer, Thomas H. Cogbill, Daniel L. Dent, Douglas B. Dorner, Russell D. Dumire, Jonathan Fryer, George M. Fuhrman, Carl Haisch, Kristi L. Harold, Thomas H. Hartranft, Jonathan R. Hiatt, Steven B. Holsten, Benjamin T. Jarman, Richard A. Moore, Don K. Nakayama, M. Timothy Nelson, Mary Anne Park, Walter L. Pipkin, Marc Schlatter, Mohsen Shabahang, Stanley Sherman, Richard A. Sidwell, John L. Tarpley, Paula M. Termuhlen, Alexandra L. B. Webb, Christopher Wohltmann, and Randy J. Woods. We offer special thanks to Paula M. Termuhlen for her steadfast and substantial support for us and for our research. For both of us, as the three waves of the research progressed, those listed above became not just collaborators, but also friends, mentors, and ultimately a "community of learning" that has made our professional and personal livers fuller, deeper, and richer in multiple ways. In that vein, Mellinger would also like to credit surgical leaders and educators including Bill Passinault, Jeff Ponsky, Tom Gadacz, Bruce MacFadyen, and Gary Dunnington as chairs and mentors who encouraged and supported the educational career focus that ultimately led to this work.

We are eager to thank the staff at Vanderbilt University Press and Shearwater Indexing for their deft handling of the manuscript. Zachary S. Gresham is a superb acquisitions editor. From our first contact with the press, Zack has been quick to respond with thoughtful, encouraging, informative, and also downright delightful commentary. For example, after sharing news late one afternoon that the editorial committee had approved the manuscript for publication, he followed up the next morning with the lead-off quip, "I hope you woke up smiling this morning." Likewise, when we moved to the formal contract portion of the process, he began a note in a way that made us smile once more: "[off camera] 'Cue the boilerplate!'" The dynamic Joell Smith-Borne was our managing production editor and thus oversaw the editing of the book's interior. Drohan DiSanto created a stunning cover for the book, based on a suggestion offered by John Mellinger. The talented Jenna Phillips spearheaded marketing and publicity for the book. Betsy Phillips, Cynthia Yeager, and Brittany Johnson also played important roles in moving the process along. Andrea Baron and Bob Schwarz of Shearwater Indexing did fine work with the index and were a pleasure to work with as well. We express our appreciation and gratitude to the entire team at Vanderbilt University Press and Shearwater Indexing.

And finally, Coverdill's career-long sociological colleague and collaborator William Finlay was a source of inspiration, unflagging support, and sage advice as the project emerged, developed, and came to fruition. He was a formal collaborator early on, but dropped off as his formidable administrative obligations mounted. The questionnaires and interview schedules for the third wave of the study benefited from thoughtful comments from the Surgical Education and Performance Group at Southern Illinois University. We also thank Sarah Ellen Williams, once a cherished undergraduate and now a promising medical student, for help entering and proofing the survey data. Jill Horn provided skillful assistance preparing portions of the manuscript and abundant cheer. To all, our heartfelt gratitude.

Explaining the Struggle
Culture, Social Organization, and
Work-Hour Reforms

I don't think the debate is about whether being really tired makes you worse at your job. I think that's very clear. The issue is whether it's better to introduce all the unintended effects of limiting work hours. Is that a more optimal solution than the tired person continuing to care for a patient? That part, to me, is unclear.

A THIRD-YEAR MALE RESIDENT IN GENERAL SURGERY

For more than a hundred years, the process of learning to practice medicine in the United States has involved an extraordinary investment of time. In a residency program, medical-school graduates work under the supervision of faculty to care for patients, experience that is required to achieve board certification in a specific specialty area. Traditionally, hours of work and daily schedules were not only long, but also largely unregulated, subject only to cultural traditions and the whims of the most senior learners, the chief residents, and the practitioners and professors who provided, structured, and oversaw medical training. A veritable raft of memoirs by those who have gone through the process offer vivid if not visceral portraits of time demands. Suzanne Poirier's (2009, 88) analysis of fifty memoirs published between 1965 and 2005 suggests that the greatest hardship of medical training is a lack of sleep, and that the "most extreme descriptions of exhaustion" stem from the demands of residencies. Miller's (2008, vii) description of his surgery residency is typical: "It has been said that if medical training is like military service, then surgical residency is Marine Corps boot camp. Postgraduate training in surgery is longer than that of any other medical specialty, five years at least and frequently longer. Tortuous on-call schedules often demand exceedingly long work hours almost unimaginable in any other profession, 100-hour work weeks being the *norm* for a surgery resident" (emphasis in original). His recollections highlight a form of collective suffering that is a prominent and consistent theme in the memoirs.

Autobiographical reflections align with recent reviews and statistical evidence. Despite reductions in call schedules and increases in vacation time since the 1960s, the typical work week for residents on the cusp of the new millennium remained "long and grueling" (Ludmerer 2015, 281). An Institute of Medicine report on sleep deprivation aptly noted that "residents work longer hours than virtually all other occupational groups" (Colten and Altevogt 2005, 145). Baldwin and his colleagues (2003, 1154) collected and analyzed data on weekly work hours from the 1998–99 training year and found that first- and second-year residents averaged 83 and 76.2 hours, respectively. Those averages conceal variation across specialties, with residents in general surgery—the focus of our book—reporting average work weeks in excess of one hundred hours. On the eve of the reforms that we will explore, nearly nine in ten first- and second-year general surgery residents were working more than eighty hours a week, the figure that was about to become the upper limit for the weekly work hours of residents (Baldwin et al. 2003, 1157).

In 2002, the Accreditation Council for Graduate Medical Education (ACGME), the professional body that oversees and accredits graduate medical education in the United States, approved a set of work hour and schedule reforms that would apply to all residents in the United States. The reforms included the following main provisions: (1) an eighty-hour weekly work limit, averaged over four weeks; (2) one day in seven free of patient-care and educational responsibilities, averaged over four weeks; (3) in-house call no more frequently than every third night, averaged over four weeks; (4) a twenty-four-hour limit on work shifts, with up to six additional hours for continuity of care and education; and (5) a ten-hour minimum period of rest between work shifts (ACGME 2004). The ACGME was to monitor compliance with the reforms, encourage residents to report violations both to their programs and to the ACGME, and begin the process of withdrawing accreditation from noncompliant programs, an act that would restrict funding for residents and render them ineligible for licensing through specialty boards after completion of the residency.

The reforms have been incendiary and are viewed by many in medicine as inconsistent with the norms of professional practice and the ideals of medical professionalism. Barone and Ivy (2004, 379), two surgical educators, described how the first meeting of the Association of Program Directors in Surgery after the implementation of the reforms had a "funeral tone" because the rules were viewed as fundamentally incompatible with surgical education and practice. More recently, Ludmerer (2015, 273) claimed that the reforms "created the fiercest controversy in medical education since the Flexner report," which was published in 1910. Hafferty and Tilbert (2015, 344), two long and keen observers of medical education, noted that "in the history of professionalism in medicine, few things have created more moral havoc about what it means to be a good physician than limits on duty hours."

Our book focuses on general surgeons, a historically long-hour specialty, which fiercely opposed the reforms and is among the least compliant (Baldwin et al. 2003; Drolet et al. 2013). We probe deceptively simple questions: Why do surgeons struggle with the reforms? Why do they continue to work long hours and view the act of doing so as reasonable if not quintessentially professional? No doubt, the reforms have generated a substantial research literature, with a recent review netting well over a thousand published studies (Philibert 2016). Studies have largely considered resident safety and well-being (e.g., Barger et al. 2005; Rosen et al. 2006), risks to patients (e.g., Desai et al. 2013; Bilimoria et al. 2016), and resident learning and professional development (e.g., Arora et al. 2008; Jagannathan et al. 2009; Bennett et al. 2017). While some attention has been given to noncompliance with the reforms (Carpenter et al. 2006; Drolet et al. 2013; Blitz et al. 2017), there has been little sustained attention to the central issues of our book, namely *how* and *why* the reforms have sparked and sustained such strong controversy.

The balance of this chapter will unfold in five sections. First, we review briefly the historical legacy of residencies in the United States, the residue of which remains quite prominent in the contemporary structure and culture of residencies. Second, we review the rise of scientific and cultural challenges to the long-hour traditions of residencies and how they set the stage for the reforms proposed and implemented by the ACGME. Third, we situate our analysis of how and why surgeons have struggled with the reforms within several literatures in the social sciences. While our analysis represents a case study of the work and training of general surgeons, it nonetheless dovetails with and contributes to several larger streams of thought. Fourth, we describe the various forms of data we collected, how we analyze that data, and our conventions for presenting the data in subsequent chapters. And fifth, we conclude with a brief overview of our authorial roles and how the substantive chapters are structured.

The Legacy of Johns Hopkins Residencies and Conditions
Prior to the Reforms

The circumstances under which surgeons work and train are critically important in shaping their responses to the reforms. Many of the most salient of these circumstances have been present for a long time, stretching back to the founding of the modern residency at Johns Hopkins Hospital in 1889, which became the model for graduate medical education in the United States (Ludmerer 2015, 17–18, 33). Despite considerable variation across time, place, and specialty, the residencies that emerged in twentieth century America have three common and enduring characteristics that are important for our purposes. A first is a blend of scientific education and direct patient care. Residents wrestle with the scientific underpinnings of pathology and therapies, but in the tradition of progressive education, they have always been "put to work" to help diagnose, treat, and care for ill and injured patients. In this early form of experiential learning, residents progress from being involved in and responsible for relatively simple forms of care, under direct supervision, to the most complex forms of care, under indirect supervision only. Residents mature into physicians by learning how to care for patients independently. Clinical skill and judgement are thought to be nurtured and developed by hands-on practice, accumulated over time, not from books alone. Residents are thus students, but they are also workers who have provided a substantial amount of patient care since the dawn of modern residencies at Johns Hopkins.

A second central characteristic of residencies is that they are structured as multiyear immersive experiences that are completely unlike most forms of graduate education. The Johns Hopkins model required that learners literally become residents of the hospital. While the residency requirement waned as the twentieth century progressed, training remained an immersive experience with long hours and frequent overnight call. Long hours are seen as educationally necessary because they allow residents to observe the natural history of disease and therapy. Being present in the hospital also maximizes the likelihood of seeing, and caring for, patients who present with relatively rare medical conditions. For example, a commonly heard expression among older surgeons during the field observations for this study (described later in the chapter) was "that the only thing wrong with every-other-night call was that you missed half the good cases." Comments of that sort are motivated by the notion that residencies are immersive experiences, where high levels of exposure and engagement properly prepare residents for independent practice. Apart from the acquisition of skills, long hours have been historically intertwined with claims about the moral responsibilities of physicians for the welfare of patients (e.g., Ludmerer 2015, 74–5). Renowned medical educator William Osler (1906, 365–88) of Johns Hopkins summed up the immersive aspect of residencies by saying that work is the "master-word" in medicine.

A third central characteristic of residencies is an enduring tension if not outright struggle between resident education and institutional service. As Ludmerer astutely notes (2015, 33), residencies are the only form of graduate or professional training situated in an institution—the hospital—in which service to patients rather than education is the primary mission. The work of residents has long been a critical component of overall patient care, with hospitals and faculty physicians both benefitting greatly from the work of residents. Without question, many instances of patient care have tremendous educational value for residents as they progress toward proficient independent practice. Also without question, residents perform service work, which includes activities that either have little inherent educational value or those that have been performed so often as to provide no additional educational benefits to the resident. As Ludmerer (2015, 209–10) put it, residents have traditionally "been required to perform an extraordinary range and amount of service duties" that could be done "equally well by ancillary staff." On the eve of the reforms, one study suggested that about 35 percent of resident time was spent on work that could be done by non-physician staff (Boex and Leahy 2003). In short, residents have long been relatively inexpensive sources of flexible, available, and skilled labor, a situation that is greatly exacerbated by the twin residency ideals of experiential and immersive learning.

A more recent change joined those three historical and central characteristics of residencies to dramatically shape the conditions of resident learning and work prior to the reforms. With the introduction of prospective payment in the early 1980s, where hospital fees often become lump sums based on a patient's diagnosis and hence their predicted use of resources calculated on the basis of "diagnosis-related groups," speed became a key objective. As Ludmerer (2015, 240) noted, "financial success depended on caring for a greater number of patients ever more rapidly," thus inaugurating what he and others call the "the era of high throughput" that has continued ever since. For residents, this implied a speed up, where they "began working up more and more patients who stayed for shorter and shorter periods of time" (Ludmerer 2015, 241), leaving residents to struggle with the twin challenges of patient volume and turnover. Under these conditions, resident education recedes and "discharge becomes the highest goal" (Cooke, Irby, and O'Brien 2010, 151). In addition, only the sickest patients are now hospitalized, which means that residents are pressed to care for sicker patients more quickly than ever before (Ludmerer

2015, 242). Importantly, all of these characteristics and conditions pre-date the introduction of the reforms, but have continued under them.

The Rise of Sleep Science and Cultural and Political Pressures for Reform

As the twentieth century progressed, the long-hour traditions of residents began to conflict with a growing and increasingly sophisticated body of research crafted by sleep scientists and practicing physicians. Research on sleep deprivation, both *acute*—due to forgoing sleep to work shifts of twenty-four or more hours—and *chronic*—due to consistently sleeping less than seven hours a night (Watson et al. 2015a; Watson et al. 2015b), suggests that it degrades a person's ability to work, learn, and retain good health. While laboratory experiments involving the effects of acute total sleep deprivation are rather dramatic, research suggests that "chronic partial sleep loss has the potential to induce waking brain deficits equivalent to even the most severe total sleep deprivation" (Basner et al. 2013, 855). As traditionally constructed, resident schedules stack acute sleep deprivation on a base of chronic sleep deprivation, and they often involve night shifts that require residents to work during their circadian nadir, the period of greatest sleepiness.

With respect to the effects of fatigue on work performance, research shows that concentration, creativity, intelligence, motivation, effort, efficiency, emotional stability, sociability, honesty, and effectiveness when working in groups "are systematically dismantled by insufficient sleep" (Walker 2017, 134–147, 297–305). Czeisler described the workplace impact of sleep deprivation in a striking manner:

> It amazes me that contemporary work and social culture glorifies sleeplessness in the way we once glorified people who could hold their liquor. We now know that 24 hours without sleep or a week of sleeping four or five hours a night induces an impairment equivalent to a blood alcohol level of .1%. We would never say, "This person is a great worker! He's drunk all the time!" yet we continue to celebrate people who sacrifice sleep. (quoted in Bronwyn 2006, 56)

Until the 1990s, scholars thought that people adapted to chronic sleep loss without adverse effects. Recent research reveals neurobiological effects that tend to go unnoticed by the affected individuals (Colten and Altevogt 2005, 138). Likening sleep deprivation to drunkenness (see also Williamson and Feyer 2000) is apt because neither group recognizes clearly their functional impairments (Basner et al. 2017; Van Dongen et al. 2003). Research further shows that we are particularly poor at discerning our fatigue-induced performance deficits during the early hours of the day, the so-called biological night (Zhou et al. 2012). In short, subjective feelings of alertness tend to say precious little about actual fatigue-induced impairments.

Sleep deprivation makes learning more difficult, an ironic pattern given that residencies represent graduate medical education. Sleep deprivation diminishes our ability to acquire or recall facts, such as textbook material and clinical information about patients, but it also hinders memory for motor operations that we perfect through practice, such as shooting a basketball or performing a surgical procedure. The magnitudes of the sleep-loss effects are large, with those who are sleep deprived having about a 40 percent deficit in their ability to make new memories relative to their rested peers (Yoo et al. 2007; Walker 2017, 53–54). Sleep helps to consolidate and strengthen newly learned memories, and sleep deprivation before, during, or shortly after learning diminishes retention (Yoo et al. 2007, 389).

Sleep deprivation also affects health. Colten and Altevogt (2005, 55) note that "the case can be confidently made" that sleep loss has "profound and widespread effects on human health." The cumulative long-term effects of sleep deprivation include an increased risk of hypertension, diabetes and impaired glucose tolerance, obesity, depression, anxiety, cardiovascular disease, stroke, a compromised immune system, increased infertility, a doubling of one's risk of cancer, and increased risk of developing Alzheimer's disease (Colten and Altevogt 2005, 55–63; Watson et al. 2015b; Walker 2017, 3, 133; Mendelson 2017). Large population-based studies have shown that age-specific mortality is higher for those who regularly sleep less than seven hours a night (Gallicchio and Kalesan 2009). Injury is also linked to sleep deprivation (Colten and Altevogt 2005, 149; Walker 2017, 140, 149–50). Here too, irony abounds, as those training for a healing profession are drawn into long-hour traditions that diminish health.

The research discussed thus far on the consequences of sleep deprivation stems from general population data or experiments with "healthy adults" in sleep laboratories. Another branch of research focuses on healthcare workers, primarily but not exclusively residents, in what are called field research studies. Without question, two studies published in the *New England Journal of Medicine* tower above all others in terms of prominence and citations (see Philibert 2016) in the debate about the work hours and schedules of residents. Both studies compared interns working in intensive care units under a *traditional* schedule, which involved about eighty hours of work each week and call shifts of twenty-four or more hours, and a *reduced* schedule, which eliminated long call shifts and kept work hours under sixty-three each week. The intervention aimed to reduce both acute and chronic sleep deprivation. In the first article (Lockley et al. 2004), the aim was to quantify sleep and attentional failures in the two groups. Interns on reduced schedules slept about six hours more per week and had fewer than half the rate of attentional failures during night work hours (11 p.m. to 7 a.m.) than when they worked traditional schedules. In the second article (Landigan et al. 2004), interns were randomized to the same traditional or reduced schedules, and any serious medical errors they committed with respect to medication, diagnosis, and procedure were recorded then rectified. Interns working traditional schedules had serious medical error rates that were 93 percent higher than those on reduced schedules. They also made 72 percent more medication errors and five times as many diagnostic errors. The study's conclusion was strong and clear: "Eliminating extended work shifts and reducing the number of hours interns work per week can reduce serious medical errors in the intensive care unit" (Landrigan et al. 2004, 1838).

While those results might seem to powerfully indict long-hour practices, they were immediately challenged. For example, three subjects in the Landrigan et al. (2014) study wrote that "worried residents and attending physicians, aware that the interns on the intervention schedule were poorly informed, took a more active role in patient care, making the majority of decisions and more closely supervising the interns' actions. This hypervigilance may have strongly biased the study toward a positive result" (Pennell, Liu, and Mazini 2005, 726). Others noted that the study's results were achieved only by means of a 33 percent increase in intern staffing, a change that could itself alter outcomes (Fessler 2005, 726; Harnik 2005, 726).

Similar ambiguities surface in other studies as well. An even-handed way of characterizing the body of field studies of residents and sleep deprivation is to say that they are mixed. For example, Weinger and Ancoli-Israel (2002, 955) write: "There is extensive literature on the adverse effects of sleep deprivation in laboratory and nonmedical settings. However, studies on sleep deprivation of physicians performing clinically relevant tasks have been less conclusive." They nonetheless suggest that "patient care *may* be compromised if a fatigued, sleep-deprived clinician is allowed to operate, administer an anesthetic, manage a medical crisis, or deal with an unusual or cognitively demanding clinical presentation" (957, emphasis added). Gaba and Howard (2002, 1249), also acknowledge that laboratory studies show "beyond a doubt that fatigue impairs human performance," claim that "despite many anecdotes about errors that were attributed to fatigue, *no study has proved that fatigue on the part of health care personnel causes errors that harm patients*" (emphasis added). In contrast, Veasey and his colleagues (2002, 1121) argued that "significant decrements exist in procedural skills in post-call surgical residents, demonstrating that this group is not immune to the effects of sleep loss." A meta-analysis of studies of sleep loss and performance among residents showed that sleep loss of twenty-four to thirty hours produced nearly a standard deviation reduction in residents' cognitive and clinical performance; those who performed at the fiftieth percentile of the sleep-loss group were comparable to those at the fifteenth percentile of the rested group (Philibert 2005, 1397–98). A typical performance among those who are sleep deprived becomes dreadful when compared with those who are rested.

Evidence-based concerns had thus been articulated by prominent scholars in the most visible journals by the early years of the twenty-first century. It would be a mistake, however, to suggest that the presence or prominence of those concerns is what led the ACGME to formulate and roll out the national reforms in 2003. Rather, the scientific debate about the impact of fatigue served to potentiate an emerging consumer movement, legal changes, and political pressures. As the long-time editor of the *New England Journal of Medicine* put it, medicine had entered into a new era of "assessment and accountability" (Relman 1988). Consumers of all sorts started to demand at least some measure of accountability from traditionally powerful individuals and institutions, including doctors and hospitals.

The consumer movement came to an explosive head with the case of Libby Zion, who died while in the care of residents in 1984 (Asch and Parker 1988). A college freshman, Ms. Zion presented to New York Hospital with several days of a fever and an earache, and her care was provided primarily by an intern and a second-year resident, both of whom were well into long shifts. Eight hours after coming to the hospital, her fever spiked and she died (Asch and Parker 1988). Her father, Sydney Zion, a prominent lawyer and journalist, helped make "her case a cause" by promoting intense legal and media interest, alleging that "you don't need kindergarten to know that a resident working a 36-hour shift is in no condition to make any kind of judgment call" (Zion 1989). A grand jury investigated her death, concluded that the residents had not acted inappropriately, and refused to indict any of the doctors involved in her care on criminal charges. In addition, no evidence was found that excessive working hours or fatigue contributed to her death (Petersdorf and Bentley 1989; Ludmerer 2015, 279). But the grand jury indicted the residency system, claiming that supervision was inadequate and that "the State Department of Health should promulgate regulations to limit consecutive working hours for interns and junior residents" (cited in Asch and Parker 1988, 772).

The grand jury report prompted the New York State Department of Health to appoint a committee of physicians to review the findings. Chaired by Bertrand M. Bell, the committee's recommendations emphasized on-site super-vision of acute care patients, limiting work to eighty hours per week averaged over a four-week period, providing one day off each week, and limiting over-night call to no more than every third night (New York State Committee on Emergency Services 1987). The recommendations were incorporated into the New York State Health Code, came to be known as the "Bell Regulations," and took effect in July of 1989.

The Bell Regulations provided a template for debates that consumed aca-demic medicine for much of the following decade. Other states considered but failed to enact regulations like those in New York. By 1993, six specialties had established weekly hour limits for residents that were to be overseen by each specialty's Residency Review Committee or RRC (Philibert and Taradejna 2011, 8). In 2000, the Institute of Medicine released *To Err Is Human* (Kohn, Cor-rigan, and Donaldson), which suggested that as many as ninety-eight thou-sand Americans die each year in hospitals from preventable medical errors. Although the long-hour traditions of residents and practicing physicians were not highlighted in the report, its release prompted the ACGME to again take up the issue of work-hour reforms (Philibert and Taradejna 2011).

The decade of debates within medicine was soon amplified by political developments. In April of 2001, a group of petitioners that included Ber-trand Bell requested that the Occupational Safety and Health Administration (OSHA) regulate the hours and schedules of residents as workplace health haz-ards (Gurjala et al. 2001). Although the request was denied, it was followed by federal legislation, the Patient and Physician Safety and Protection Act of 2005, proposed in the House of Representatives by John Conyers in November of 2001 (HR 1228) and in the Senate in 2002 by Jon Corzine (S 1297). These political developments were accompanied by additional position statements by the American Medical Association, which implored the ACGME to enforce work-hour limits and ensure that noncompliance would be monitored and corrected, and the Association of American Medical Colleges, which argued that "prudence favors the establishment of a reasonable upper limit" (cited in Philibert and Taradejna 2011, 9).

In June of 2002, the ACGME approved work-hour and schedule reforms that would apply to all medical and surgical residents in the United States. The reforms took effect on July 1, 2003, and "acknowledge scientific evidence that long hours and sleep loss have a negative effect on resident performance, learning and well-being" (ACGME 2004). Although the ACGME's reforms diminished pressure for federal legislation and oversight, they were none-theless viewed in residency programs as a debatable political mandate with insufficient empirical support. For many, the "scientific evidence" cited by the ACGME that linked long hours and clinical performance was uneven and suspect (Rosenbaum and Lamas 2019, 969). Nor had there been any systematic, evidence-based effort to establish how *particular* reforms—like eighty-hour work weeks or twenty-four-hour limits on shifts—would bear on resident development, patient care, or safety.

To be clear, we have always been sympathetic with efforts to improve the working and educational conditions of residents, and agree with Philibert when she says that "to deny the negative impact of long work hours, sleep loss, and fatigue in residents is folly" (2016, 797). However, policy changes must be explored carefully and with an open mind, as unintended consequences—as suggested in the epigraph that led off the chapter—can accompany and offset improvements. In an important article on resident socialization and the reforms, Brooks and Bosk (2012, 1630) thoughtfully noted that their analysis "emphasizes the importance of understanding the existing occupational culture when creating and executing policy, especially when those regulations challenge many of the norms of that culture." We wholeheartedly agree. Our analysis identifies and explores the relevance of additional dimensions of occupational culture overlooked by Brooks and Bosk (to be discussed later in the chapter). We also highlight the critical but unexplored role of social organization as a key contextual condition that has shaped how surgeons have experienced and assessed the reforms. Culture and social organization operate as interlocking social forces that leave surgeons to struggle with reforms that might otherwise seem to have obvious merit to cultural and organizational outsiders.

A Case Study with Broader Relevance

In the chapters to follow, we describe and analyze the working conditions and circumstances of general surgeons in the United States as we explore and explain how and why they struggle to fully embrace and enact the work-hour reforms. It is, no doubt, a case study of how the reforms have played out in one important medical specialty over nearly two decades. While focused case studies have a long and venerable tradition in the social sciences, they immediately raise questions. What about broader theoretical and substantive issues in the social sciences? Does the analysis dovetail with, and contribute to, any of those areas? And what about other medical fields and other places? Have other specialties, and those in other parts of the world, had the same struggles for the same reasons? Here, we take on both issues, and start by showing how our analysis links to several broader issues before turning to the issue of other medical specialties and national contexts.

GENDER AND AN OCCUPATIONAL CULTURE OF FATIGUE

In *Dangerously Sleepy: Overworked Americans and the Cult of Manly Wakefulness,* Derickson (2014) provided a series of historical case studies of blue-collar work—occupations like trucking, steelworkers, and railway workers—in support of a broader argument about culture and gender. For many such workers, the stamina needed to endure long days, nights, or both on the job, coupled with the overwhelmingly if not exclusively male character of those occupations, forged links between long work hours, bread winning, and masculinity. Although it was not explored by Derickson, the practice of medicine and residency education are strikingly similar. For many years, participants in the Johns Hopkins residency model were exclusively male. Rowena Spencer, for example, became the first female surgery intern at Johns Hopkins Hospital in 1947, nearly sixty years after the founding of the surgical residency (Nitkin 2019). She went on to become the first female surgeon to practice in her native Louisiana. Even today, women represent less than a quarter of surgeons in the United States (Haskins 2019). Residencies last at least three years, and five or more for surgery, and are often followed by fellowship training. All of this falls during the years that women are most likely to have children. Even under the reforms, the hours and schedules of residents remain long and demanding, a pattern that is clearly evident to medical students who rotate onto surgical services. Those who enter practice, as we describe in the next chapter, are often obliged to work long hours and to cover call for days at a time.

Sociologists would consider residencies, and the broader practice of medicine, to be highly gendered institutions, which means that gender is present in the processes, practices, images, ideologies, and distributions of power (e.g., Acker 1992). Residencies were once restricted to men only, remain in many specialties (like surgery) numerically dominated by men, and are structured in such a way that they are most compatible with the typical life courses and cultural obligations of men as they command time during prime years for child bearing and caring. Moreover, many medical specialties have been culturally tagged as befitting men, not women, a pattern explored with care by Cassell in her groundbreaking *The Woman in the Surgeon's Body* (1998). It thus makes sense to hypothesize that women, who have long operated at the margins of surgery, might view the reforms differently than their male counterparts. Are the struggles that we explore primarily or even substantially different for men and women residents and attendings? Is a shift to a somewhat less onerous set of policies for work hours and schedules a threat to a traditionally masculine work world? Is that what sparked struggles if not resistance?

In the only other book-length study of the reforms, *Challenging Operations: Medical Reform and Resistance* (2011), Kellogg explored sources of resistance to the reforms. She employed comparative ethnography to study three general surgery residency programs from slightly before the 2003 reforms took effect through the end of 2004. She also conducted interviews, largely but not exclusively with residents, and directly "asked residents whether or not they supported a work-hours reduction in their hospital" (87). At the outset, 77 percent of residents supported the reforms, a figure that included all interns, most female residents, and a minority of male residents. She noted that "virtually all" attendings opposed them.

For Kellogg, resistance to the reforms was grounded in a culture, a status system, and social positions. The culture, which she dubbed the Iron Man culture, overlaps substantially with what Cassell (1998) described earlier as the Iron Surgeon. In short, long hours and little concern about fatigue were central to the Iron Man culture (49–72), a pattern that reaches back to the early days of residencies at Johns Hopkins. Those who could approximate its heroic demands were afforded high status in residencies. However, residents were differentially positioned to enact the culture, and women, in particular, were largely unable to attain the Iron Man ideal. Similarly, a minority of men who aspired to a more balanced approach to work were joined by those who sought a more patient-centered work style in supporting the reforms (73–91). Those unable or unwilling to pursue or realize Iron Man status thus supported the reforms.

Kellogg gives only passing attention to how surgeons experience and interpret their work and why some might struggle with the reforms. In only a few pages (64–68), she presented what she called "legitimating accounts," framed as ways of interpreting the long-hour culture and practices "as normal rather than strange." Importantly, the three accounts—ensuring continuity of care, learning by doing, and living the life of a surgeon—are *rationales* that defend long-hour traditions, not *explanations* for behavior. Behavior and outlooks were seen as driven by the Iron Man culture, status processes, and social positions, not workplace experiences.

Kellogg's primary aim was to explain why reforms seemed to fail in two residency programs while largely succeeding in a third. She advanced a "micro-institutional" approach that focused on resources available in one program but lacking in the other two. Of central importance is the availability of "relational spaces," places in the hospital that afforded residents the chance to gather, share support, develop strategies for working in new ways, and thereby overcome resistance. These safe spaces nurtured reform as those who opposed the reforms accosted and tried to stigmatize supporters (104, 115–131, 135–136). The proportion of women in the program also mattered, as programs with more women had difficulties implementing the reforms because men united and formed a wall of resistance (140–145). Culture, status, social categories, and space combined to form the crux of Kellogg's argument.

As she concluded her book, published when the reforms were in their ninth year, she correctly noted that the two programs in her study where reform floundered "are not the exceptions but the norm" (165). Given that her research window closed in 2004, it is unclear whether the one program remained a reform stronghold or regressed into resistance. Our view is that the primary reasons why surgeons have struggled with the reforms elude Kellogg's analysis, as the sheer magnitude of national resistance to the reforms hints at something much more systemic than a dearth of relational spaces to nurture reform and reformers. We believe that the issues she dismissed as "legitimating accounts," as mere rationales for concern about the reforms, represent matters of fundamental importance that have sparked years of ongoing struggles.

We draw inspiration from Kellogg's scholarship by attending carefully to culture and gender. We focus much more fully on the workplace experiences and interpretations of residents and attendings; we also explore in depth the organization of residencies—social structure, in sociological language—and how it might bear on thought and action. Culture, too, is further explored, as other occupational cultural traditions—not just or even mainly the Iron Man ideal—shape the prospects of reform. We argue that surgeons claim that fatigue rarely impairs, is not a substantial risk factor for patients, and that the work-a-day world of "real life" surgery requires surgeons to work while fatigued. Surgeons believe that residents must encounter and learn to assess, manage, and work while fatigued during residency because they will need to do all of those things in practice. This culture of fatigue—beliefs and behaviors regarding working while tired—undermines a main rationale for the reforms. In the conclusion, we argue that the prospects for work-hour reform hinge to a significant degree on whether the culture of fatigue can be countered effectively by additional evidence, both general and specific to individuals, about the effects of fatigue on cognitive and physical performance.

We further argue that although surgery remains gendered in many ways, beliefs about the experience and consequences of working while fatigued and the perceived necessity of doing so do not vary for men and women, nor do most other forms of belief and behavior related to the reforms. We explored carefully the possibility that gender matters in virtually all of our analyses, both quantitative and qualitative, in every chapter to come. In the analysis of our survey data, our consideration of gender is clearly evident in the tables we present. In the qualitative data from the interviews and ethnography, we systematically explored the possibility that gender shaped the views and experiences of residents and attendings with the reforms. As with the survey evidence, we found no such support. For stylistic reasons, we do not repeatedly belabor that fact, and instead present the common views of both men and women. As the evidence is presented across the subsequent chapters, it will become quite evident that women and men struggle with the reforms in similar ways and with equal passion and frustration.

FUNCTIONAL INTERCHANGEABILITY, INTUITION AND TACIT KNOWLEDGE, AND WORK ROUTINES

The word bureaucracy is often associated with unpleasantness: red tape, top-heavy inefficiencies, and cold indifference to special circumstances. Those challenges aside, one of the chief and very real virtues of bureaucratic organizations is the separation of an organizational role from an incumbent of that role. Roles that can be well characterized with a thorough job description and filled with capable individuals allow an organization to continue to function effectively when any given role incumbent departs. When a person can seamlessly substitute for another without much, if any, loss of capability, functional interchangeability has been achieved. Functional interchangeability is important in all organizations when workers quit or retire, but it is critical when organizations require round-the-clock staffing for some roles. Health care roles, especially in hospitals, are among those where functional interchangeability is vital.

In his path-breaking analysis of time and organizations, Zerubavel (1979, 42–49) argued that hospitals have traditionally viewed changes of personnel— and thus the transferring of responsibility for patients—as a "necessary evil." They have historically attempted to minimize discontinuities in patient care by reducing the frequency of shift changes, by fostering flexible but long work schedules among physicians, and by emphasizing the importance and function of patient charts. Importantly, Zerubavel argued that "the belief that medical responsibility is not mechanically transferrable from one physician to another also *precludes temporally rigid work schedules* which are based on fixed leaving times and which allow for abrupt assumption and suspension of duties and responsibilities" (49, emphasis added). In addition to temporal flexibility, Zerubavel suggested that the patient chart served as a "major facilitator" and an "effective mechanism" that permitted one caregiver to reliably substitute for another, thus achieving functional interchangeability (45–46). Flexible work schedules combined with the patient chart to permit the realization of functional interchangeability among the physicians and residents observed by Zerubavel.

Alongside the notion of functional interchangeability, there has long been interest in the presence and prominence of intuition and tacit knowledge in many forms of work. Careful analyses of work spanning a wide range—from mechanical repair work (Harper 1987) to the design and fabrication of nuclear weapons (MacKenzie and Spinardi 1995)—have highlighted the importance of intuitions and tacit knowledge that might be difficult if not impossible to articulate, let alone transfer smoothly and fully from one person to another. Along these lines, Wilensky (1964, 149) argued some years ago that professional knowledge is "to some extent tacit" and that professional work could produce understandings or insights "which we cannot fully report." Polanyi (1962, 601) likewise argued that "there are things that we know but cannot tell," a point echoed by Freidson (2001, 24–35).

Studies of medical decision-making and action suggest a prominent role for what amounts to intuition and tacit knowledge (Groopman 2007; Mickleborough 2015). Abernathy, a surgeon, and Hamm, a cognitive psychologist, describe in *Surgical Intuition* (1995) that expert intuitive action tends to be fast, generally accurate, flexible, but subjectively unexplainable. In moments of that sort, it is not evident that any explicit "reasoning" is guiding action; rather, these moments have been called "knowing-in-action" (Katlic and Coleman 2018). Action often involves, in short, the sorts of understandings described years ago by Polanyi, Wilensky, and others. One challenge in medicine is that biology varies, as does the biology of pathology, which means that the preset algorithms and practice guidelines that have risen in medicine will only apply approximately to a given patient (Groopman 2007). To compound the matter, it has long been known that there is considerable variation in how seemingly identical patients respond to therapies (Eddy 1988). All of these issues combine to make functional interchangeability a difficult if not fraught undertaking when patients have complex or potentially confusing medical conditions. The mere fact that physicians and residents come and go does not, of course, establish the attainment of functional interchangeability.

The reforms offer a rare opportunity to examine the consequences of a dramatic shift in how time is formatted and understood in a professional setting. This national and natural experiment in work hour and schedule reform allows us to explore carefully the transfer of information and responsibility for patients from one caregiver to another. Is that transfer smooth and effective? Is it greatly facilitated by patient records, and impeded by temporal rigidities, as Zerubavel anticipated? Our analysis sheds new light on the old problem of functional interchangeability among professionals and how a shift to a more rigid approach to time and the use of patient records bear on that process.

We find that shorter shifts, fewer weekly work hours, and mandatory time away from the hospital might help reduce fatigue, as many surgeons acknowledge, but that those changes introduce other risk factors. The reforms prompted more transitions in care, where information about patients and responsibility for them is transferred from one caregiver (or team) to another during what is called a patient handoff (also called a hand-over, check-out, or sign-out). These transitions are thought to be problematic because pertinent information about patients can be omitted, difficult to convey, misunderstood, or forgotten. We argue that lapses of this sort stem, in part, from inherent difficulties in transferring complex information, but also from cultural patterns, whereby residents tend to rush through transfers, often in exceptionally distracting contexts. In addition, the reforms reduced overnight call and encouraged the widespread adoption of formats for covering patients at night—called night float and cross coverage—that lessen familiarity between residents and patients. Those staffing night float and engaging in cross coverage do not know their patients well, are much less involved in the care plans for those patients, and thereby tend to behave in ways that suggest they are only "secondary" caretakers.

These problems are compounded by substantial limitations in medical records. Our evidence suggests that the least experienced members of surgical teams—the interns—are the primary authors of daily patient notes, and that notes are less than fully complete or updated as care plans or patient conditions change. Other key documents, like operative notes that summarize procedures, also tend to be minimalist documents due to a mix of legal concerns and an occupational culture that does not value long, detailed accounts. Both patterns mean that a new caregiver who is unfamiliar with a patient cannot simply review the medical records to quickly and effectively grasp a patient's condition and course. Put differently, much can be lost across transfers of care, as those most involved and familiar with a patient know more and can use that knowledge to more easily interpret and respond to changes in a patient's condition. All of this, of course, is critical when patients are complex and unstable.

Our analysis thus sheds light on how organizational routines and elements of occupational culture combine to impede the realization of functional interchangeability. At present, care providers are not interchangeable in a seamless way, and this pattern and conviction contribute substantially to the struggles that surgeons have with the reforms. In making these arguments, we contribute to literatures on organizations, the character and role of intuition and tacit knowledge in professional work, and occupational culture.

ETHICS, PROFESSIONALISM, AND THE WORK-HOUR REFORMS

Ethical issues have long been intertwined with medical education and practice. Our description earlier in the chapter of the state of residency education prior to the reforms was hardly idyllic, as immersive experiences, long hours, and an abundance of noneducational service work made residents' lives difficult. The situation intensified with the emergence of cost-containment policies in the early 1980s, when residents were beset by even higher patient volume, turnover, and acuity. This confluence of pressures prompted the penning of books with titles like *Getting Rid of Patients: Contradictions in the Socialization of Physicians* (Mizrahi 1986), suggesting that medicine was no beacon of ethics and professionalism. Residency follows medical school, where researchers have documented a consistent and concerning moral trajectory among students since seminal studies such as *Boys in White* (Becker et al. 1961) and *The Student-Physician* (Merton, Reader, and Kendall 1957). Despite substantial changes over time in the content of medical curricula and the social characteristics of medical students, studies consistently show that as medical training progresses, students begin to objectify patients more often and more fully, ethical orientations begin to wane, and idealism is replaced by cynicism (Wendland 2010, 18–21). Patients with complex stories, hopes, and dreams become the "gallbladder" or the "cold limb," reduced to their affliction alone. In a context like this, the ethical statements of medical societies and scholarly and practical efforts to address ethics and professionalism might seem quaint.

Although we find evidence of objectification, cynicism, and continued overwork, we also find substantial evidence that despite our era of "high throughput" healthcare, both faculty and residents often spoke about professional values and obligations and felt distressed when aspects of the work-hour reforms appeared to complicate or compromise patient care. In these ways, ethical orientations and professionalism clearly persist, and were falsely pronounced dead some years ago. The reforms generated new tensions that shed considerable light on ethics and professionalism in medicine. Importantly, these tensions arise as residents and faculty engage with patients as they learn and practice medicine. They arise, in short, with considerable reg-ularity in real-life medical encounters, and are thus not the sorts of abstract, largely hypothetical matters often featured in discussions of ethics and pro-fessionalism. The beliefs and behaviors we explore align well with the notion of professionalism as a "normative belief system" about how best to organize and deliver care (Wynia et al. 2014).

Consider stay-or-go decisions, which became a routine matter for residents who reach the maximum hours permitted for either a single shift or the weekly total of eighty hours. A resident who reaches a limit often faces the unhappy choice of either exceeding the cap by staying for patient care or leaving and risking the perception if not the reality of abdicating professional responsibil-ities to patients and fellow caretakers. With weekly limits, those who exceed eighty hours in one week can remain within the limits if they can subtract— by coming in late, leaving early, or taking a day off—in subsequent weeks to create an average of eighty hours a week over a four week period. We show that residents sometimes do subtract hours, but not often when they need to, not in a predictable or substantial way, and not without trepidation, as efforts to subtract hours expose residents to the risk of being viewed as weak, lazy, or inefficient. Staffing constraints and the daily rhythms of work also served to deter trimming. Although adding hours bolsters professionalism and the sense of putting patients first, subtraction does not, even though it can help residents honor the eighty-hour work week average.

Residents rarely adopt a strictly clock-driven approach to leaving, but rather exercise discretion guided by notions of proper care, competence, efficiency, and something akin to a playground culture, the no-dumping rule. As they make these choices, they are clearly and consistently influenced by their per-ceived obligations to patients. The long-standing notion that "patients come first" surfaced repeatedly in how residents described their choices and in our observations of the behavior of residents. It was also a central concern among faculty, who worry that care can be compromised when caregivers are overly mindful of the clock. Without question, the decisions and behavior of residents are driven by concerns about care, even though they also display evidence of a mechanistic and depersonalized view of humans and substantial cynicism. These orientations are not mutually exclusive, a pattern we believe is insuffi-ciently understood in the literature on ethics and professionalism.

Perceptions of competence, familiarity, and availability also bear on stay-or-go decisions. Few residents facing an hour limit leave an unstable or com-plex patient in the hands of a less-experienced resident, or one unfamiliar with the patient. Nor do they routinely pass off care activities that need to be accomplished in a timely way if others are unavailable to provide immediate assistance. All of these beliefs and behaviors regarding stay-or-go decisions show that the notion of proper care is a highly salient guidepost among residents.

There is substantial evidence of what Szymczak and Bosk (2012, 345) called a "culture of efficiency." While efficiency has several meanings, one key meaning is that an individual resident be organized and capable of dispatching a long list of patient-care tasks expeditiously. Efficient residents have that capability. It also means that residents cooperate to manage workloads and take appropriate and timely action to accomplish work, nip problems in the bud, and manage those that surface. Szymczak and Bosk claim that "a 'training for efficiency' (TFE) ethos is the predominant value organizing the professional and occupational culture of residency" (355). The reforms have compressed work for many residents, as the same amount of work must be completed in fewer hours. Residents must be efficient and are evaluated on that capability. Because exceeding permitted hours to finish work can be interpreted as inefficiency rather than the natural consequence of high workloads, residents underreport their hours to avoid being labeled inefficient or drawing attention to themselves (Szymczak et al. 2010, 345, 373). They also exceed permitted hours because there are situations where familiarity with a patient allows a particular resident to complete some form of patient care more quickly. In that case, residents use a group notion of efficiency to guide stay-or-go decisions and will often exceed those limits if it diminishes time requirements or improves care.

There is also no question that stay-or-go decisions and behavior are shaped by something like a playground culture, the no-dumping rule. Those who dump pass work along to others that is interpreted as work that *could* and *should* have been accomplished by the originating resident. Those who dump fail to do their "own" work and risk being stigmatized and targeted for retaliation. Of course, not all work that is passed off constitutes dumping, and allegations of dumping are often hasty and based on conjecture. The only surefire way to avoid allegations of dumping is to disregard hour and shift limits and pass off little or no work. Dumping is believed to stem from character flaws, a poor work ethic, inefficiencies due to inadequate medical knowledge or procedural skill, or an inability to organize one's work effectively. All are serious, potentially career-ending problems.

Concerns about care, competence, efficiency, and the no-dumping rule combine to shape stay-or-go decisions and behavior. Some, like care and competence, are clearly related to classic notions of ethical and professional behavior for physicians. Efficiency, however, centers more on sustaining and maintaining credibility and avoiding having one's abilities and work ethic scrutinized. The no-dumping rule joins with concerns about efficiency to push us even farther from classic notions of ethical and professional behavior. All serve to create challenges for those who wish to respect and abide by the reforms. They also reveal how occupational cultures and the social organization of work and training interlock to create headwinds for the reforms.

Violating the hour limits is in some cases strongly motivated and justified on the basis of doing what is seen as right and proper for patients. But "doing right" often pairs with "doing wrong," as those who exceed the hour limits face the fraught choice of lying or reporting violations, thereby inviting feared scrutiny of themselves, their resident team, and their program. The reforms thus reveal the operation of ethical principles in the work and training of residents; they also precipitated a series of ethical and professional predicaments worthy of our attention. We argue that for many, the broad values of honesty and selfless devotion to patients—to always put *patients*, not the *clock*, first—are now at a loggerhead (Carpenter et al. 2006; Bryne, Loo, and Giang 2015). Autonomy and authority, central to conceptualizations of professionalism in both sociology and medicine (Michalec and Hafferty 2013), have been squeezed by the clock.

MEDICAL SPECIALTIES, OTHER COUNTRIES, AND THE WORK-HOUR REFORMS

Despite the substantial body of data that we collected, drew upon, and will describe in the next section, it nonetheless remains the case that there is much we did not explore. Two issues are especially noteworthy. One involves the fate of the ACGME reforms in fields other than general surgery. As we formulated our research, it was apparent that medical specialties had distinctive work traditions, and that some—like pathology and dermatology—had historically worked less and were not poised to struggle with the reforms. Evidence on work-hour compliance confirms those suspicions (Drolet et al. 2013). We opted to focus on a single specialty the second author practices, and one the first felt he could muster the time and resources to grasp and explore in detail. It is also the specialty that has historically worked the longest hours and has had among the greatest struggles with the reforms. While residents and attendings in other specialties have heard, read, and seen merit in our analyses and arguments, it nonetheless remains unclear to what extent our findings reflect experiences in other medical specialties.

Our reading of the literature suggests that residents and attendings in other specialties have struggled in much the same way and for the same reasons, but three differences are most salient. First, studies that have explored links between the quality and safety of patient care and the reforms suggest significant differences between medical and surgical specialties (Philibert et al. 2013). Put simply, studies of internal medicine tend to find that the reforms have improved the quality and safety of patient care, whereas those of surgery tend to find the opposite. Second, surgery is distinctive because of its attention to operative volume as a proxy for preparedness to practice independently following the residency and emphasis on perioperative care, the care patients receive before (preoperative) and after (postoperative) surgery. Concerns about operative volume and resident involvement in perioperative care, and how both might be influenced by the reforms, surely sets surgery apart from other specialties. And third, there is evidence that the consequences of reductions in what we will describe as continuity of care—of being involved in a patient's care from presentation to discharge—might be more important for surgical than medical specialties (Philibert et al. 2013). Continuity is thought to be important for the quality and safety of patient care and for a resident's development of clinical judgement. These differences make us suspect that some of the struggles we will explore are at least somewhat more pronounced among surgeons than those in other specialties.

A second issue is that we limited our attention to general surgery programs in the United States. Without question, other countries have also crafted and rolled out policies constraining the work hours and schedules of residents and, in some cases, practicing physicians. By focusing on the work and training of surgeons in the United States, we do not mean to imply that limitations on work hours and schedules would present exactly the same challenges for surgeons in different cultural, political, and organizational contexts. Denmark, for example, limits all physician work weeks to thirty-seven and a half hours, New Zealand allows seventy-two hour weeks, and European countries allow forty-eight (Baldwin et al. 2003; Ulmer, Wolman, and Johns 2008; Moeller, Webber, and Epstein 2016). In Canada, restrictions on residents' work hours have been in place for even longer than those in the United States (Romanchuk 2004). Concerns about limited hours are present in other countries, but they are too varied and complex to credibly review or present here (e.g., Jagsi and Surender 2004; Chikwe, de Suoza, and Pepper 2004; Temple 2014; Parshuram et al. 2015). Our conviction is that comparative studies are needed to assess cultures of professionalism, fatigue, and efficiency, along with the enabling and constraining aspects of the social organization of training and practice (Hafferty and McKinlay 1993). Our hope is that a careful consideration of one specialty in one country will provide a foundation from which to launch a broader comparative study.

Mixed-Methods, Multi-Center, and Multi-Wave Evidence

Our book draws upon a substantial body of original data: ethnography in a single general surgery residency program and three rounds of surveys and interviews with residents and faculty in a diverse mix of general surgery programs. The data combine depth and breadth, qualitative interviews and observations as well as survey data, from residency programs that varied in size, structure, visibility, and location. The qualitative observations offered by previous scholars (Szymczak et al. 2010; Kellogg 2011; Brooks and Bosk 2012; Szymczak and Bosk 2012), who we touched upon in our earlier sections, are valuable, but they come from just a few programs in urban areas that tend to have "elite" standing. They risk illustrating local cultures that might differ substantially from those in other regions or in other types of programs. In contrast, we cover a broad and diverse range of residency programs in the United States.

In the ethnographic portion of the project, Coverdill secured and took advantage of access to an academic general surgery program and all of its services and arenas of work and education. That included operating rooms, the hospital floors, clinics, morbidity and mortality conferences, educational sessions, the surgical simulation laboratory, departmental meetings, and so forth. He had access to two hospitals (with Level 1 adult and pediatric trauma), a nearly 500-bed adult facility and a children's hospital with about 150 beds. Both were in a metropolitan area in the southeastern United States with a population of about six hundred thousand. The program had twenty-five categorical surgery residents spread across the five postgraduate years (PGYs). It did not require a year or more of research, although a few residents each year typically took a research year. This prong of the project began in 2007, continued through 2011, and included more than one thousand hours of observation. All observations were typed into fieldnotes within one day.

Access to the fieldwork site was facilitated by the program director and the head of the Surgical Research Service, who helped Coverdill make introductions and secure approval from their institutional review board (IRB). The project was described at the beginning of a morbidity and mortality meeting, which was mandatory for all residents and attendings, and Coverdill responded to questions and concerns about the project. At that meeting, and then as residents and attendings joined the surgery department, Coverdill obtained consent to observe their work and training. The research role—to tag along with residents, attendings, and teams—was similar to the well-institutionalized role of shadowing in medicine. On the rare occasions when a question was raised or there was a chance to offer an introduction, he said this: "I'm Jim Coverdill, a professor at the University of Georgia. I'm here to observe the work and training of surgeons. Do you mind if I observe today?" No patient, family, staff member, resident, or attending ever objected.

The ethnography was valuable for two primary reasons. First, it allowed him to gain first-hand experience with the work settings, work practices, and workloads of faculty and residents. He was able to observe, for example, the division of labor between an attending and one or more residents during and then after a procedure in the operating room. He rounded with teams, observed the allocation and execution of floor work, and learned how incredibly different services were in terms of the expectations of attendings, staffing levels, workloads, and so forth. Second, it permitted direct observation of key work practices such as handoffs of patients, shift changes, and documentation in the medical record. For example, in the medical literature, the passing of information, responsibility, and unfinished work in a handoff was described as a complex technical act prone to failure. Observing what was actually done provided a key check on what residents and attendings would say during interviews and report on surveys.

The ethnography took place in the middle years of a broader effort to collect survey data and interviews with faculty and residents in programs across the United States. In 2004, 2009, and 2014–15, we collected questionnaire and interview data from residents and attendings in general surgery residency programs that varied in terms of academic and community orientations, the number of residents, urban and rural locations, and high or lower prestige and national reputation. There were nine programs in the first wave, fifteen in the second, and thirteen in the third, representing twenty-five distinct programs (six participated two or more times) located in seventeen states and all four continental time zones in the United States. Additional follow-up interviews with residents interviewed during the third wave were conducted early in 2018 to bolster our data on delayed departures. Overall, we amassed 1,421 completed questionnaires and 258 semi-structured interviews, approximately split between residents and faculty. Response rates were high, with a cumulative rate of 73 percent for the questionnaire results.

Programs were identified and approached in the same way during each wave of the study. We believed that a random sample of programs would fail, as busy residents and faculty would be insufficiently motivated to participate. Instead, programs were chosen on the basis of both program traits—an effort to obtain a diverse mix of programs—as well as relationships—that the program director be known to Mellinger as a supporter of research who could become a local champion of the study. We thus secured the collaborative assistance of an attending in each program who obtained local IRB approval and managed data collection in their program. Surveys were distributed and completed, most typically, in a group setting, such as during an educational or program meeting. Completed surveys were enclosed in envelopes prior to being turned in to ensure confidentiality. The final question on each wave of the survey asked the participant if they would volunteer for an interview with Coverdill, where their participation and comments would be confidential. Volunteers completed separate contact information forms that were, again, sealed prior to collection. Our site collaborators helped collect the data, but were not privy to survey responses, who volunteered for interviews, and what participants said during interviews. Data were mailed to Coverdill for entry and analysis.

The surveys and interviews were constrained by our understanding that surgeons have little time to participate in research. In each round, we used paper survey forms, which amounted to a single sheet of paper with a front and a back filled with questions. Paper forms allowed the surgeons to verify that it was indeed a short survey before devoting ten to fifteen minutes to complete it. Interviews were described as fifteen to thirty minutes in length, and were nearly always clipped at thirty minutes even if a participant wished to talk more. The interviews provided rich information despite their relative brevity. Nearly all were conducted by telephone and with consent were recorded and transcribed verbatim. In our analysis of the interview and observational evidence, residents are distinguished by "postgraduate year" or PGY and gender; attendings are simply distinguished by gender. We thus use short notations, such as PGY3-M for a male third-year resident and A-F for a female attending, when presenting quotations.

The survey data allow us to explore prevailing patterns and how they might differ across types of programs, experience levels, and gender. The interview and observational data allow us to explore carefully how faculty and residents understand issues and why they behave as they do. Compared to previous sociological studies by Kellogg and Bosk and his colleagues, we collected and drew on evidence that is more national (programs span from one coast to the other), more varied (from prestigious academic centers with national reputations to those with a local reputation and a community focus), more inclusive methodologically (survey data along with observations and interviews), and of longer duration (not just early responses to new rules or during a two-year time period).

Authorship and Roles

A few words are in order about our division of labor and contributions to the text. The first author, Jim Coverdill, a sociologist, took the lead in the research design, crafting the survey and interview questions, conducting all interviews, and performing the statistical and qualitative analyses. He also conducted the ethnography, wrote up the field notes, analyzed that evidence, and wrote every chapter of this book. Throughout the project, medical school IRBs constrained John Mellinger's role, as they wanted only the external sociologist to collect and analyze the data to eliminate the possibility that a surgeon with authority over residents could identify and potentially respond to participants. We of course discussed issues and collaboratively vetted our research plans and then drafts of the results, but the analysis and voice remains Coverdill's.

That might make it seem as though Mellinger played only a minor role. Nothing could be farther from the truth. From the very beginning of our collaboration, Mellinger was a wonderful source of insider insights, a critical sounding board, and an extraordinarily effective networker and recruiter as we sought to identify and include residency programs in the study. Quite literally, the research would not have gotten off the ground, much less been sustained for nearly two decades, without him, and the quality of the work was elevated by his keen observations as a scholar, skilled surgeon, and award-winning medical educator. In much of the text, Mellinger's presence is implied through those roles, but the words that readers encounter were penned by Coverdill. That changes, however, near the end of subsequent chapters, where Mellinger contributes a reflection. In some cases, he comments on the broad themes discussed in the chapter; in others, he provides a recollection of his time as a resident or his work as an attending surgeon that dovetails with the chapter's main themes. The reflections enrich the material provided in each chapter and provide an insider's voice. One of us is a sociological outsider, the other a surgical insider, but together we explore and explain how and why surgeons have struggled with the work-hour reforms.

CHAPTER 1

Fatigue as Impairment or Practical and Educational Necessity?

When I get into practice, I'm going to have to know, at 2 a.m. when I'm on call, that I have the skill to manage that. I think unless you have practiced being sleep deprived, you are not going to be able to think well on your feet. Like most things, you get better at it as you do it more. You just do what you have to do, both to get your education and to take care of your patients. (PGY4-F)

Fatigue has moved closer to the center of the educational and policy stage than ever before. The ACGME began to require on July 1, 2011, that residents and faculty members be educated to recognize signs of fatigue and engage in fatigue mitigation (ACGME 2010). At that same time, shifts for interns were limited to no more than sixteen hours, a threshold recommended by the Institute of Medicine on the basis of research that suggests performance wanes after that much wakefulness (Ulmer, Wolman, and Johns 2008). These policies were designed to upend long-standing patterns of fatigue-related belief and behavior, but do not go far enough for some sleep scientists and advocacy organizations (Preston et al. 2010), who wanted sixteen-hour caps for *all* residents, fewer periods of call, and other constraints. These changes highlight relatively new and unambiguous convictions: fatigue is an impairment that jeopardizes both physicians and patients; fatigue can and should be minimized if not avoided entirely; education about fatigue means learning to recognize and avoid it. Some argue that no fatigued surgeon—in training or in practice—should be allowed to perform elective surgery (Nurok, Czeisler, and Lehmann 2010; Czeisler, Pellegrini, and Sade 2013).

Few outside the medical world appear to view those positions as outlandish. Why, after all, would anyone want to work shifts as long as twenty-four or more hours when the national norm for full-time work is eight? Why would anyone insist on having surgeons-in-training—or practicing surgeons, for that matter—work such long hours? And how many of us would choose to be operated on by a fatigued surgeon? Evidence from a national survey of adults bears on these issues, suggesting that 96 percent believe that work shifts for resident physicians should not exceed sixteen hours (Blum et al. 2010). If respondents learned that their doctor had been awake for more than twenty-four hours, then 85 percent would "feel anxious about the safety of their medical care" and 80 percent would "want to be treated by a different doctor" (Blum et al. 2010, 5). Moreover, a Kaiser Family Foundation (2004) national survey found that 74 percent believed that "overwork, stress, or fatigue" among health professionals was a "very important" cause of preventable medical errors. Public opinion would thus appear to run counter to the long-hour traditions of physicians.

Our aim here is to elucidate contemporary fatigue culture, a set of beliefs and behaviors associated with fatigue and working while tired. As Schein (2004) argued, cultural understanding facilitates change, as it is rarely effective to simply declare a culture "wrong," especially one that is long standing and widely held. General surgeons have traditionally worked among the longest days, and most hours, of any medical field, and they continue to do so (Baldwin et al. 2010). In public forums, surgeons have opposed the reforms primarily because of the perceived value of continuity of care for both learners and patients and the risk of discontinuities induced by patient handoffs (Fischer, Healy, and Britt 2009). Those issues are examined in the next chapter.

Resistance may also stem from broader aspects of surgical culture. One study of residents noted an "underlying culture within the surgery environment that is different from that in other specialties, and which may involve less willingness to accept the natural limitations of human performance" (Woodrow et al. 2008, 465). In particular, the authors identify an "optimism bias" (Weinstein 1989), which leads surgeons to believe that others suffer from fatigue in ways that they do not. Those patterns correspond with the ethnographic observations of Cassell (1991; 1998, 103), who argued that surgical training inculcates a "stoic ethos" that abhors physical weakness and denies the surgeon's bodily needs. A survey of program directors in general surgery (Willis et al. 2009) bolsters those results by showing that fatigue was the lowest-rated factor among eleven barriers to quality care and was thought to have little bearing on surgical performance. Continuity of care, an issue we probe in the next chapter, was second-rated, with 83 percent saying that it was "very important," behind only "poor fund of medical knowledge." Fatigue was seen as a very important barrier to quality patient care by only 17 percent of program directors. This culture may well foster resistance to the reforms.

In this chapter, we explore fatigue culture among surgeons. We probe beliefs and behaviors regarding fatigue with an eye toward what they entail and what role they play in surgical training and practice. We draw upon a roster of twelve survey items and three main interview questions, suggested by the fieldwork, which were followed by probes to expand and clarify responses. The first asked whether participants believed that duty periods in excess of sixteen hours diminished cognitive or physical aspects of surgical performance. This question related directly to a shift-length threshold that became a rule for interns in 2011. The second asked participants how they might explain to the public how surgeons can remain skilled and safe after working twenty-four or more hours. A third asked surgeons to reflect on the value and feasibility of specifying specific hour limits—like a sixteen hour limit for interns, a twenty-eight hour maximum shift length for residents in their second or subsequent year, and an eighty hour per week limit for all residents—in a way that aligns with restrictions on airline pilots and those who drive buses and large trucks. The questions sparked extensive commentary on experiences with, and beliefs about, fatigue and working while tired.

Survey-Based Insights into Fatigue Culture

The third wave of data collection contained a roster of twelve questions that were suggested by what was learned in earlier interviews and field observations. Results are presented in Table 1.1. For each question, response options ranged from "strongly disagree" to "strongly agree," but for ease of interpretation, results were simplified to reflect the percentage of each group who "agreed or strongly agreed" with each questionnaire item (a practice we will use in subsequent chapters as well). The statistical significance of the difference between the responses of residents and faculty was assessed with a standard chi-square test statistic (a practice we will also use in subsequent chapters). Each row in the table lists the exact wording of each question; each question is assigned an item number to ease the presentation.

Items 1 through 4 probe the perceived consequences of fatigue for emotions, technical skills, speed, and cognitive operations. Substantial percent-

TABLE 1.1. Fatigue-Related Beliefs and Behavior among General Surgery Faculty and Residents

Item	Exact Question Wording	% Agree or Strongly Agree	
		Residents	Faculty
1	Fatigue affects my emotions—things like patience, empathy, and cheer.	82	74*
2	Fatigue affects my technical skills—things like tying knots, manipulating instruments, and dissecting a tissue plane.	45	23*
3	Fatigue affects the speed at which I can work and make decisions.	80	52*
4	Fatigue affects my attention span, memory, and the quality of my decisions.	74	38*
5	Fatigue that may affect my emotions, technical skills, speed, attention span, memory, or the quality of my decisions does not diminish significantly my ability to provide good patient care.	84	88
6	I have pushed myself to continue my patient-care duties despite being fatigued.	90	97*
7	In practice, there are times when surgeons must work while fatigued.	97	98
8	As you gain surgical skill and experience, you work and react more in a patterned or automatic way that's less affected by fatigue.	79	82
9	Surgeons can learn to work safely and effectively even when fatigued.	78	82
10	Proper training requires that residents have at least some long workdays to experience fatigue in order to learn their limits and how to adapt to fatigue.	79	85*
11	Naps are an effective deterrent to fatigue-induced impairment.	50	53
12	I regularly take naps during long shifts to reduce fatigue.	22	27
	Sample Sizes	*291*	*279*

Notes. An asterisk (*) next to the second percentage for a pair of contrasts indicates a significant difference in the percentages at the .05 level; a plus sign (+) indicates significance at the .10 level (from Pearson's chi-square tests).

ages of residents, in particular, agree that fatigue affects their emotions (item 1), the speed at which they work and make decisions (item 3), and their attention span, memory, and decisions (item 4). In each case, faculty were slightly (as in item 1) or substantially (as in items 3 and 4) less likely to agree, with the differences ranging from 8 to 36 percentage points. Technical skills stood out as distinctive, as only 45 percent of residents and 23 percent of faculty agreed that their technical skills were affected by fatigue (item 2). Together, the items suggest that both groups believe that fatigue matters, to at least some degree, for one or more aspects of surgical work.

What is remarkable, however, is the largely similar response that residents and faculty gave to item 5, which asked if fatigue-related changes diminished significantly their ability to provide good patient care. In short, 84 and 88 percent of residents and faculty, respectively, believe they continue to provide good patient care even when they are fatigued. That result is substantially similar to what is found for item 9, which posed a largely equivalent question. The vast majority of residents and faculty do not believe that fatigue undermines their ability to provide good and safe patient care. They may do so with less cheer, speed, and cognitive ease, but the care they provide is nonetheless thought to be adequate.

Three other patterns stand out. First and foremost, practically all residents and faculty believe that there are times when surgeons must work while fatigued (item 7). Nearly similar percentages report pushing themselves to continue working despite being fatigued (item 6), although the percentage is slightly higher for attendings than for residents. These results point to the conclusion that surgeons believe that long hours and fatigue are, at least at present, occupational facts. Second, items 8, 9, and 10 suggest that training and fatigue can, and perhaps must, mix. Both groups believe that increased skill and experience help to offset fatigue (item 8) and that it is possible to learn how to work safely and effectively when fatigued (item 9). Similar support is evident for item 10, which asks if residents need to experience fatigue in order to learn their limits and how to adapt to fatigue. These items suggest that encounters with fatigue are educationally valuable, that fatigue can at least partially be offset by accumulated skill and experience, and that it is possible to learn how to work when fatigued. A third and final pattern involves naps, which have been touted by the ACGME as a key fatigue mitigation strategy. Items 11 and 12 show that about half of residents and faculty agree that naps are an effective way to mitigate fatigue. However, only about a quarter of each group agrees that they regularly take naps to reduce fatigue, which suggests that naps fall short of being a widespread and effective strategy for countering fatigue.

We extend the basic analysis presented thus far to consider gender, experience, and whether the surgeon was located in an academic or community-based program. Consider first the role of gender, which is presented in Table 1.2. Among attendings, the strong pattern is one of similarities, not differences, with only items 4, 8, and 11 even hinting at potential gaps. Among residents, the pattern is even stronger, as only two items (6 and 12) differ significantly for men and women, but those differences are substantively minor. Fatigue culture appears to be understood and experienced quite similarly for men and women, regardless of rank.

TABLE 1.2. Fatigue-Related Beliefs and Behavior among General Surgery Faculty and Residents by Gender and Experience

		% Agree or Strongly Agree					
		Attendings		Residents			
Item	Brief Question Wording	Men	Women	Men	Women	PGY1-2	PGY3-5
1	Fatigue affects emotions	74	73	82	83	88	78*
2	Fatigue affects technical skills	25	18	44	45	51	40+
3	Fatigue affects speed	49	58	80	82	86	76*
4	Fatigue affects my attention and decisions	41	29+	75	75	76	73
5	Fatigue that may affect 1–4 does not diminish patient care	87	90	85	83	91	78*
6	I have pushed myself despite being fatigued	96	100	88	95*	87	93
7	In practice, surgeons must work while fatigued	98	97	97	99	98	97
8	Experienced surgeons are less affected by fatigue	84	75+	77	82	78	80
9	Surgeons can learn to work safely and effectively even when fatigued	83	81	79	78	71	83*
10	Proper training requires that residents experience fatigue	85	86	78	81	72	84*
11	Naps are an effective deterrent to fatigue impairment.	57	41*	53	45	59	43*
12	I regularly take naps to reduce fatigue.	30	22	25	16+	18	24
	Sample Sizes	*203*	*73*	*178*	*108*	*122*	*164*

Notes. An asterisk (*) next to the second percentage for a pair of contrasts indicates a significant difference in the percentages at the .05 level; a plus sign (+) indicates significance at the .10 level (from Pearson's chi-square tests). The items are the same and in the same order as in Table 1.1, but the wording is shortened here.

The pair of columns on the right side of Table 1.2 show that less experienced residents, on the other hand, do differ from their more experienced peers on seven of the items, but no difference is more than 16 percentage points. All differences are in the direction of less experienced residents being more sensitive to losses from fatigue (items 1, 2, and 3), more concerned about safety and the need for long hours (5, 9, and 10), and more appreciative of the value of napping (item 11). As we see it, these are relatively minor differences that fail to suggest sharp divisions among residents.

We also explored the relevance of experience among attendings and program type but do not present those results because they showed little of interest. Among attendings, those with one to ten years of experience were nearly indistinguishable from their more experienced peers, with the one exception that they were slightly more supportive (90 versus 80 percent) of the notion that proper training requires that residents have some long workdays (item 10). Likewise, those in academic programs are very similar to their peers in community programs, with only one somewhat perplexing difference emerging: those in community programs are more likely (57 versus. 46 percent) to believe that naps can be effective in deterring fatigue-related impairments (item 11).

Without question, the survey results stand in stark contrast with the official position of the ACGME that casts fatigue as dangerous for patients and providers and therefore something to be minimized if not avoided entirely. We now draw on the interview and observational evidence to better grasp the views of surgeons, developing the analysis in three main sections, each of which represents a cornerstone of fatigue culture. We begin with what we view as the most critical component of fatigue culture, namely the conviction that the "real life" practice of surgery requires an ability to work while fatigued. This core conviction, we argue, interlocks with and buttresses other aspects of fatigue culture. In the second, we describe typical understandings of fatigue. For most, fatigue matters, but falls short of being an impairment or a substantial risk for patients. The third section explores how surgeons believe they must encounter and experience fatigue in training in order to learn what it does to them, how to adapt to fatigue while working, and to probe their limits to working while tired. Encounters with fatigue are widely viewed as an educational necessity. In this section, we conclude with a brief overview of a dissenting view, as there is a distinct minority of surgeons who believe that hour limitations are needed to upend a surgical culture that encourages them to ignore fatigue.

"Real Life" Requires Surgeons to Work Fatigued

One of the most emphatically and uniformly expressed beliefs among residents and attendings is that the practice of surgery generally *requires* the ability to work while fatigued. Unlike residents, there are no hour restrictions on attendings, nor is there much if any oversight of hours in most practice settings. When asked about their work hours and schedules, attendings described schedules that varied. Some worked more than others; some days were longer than others. But in many cases, the schedules were starkly inconsistent with the work hours and schedules of residents. Consider the following comment, which mixes observations about "real life" and work-hour reforms:

> Real life work is not sixteen or even twenty-four hours! We all know that. If we're going to train somebody to do a job, you have to train them for real-life situations. It's okay to ease them into it and not just throw them in or make them work very long hours with a lot of stress. But it's not appropriate to falsify or fanaticize a make-believe world in training that is not the real world that they're going to live in in the future. . . . I wake up at five in the morning. I usually finish my last note around ten thirty at night. And then I take call every other night. There are only two surgeons. So yeah, I've had to learn how to deal with fatigue. I think that from the standpoint of today's educational gurus, proper training and fatigue don't mix. Fatigue is very clearly a bad word! But that's fantasy. (A-M)

Few surgeons who were observed or interviewed worked this much on a daily or weekly basis. Most typically, expressions were of this sort:

> I've had a number of days in the last month where I've had to work until two or three in the morning. Then, I get back up at six and come in to do another day of work. That's the way it goes! You accept that as part of your job. (A-M)

In this and many other cases, extremely long days are more the exception than the rule, but the possibility of spikes of this sort are widely recognized as "part of the job."

Time demands are driven by three main factors: practice structures; a shortage of surgeons; and the expectations of patients, referring physicians, partners, and hospitals. Practice structures are key, as they frame how often surgeons are on call and what responsibilities they assume. Consider the following practice structure:

> I'm one of three partners. We cover twenty-four-hour emergencies and trauma for five hospitals. We have no choice but to work long hours. There has to be a name on the schedule for every minute. During vacations, during times when there has been a conference, I have done five and six day stints in a row. After I've been on call all weekend, a seventy-two-hour shift, I'm then the operating doctor—I'm the person doing elective cases. So, it's just a necessity that the person who was on call all weekend is the one who at 7 a.m. on Monday will do a load of something like elective hernia cases. I feel that I've become very accustomed to sleep deprivation. (A-M)

The division of labor among the three partners is partly imposed by others, such as the need for a name on a schedule. But it also reflects choice, where a weekend of call is followed by a day of elective cases that presumably could have been shouldered by another partner. An extra burden for one partner means cherished time off for others. Quite a few surgeons described mixed practices, where they do, for example, general, vascular, and transplant surgery. Transplant surgeons tend to schedule a good bit of nontransplant surgery around what is predominantly an unpredictable main line of work. One attending described the challenge:

> I do a fair amount of elective surgery, but I also do [solid organ] transplant, which is purely not scheduled. So if I have a full day of elective surgery and then lo and behold I've got a transplant to do that's going to start tonight as well—well, that's just the way it is. If someone said to me, "No, Dr. [X], you can't do elective surgery, because you have to be on call for transplants," then I wouldn't be able to make enough money to make my practice work by just hanging around on call. (A-M)

This too is understood as "part of the job," but it is driven by the types of surgery performed. Those who specialize in endocrine, colorectal, bariatric, or breast surgery, for example, were widely thought to have few late-night emergencies, minimal call obligations, and shorter workdays. Those are recognized as "lifestyle" fields that rarely require surgeons to work while tired. Other sub-specialties, such as cardiothoracic, vascular, and transplant, along with practice in general surgery, are widely viewed as involving unpredictable and often long workdays. A faculty member in a community program described how "it's your bread-and-butter general surgeon who is your front line soldier in surgical care emergencies that gets the most calls in the middle of the night" (A-M).

The supply of surgeons and expectations on the part of patients, referring physicians, hospitals, and partners also play key roles in sustaining long days. As they discussed work hours, surgeons noted that the need and demand for surgery is going up, not down, and that there has been no offsetting influx of new surgeons. There is, in short, no bench of relief surgeons who could shorten the hours of those in the game. One summarized the matter this way: "Like it or not, we do not have an adequate workforce to prevent a situation in which surgeons are going to have to, at least occasionally, work while fatigued" (A-M). Expectations are also in the direction of completing scheduled procedures, even if fatigue emerges.

Have you had any occasions in your practice where you basically told a patient, "I can't do your procedure because I've been up all night and I'm too tired"? I can recall two occasions. It was later in my practice—probably after being in practice for fifteen years or whatever. It's hard to do and by no means the norm here or any-where. There are patient and referring physician expectations that we be available. It's difficult for everybody. Patients get off work to have these planned things. It's not always easy to reschedule. There is only so much operating time in a day, and slots get booked up. If you throw away what you have set aside, it may be a while before you can find that time again. (A-M)

Another surgeon noted how "there's an expectation from patients that you're not supposed to get tired!" (A-M). Partners can sometimes be asked to help, but there are limits to that, as they also have their own cases to manage. As one surgeon put it, "passing cases off to partners is not the norm, and I don't think it would work out well if it happened very much!" (A-M). Expectations also come from hospitals, largely in the name of efficiencies. In one case, an employed surgeon noted the hospital's inability to flexibly adapt to his fatigue:

There's no tolerance for fatigue built into the system. They're not going to em-ploy an extra thoracic surgeon because there might be situations where I'm tired—whether it's because I'm sick, because my children have been up all night, or be-cause I've been operating all day. No way. Suck up and do it! (A-M)

In a similar way, other surgeons noted that operating-room schedules had changed in recent years, and were increasingly managed to maximize efficiency.

I'm getting pressure now from the hospital to do really long days in the OR. In-stead of allowing me to say, "I'd rather do my difficult cases in the morning," I'm getting pressure from the hospital to operate all day long, just one day a week. Well, when you're the last patient on the list, how does that make you feel? Now your doctor is tired. . . . They want the OR humming and don't care! (A-F)

Block scheduling in this way may foster efficiencies, as an OR can be prepared and staffed in a suitable way for a particular surgeon; minimizing occasions when cases are re-scheduled due to fatigue is also clearly related to efficien-cies. However, both fail to respect and acknowledge the possibility of fatigue.

We have given primary voice thus far to attendings, as they are best posi-tioned to speak to the issue of real-life practice and the culture of fatigue. How-ever, residents work side-by-side with attendings, and see them come and go as days and weeks unfold. They also imagine their futures on the basis of what they see and the practice setting to which they aspire. In conversation, residents are uniformly quick to note that attendings do not have hour restrictions and that long days are common. Given the diverse sample of residency programs in our data, some residents aimed to practice in small cities and rural areas, places that tend to imply sparse staffing and the need to do what must be done when the need arises. One resident, who aspired to small-town practice, described her father's experience:

> My dad was a general surgeon and we lived in X [a town with a population of less than ten thousand]. He was the only general surgeon for two hundred miles for seventeen years. In a perfect world, yeah, it would be nice for him to have not worked some nights, and for somebody fresh to be available, but that just wasn't an option. I just don't think that's feasible. (PGY4-F)

Residents sounded much the same as attendings in claiming that the real-life practice of surgery requires the ability to work while fatigued. That conviction disposes residents to view hour restrictions as needless constraints, and to exceed hour limitations—even when told not to—because doing so aligns with their imagined futures. Note how, in describing her work, the following resident looks to an imagined future:

> My residency is fairly supportive—people help each other to go take a nap or go home. But I think as surgeons who are entering private practice, you don't necessarily know if you'll have that guarantee, so we push ourselves. We know that people tell us to take breaks and everything. But many of us think, "what happens when we're no longer residents?" Nobody is telling me that I'm going to be able to be done in 24+4 hours, so we need to be able to do that. We have people who take call for an entire weekend. You see them getting more and more tired where they've been woken up with consults and having to come in and operate. They'll do shifts of seventy-two hours where they take call. We have other surgeons we work with who actually do weeks of call, a week block at a time. Depending on what kind of practice setting you go into, there's the potential that it won't just be a twenty-four-hour shift that you are expected to be awake and answer phone calls for. . . . You look at them and say, "I may have to deal with that someday." (PGY4-F)

As this comment suggests, work-hour violations, as we show in later chapters, are not best understood as instances of simple coercion by attendings driven to get more work out of their underlings. In many cases, violations stem from anticipatory socialization into a culture of fatigue viewed as essential for professional practice.

Fatigue Matters, More or Less

The dominant view of residents and faculty members is that fatigue matters, having deleterious effects on emotions, cognitive capacity, and fine-motor skills. Patience, empathy, cheerfulness, efficiency, and speed were repeatedly mentioned—and observed in the fieldwork—as traits that waned as fatigue mounted. With fatigue, work becomes burdensome. Thought processes slow. Things that are easily and quickly dispatched when fresh take longer. And in a way that aligns with the survey results presented earlier, technical skills diminish, but many consider them only marginally affected by fatigue. Grumpiness and a loss of speed are quickly acknowledged in a way that a loss of proficiency with instruments and one's hands is not. Grumpy and sluggish surgeons may not be their best, but they are still capable.

Residents, in particular, do not trivialize fatigue, and are quick to acknowledge it and describe their experiences. One recounted a recent shift and what it entailed:

> *Is it your experience that long shifts diminish cognitive or physical aspects of surgical performance?* I think so. I think there comes a limit as to how many hours you can physically be awake and working. For example, I worked Saturday. I took call without an intern. So I was by myself all day and all night Saturday. By Sunday morning after being up all night and not sleeping at all I wasn't on my game as much as I would've been twelve hours before. So I think there's a limit to what we can manage. *Could you illustrate that a bit? What aspects of your game do you think get eroded when you're working that long?* Your attention span is a little decreased. Your alertness is decreased. I think your technical skills are hindered just a little bit. Not because you can't do it, but because you just want to get it over with. . . . But technically I think you're just a little slower and maybe not as attentive to fine detail as you would be if you were well rested. (PGY2-F)

Most comments mentioned a loss of speed, typified by the following observation:

> For me, being really tired means that things that would be second nature for me I have to think about more. It's like my mind gets stuck and slow, like a computer with viruses or something. (PGY4-F)

Many spoke of reaching a point where they "want to get it over with," as in the comment above, or, in another, "focused on churning the work out and getting done" (PGY3-M). At a certain point, an adequate decision or action suffices, and any pretense of optimal care vanishes. In this connection, several residents described how they did more "phone call management"— making care decisions over the phone rather than going to see the patient— when awakened at night:

> *Could you give me a better sense of the kinds of things that become more challenging as a shift gets longer?* Certainly, if you are in house, I find it really hard when I'm sleeping and then get a call from a nurse. I find it hard to drag myself out of bed to go see something that I should probably go and see. But you try to rationalize things in your own mind so that maybe it's not significant and doesn't really need anything more than an answer over the phone rather than going to see that patient. (PGY4-F)

Fatigue can also make it difficult to recognize the importance of particular pieces of information. As an illustration, one resident (PGY3-M) described being in the operating room at 7:30 a.m. after what he called an "unbelievably brutal" night of call. The case was an arteriovenous (AV) fistula on a patient with end stage renal failure—an elective operation on blood vessels that aims to prompt a vein to grow larger and stronger to create a better, long-term access point for hemodialysis. Before the attending entered the room, the anesthesiologist announced that the patient's potassium level was seven. The resident explained how he heard the value but did not respond, even though he knew full well that it was a potentially fatal lab value. Once in the room, the attending immediately canceled the case after hearing the lab value and questioned the resident's medical knowledge. For the resident, it was fatigue, not a lack of medical knowledge, that slowed his comprehension and response.

Faculty focused on similar themes as they described fatigue, but offered a distinctive twist. Nearly all paired comments about fatigue-induced losses of efficiency, fine-motor skills, and good humor with statements about how such losses had little-to-no bearing on what really matters—patient outcomes and safety. Residents often voiced the same sentiments, but rarely coupled the issues as tightly. Consider a typical comment:

> *Is it your sense that long shifts diminish cognitive or physical aspects of surgical performance?* Well, I feel like there may be data that show that in certain tasks, like if you're putting pegs in a pegboard or something. But when you're doing surgery, if you're really tired, you're going to be more likely to break the suture when you're tying the knot. And is that significant? I don't know. Does it take you a little bit longer? Do you have to maybe dissect that tissue plane a little bit more

slowly? But I don't see where people are cutting and making holes in bowel that they otherwise wouldn't have if they were well rested. Do you see what I'm saying? *So there may be some loss, but it's not enough to think that it represents a danger?* Right. It's not like you're falling asleep and having a car crash in the OR! (A-F)

Attending surgeons believe there are, most typically, no victims of fatigue. Another described fatigue similarly, emphasizing a loss of speed and cheer without any real loss for patients:

Do you think you are about as good after you've been up that long working as you are earlier in a shift [we were speaking mid-morning after the surgeon had been in the hospital all night and had just completed a scheduled 7:30 a.m. case]? No, there's no way! I mean, does that mean it might take me an extra five, ten minutes to do the same case? Maybe. Does that mean that I'm grumpier and less pleasant to work with? Sure. Does that mean that my thought process isn't as clear? Sure. I mean, you're not superhuman. It has to be worse. But not worse to the point where patients are in danger or outcomes are adversely effected and things like that. (A-F)

Residents commonly echoed those sentiments, but occasionally expressed concerns about how fatigue-related deficits might be consequential. As residents described them, mistakes in plans, paperwork, or medical records that might in theory harm patients were usually subject to oversight by others and could thus be caught before becoming consequential. A chief resident noted how this could lead to mistakes after rounding on patients:

If you're rounding on a service, and the rounds generate a list of fifteen or twenty things to do, I think details can fall through the cracks a little more easily when you are really tired. Are they life threatening? Probably not. Do they get caught by someone else? Maybe. But I think you're less on your game when you're really tired. (PGY5-F)

In addition, quite a few residents recounted instances of fatigue-related memory lapses. Consider an example from another chief resident:

As a junior resident, especially, there were some very busy nights on call. You push yourself to the point where you become really sleepy. I have ordered stuff before on call that I don't remember having ordered. Some nurse calls on a verbal order. I'll come in the next day. I happen to notice on the chart, "verbal order for X." I'm like, "that wasn't a bad idea, but I don't remember saying that. I don't remember fielding that phone call." That's kind of scary! (PGY5-M)

The comment about whether missteps of this sort were life threatening—"probably not"—or caught by someone else—"maybe"—implies a level of fear that faculty members either did not harbor or refused to voice. So also does the expression "that's kind of scary!" Faculty members generally expressed blunt, categorical views, such as "I've been in this business for twenty years and have never seen a problem because of resident fatigue" (A-M). Those who were less categorical fingered training, not fatigue, as the proximate cause of patient-care problems:

> There are very few mistakes, in my experience, that are due to the number of hours worked at a hospital. What causes errors is a lack of experience and training. So it's my intern and they've just never been told to do X, Y, and Z. Once you're taught, it doesn't make a difference whether you're tired or not. Some people are more tired just coming in first thing in the morning; they actually get better as the day goes by! (A-M)

Overall, surgeons believe that fatigue tends to have deleterious consequences. For most, however, fatigue does not represent an *impairment* that threatens the well-being, outcomes, or safety of patients. One faculty member, after describing fatigue-induced changes in performance, framed the matter in statistical terms: "There is some degradation. But do I think it's a statistically significant degradation? The answer is no" (A-M).

Learning to Work Fatigued

We consider here the third and final cornerstone of fatigue culture: the belief that surgeons *can* and *must* learn to work while fatigued during their residency training. The prevailing view holds that surgeons can learn to function effectively when fatigued, that residency is the best time to acquire that capability, and that working while fatigued becomes easier as surgical and medical skills increase. These are widely held notions, but they have detractors who claim that fatigue culture blinds surgeons to their own limitations. We consider the dominant view first and then turn to dissent.

In the interviews and observations, it was common for surgeons to mention self-selection. The idea is that "everyone knows" surgery is a long-hour field, and medical students who are unaware of that tradition are disabused of their ignorance early in their first surgery rotation. During the fieldwork, a common topic of discussion among new groups of medical students on a surgical service was time—how early days started, how long they were, and how utterly grueling surgery was compared to other rotations. As one resident in the fieldwork put it, "surgeons self-select because you clearly see what surgery is like as a medical student—it'd be crazy to choose surgery if you needed a lot of sleep!" (PGY2-M). An attending spoke about self-selection in a characteristic way:

> Some people have better hands. I think we'd all agree on that. Part of surgery is learned, but I think part of it is an ability that's not just learned. I think the same can be said for fatigue—that some are better at it, at managing it and dealing with it, than others. I think managing fatigue is definitely something that you learn by encountering it. But it's something that you have coming in too. It's not something that everybody can do. (A-M)

A mixture of self-selection and learning is fundamental, as some are thought to be unable to function capably when fatigued, and stories about such people were common.

A central aspect of the occupational culture of surgeons is a focus on experiential learning, with many, especially in the fieldwork, claiming versions of this sentiment: "you don't learn surgery or how to be a surgeon from a book." In this connection, a widespread belief is that the experience and consequences of fatigue can be altered—and to a large degree minimized—by conditioning, experience, and to some extent an academic awareness of fatigue.

> *Would you say that you can learn how to recognize the signs and symptoms of fatigue and how to work capably while fatigued?* Yes, I do. I totally do. Can you make that more academic and educated by giving residents an hour or two of a seminar and present here's what happens when you become fatigued? Sure. If you're on call and you know that this could be a busy night, but things are quiet right now and tucked in, then try to take a nap! You can be told that—and they are—or you can kind of learn it by living it. Probably going forward, being told it more often would be a good thing to do, but that's no substitute for experience. Everyone will learn how to deal with long days. Yes, you certainly learn how to function when tired, and that's pretty much the same for everything we do—encounter it, learn from it, become better at it. (A-M)

Academic presentations about the consequences of fatigue and strategies to mitigate it were mandated by the ACGME in 2011 and are shared with all residents and attendings. They are, however, seen as "no substitute for experience." Learning to work while fatigued was often compared to the training of elite athletes and soldiers.

The military trains their people under extreme conditions so they can tolerate it when they go to Afghanistan. For the Tour de France, riders train under extreme conditions. They know how hard they can push, when they need to rest, and how to rest efficiently. I think it is a skill that you learn through experience. I think that physicians, and surgeons in particular, have learned how to apply the mental and physical concentration when it counts to get the job done. (A-M)

To a significant extent, then, surgeons maintain that fatigue can be countered through physical and mental conditioning gained through experience.

Both residents and faculty members also believe that fatigue can be offset by deeply established skills acquired over time. A resident put it this way:

My experience has been that many people are struck by how long surgeons work, and wonder how anyone could be skilled and capable after working for twenty-four or more hours. Can you explain how that's possible? Well, it's kind of like riding a bike. Even when you're tired you can still get on a bike and ride it. And that's kind of like surgery. Once you've obtained skills at a certain level, you can still perform with fatigue but your critical-thinking and, maybe, problem-solving skills are a little less, but you're still able to get the job done even with fatigue. But I think you need to be trained at that level where your skills come, kind of, automatically. A resident wouldn't be able to do complicated cases with fatigue as well as the attending surgeon would because they have mastered the skill and it's more automatic to them. (PGY4-M)

Another resident emphasized that the kind of skill that offsets fatigue could be more nearly general medical knowledge than a set of procedure-related movements or steps.

I think in a general sense that if you get too tired and run down, it is easy to forget things and incorrectly write things, especially I would say as an intern or a two [second-year resident] when things are often times not as much in a context in your head. They are more of a list of things. (PGY4-F)

A faculty member voiced a similar belief, couched as a general advantage of experience:

I think there's no question that an excessive period of time, particularly for people with minimal knowledge, is probably not as safe. As you gain more knowledge, you react more by a patterned or automatic reaction than trying to compute it cognitively. So I think a senior resident probably has a better capability of pulling a twenty-four-hour shift than a junior resident who's overwhelmed and lost, but less so than an attending. (A-M)

Key to the skill-offsets-fatigue belief is the emergence of automaticity (Moulton et al. 2007), whereby capability develops to the point that skillful task performance requires little-to-no effortful control. During the fieldwork, it became obvious that experienced surgeons can and do perform complex operations while discussing any number of topics. As in many endeavors, what seems complex and difficult for newcomers can become easy for those with substantial experience. What is not clear, however, is whether fatigued surgeons manage unexpected or novel situations well, shifting out of automaticity and "slowing down when they should" (Moulton et al. 2007). One surgeon, when asked about this, responded as follows:

> As you go through your surgical training, it becomes a matter of pattern recognition. You've seen this pattern of disease enough times. There are very few really bad red herrings that can get you into trouble in the course of your surgical career. And so much of it is just pattern recognition in the OR and things that are relatively rote. So I think you can do some of those things when you are a little fatigued without degrading the patient's care. (A-M)

The expression "some of those things" in the last sentence of the comment leaves room for exceptions, but the main emphasis is on routine patterns, what a surgeon in the fieldwork eloquently called the "algorithms of experience." This position, however, is not in step with much of the next chapter on patient handoffs, where "relatively rote" is downplayed by surgeons in favor of "often idiosyncratic." We will explore this issue more fully in that chapter.

All surgeons emphasized that the best time to encounter and learn to manage fatigue was in residency, when support is present, not during practice, when support may be in short supply. Residents anticipated having to take long call and work long days when they began practice. For example, expressions of this sort were common: "Forcing residents to work all night is good because when you graduate and you're an attending surgeon, it's not a nine-to-five job" (PGY4-M). Another described how long shifts provide essential preparation for practice:

> There's value to learning how to take care of call for more than twenty-four hours. We need to have at least a taste of that experience, because poof—we are attendings! And if you've never had the experience of taking call for more than sixteen

hours, and then all of a sudden you are expected to take twenty-four-hour call or more by your partners and the group you are working in, that's bad. I'd feel under prepared. You need to know what that's like. A bit of constraint is good—certainly I don't think we should be taking thirty-six-hour call every three nights. But once a week? That's not that bad. (PGY3-M)

Faculty members recounted practice requirements—or pointed to them during the fieldwork—to justify exposing residents to fatigue as an educational necessity.

There are times when you go for thirty hours. You're on call, it's a bad weekend, and you're operating. If you're not trained to go through that, when you actually get to the real life environment, you won't function well and you're going to be a danger to your patients. So that amounts to a lack of proper training. (A-M)

It would be difficult to overstate how critical the real-life theme is for fatigue culture. Attending surgeons and residents consistently argued that it is imperative that residencies prepare new surgeons for the schedules and hours they will encounter in real-life practice. Many used the disconnect between hour protections in residency and a lack of protection and support in practice as grounds for opposing the reforms as "fantasy" that might yield unwanted and unintended consequences. Consider, for example, this argument:

I fear that the work hour restrictions are going to increase the chance that patients will have adverse outcomes due to attending physician fatigue. We're creating an environment in which residents don't have to learn fatigue mitigation strategies. I learned to deal with fatigue as a resident during my long work hours. I learned how to take short, twenty, thirty, maybe forty minute naps that would re-energize me, enable me to get by and to be functional. I learned when I had had enough and couldn't go on anymore because I was pushed to my limits at times. By failing to put residents in those positions now, at least to the degree that we used to, I fear that we're going to not only hamper their educational experience because they're not getting as many cases, but even more fundamentally, we're failing to train them how to overcome and work through fatigue. It's just like any other type of training—you get better through experience. (A-F)

Without question, the ideas presented thus far about the need to learn to work while fatigued dominate the culture of fatigue. A small minority of surgeons, however, voiced strong concerns about this culture. For them, the culture includes more than beliefs about how surgeons must encounter and learn to work capably and confidently while fatigued. It also includes beliefs about surgical toughness and how those who fail to push through fatigue are flawed or, in common parlance, "weak." These beliefs clearly dovetail with those described by Cassell (1998) and Kellogg (2011). In this connection, some residents described how they would "plow on to appear tough—that's really common, really common—even when I was really sleepy" (PGY5-M). Others directly noted the attribution of weakness:

> A problem with self-assessment and no limits is that no one is going to admit to being too tired—or they're going to be reluctant to do that because they'll look weak. We fight through being tired. You learn to work through it and ignore your fatigue. *Is admitting to being tired a sign of weakness?* Yes, absolutely! I think we fight fatigue for other reasons too—it's a sign of ownership and feeling of responsibility to take care of your own work. I think it's common in medicine, but I think it applies even more so to surgery. (PGY2-F)

Several attendings echoed those ideas, noting that "there's no question there's machoism in our response to fatigue—you know, the I-can-do-it-I'll-be-fine way we respond" (A-M) and that "to ask for help or to tell someone we're too tired is a sign of weakness" (A-M). Concerns about attributions of weakness and a desire to uphold the tough-surgeon ideal incline surgeons to ignore signs and symptoms of fatigue impairment. For this minority of surgeons, externally imposed limits on hours are essential. Consider the following comment, which is typical in suggesting that constraints need to be blended with elements of flexibility:

> The rigidity of hour limits is a problem for surgery, but to me, limits are reasonable because we are very bad at policing ourselves in terms of fatigue. I think the culture's better now than it used to be. It's this whole continuity-of-care thing, especially among those of us who trained a little bit earlier. We pride ourselves in making sure we don't leave with things undone—you don't leave a sick patient for somebody else to take care of. It would take a dramatic culture change for us to be able to police ourselves about fatigue—so that people don't think they have to keep going when they are too tired. They would not feel that they would be punished or looked down upon if they admit that they're tired or feel unsafe. So we probably do need external stop signs and less discretion. But some kind of flexibility needs to be built in for patient safety, for purposes of education, and because there will always be times when there just isn't anyone else who can take over. (A-M)

When compared with typical comments about fatigue, this is a remarkable statement, and one that may eventually come to be embraced by a larger portion of surgeons. Key to the comment is a concern about continuity of care, a core issue that we address in the next chapter. It joins fatigue culture as a second primary reason surgeons struggle with work-hour reforms.

Reflection: Gentlemen, This Is What You Signed Up For

The first month of my internship year was spent working in one of the busier emergency rooms in the country. The staffing was a second-year resident and myself. We worked twenty-four hours on, twenty-four hours off for the full month. It was not unusual for me to personally see seventy patients over the twenty-four hours, which could include up to a half dozen or more major traumas. I remember at times simultaneously seeing and processing seven patients at a time. Trying to gain all the learning I could out of those interactions was exhilarating as well as terrifying. There were times I would realize twelve or more hours into a shift that I hadn't stopped once, and really needed to find a bathroom. Sleep was rare; pauses in the pace gave us a chance to "catch up" on the paperwork, which it literally was at that point, some thirty-five years ago now.

A significant help as I tried to process the quantum leap in workload complexity this represented compared to anything I had experienced in medical school was the presence of medical students. A frequent and time-consuming task we would encounter were the proverbial "AOB head lacs"—intoxicated patients (AOB meaning alcohol on breath) who fell or had an altercation and suffered a facial or head laceration that needed repair. Students were delighted to gain experience sewing up such patients after we had made sure they didn't have more significant underlying injuries. Not getting tied down in such procedural elements of ER activity made it possible for me to keep seeing, triaging, and making dispositions of the steady stream of patients who would come in over the course of the shift. Perish the thought that I wouldn't have the eager students there to help! Unfortunately for me, being assigned to that rotation in July at the beginning of the academic year, my rotation in the ER overlapped precisely with the students' summer break from medical school duties.

It wasn't until a couple weeks into the experience that I had my first real brush with the physical effects of fatigue. One day I was in our apartment, asleep on the couch during my twenty-four-hour off period. The period of the month where the students were no longer available had just ensued. My wife heard me yelling in my sleep from the couch in a virtual hallucination, repeating the phrase, "I need my students, where are my students?" She woke me up, we had a good laugh, and life went on, with or without the students.

Later that month, after a particularly busy twenty-four hours, we were having our "sign out" with the ER director. It was beneath him to speak directly to me as an intern, and my only interactions with him in general were to hear what he said to my second-year resident as he thumbed through the charts of every patient record generated by us from our shift. There would almost never be comments of praise, but there was plenty of feedback if we missed giving a patient a tetanus shot, or failed in other ways, which he had an uncanny eye for finding in our scribbled notes regarding our patients' care. On this particular day, my colleague and I must have looked a bit more tired, disheveled, and discouraged by the pace of our prior twenty-four hours than usual. Without lifting his eyes from the records in front of him, he calmly and evenly said to us, "Gentlemen, this is what you signed up for."

I went on over the course of that year and my subsequent years of training to learn to face and manage fatigue in the course of my duties. Generally speaking, I found that I and my colleagues seemed able to work in difficult and exhausting settings when we had to, and that the "band of brothers/sisters" mentality I shared with my fellow residents allowed us to cope well with long shifts and the pressures my first month of internship had baptized me into. Occasionally I would see colleagues seem to shift or shunt work to others when they were tired or stressed, but generally this seemed to most of us to correlate with character patterns in such individuals rather than physical limitations. Periods of every-other-night call or particularly busy shifts often became more of a badge of honor than a perceived liability, and over time, bred a certain confidence in the face of adversity and challenge that seemed almost a psychological necessity to keep doing what we felt were meant to do.

As I reflect back on those initial experiences now, I see a more systemic side to the issue of surgeon fatigue and its management, one that I don't think I understood then. It is no less true now than it was when I trained that our entire healthcare system relies heavily, particularly in high need and low resource areas such as our major urban centers or even the Veterans Health Administration (VHA) system, on the labor provided by medical and surgical trainees. Most surgeons in practice routinely work well over sixty hours per week, and eighty or more hours is not infrequent. For the foreseeable future, and in all likelihood in a more acute way in years to come (if the workforce prophets are correct), it will be necessary for surgeons, particularly general surgeons and those committed to the front line, broad, and urgent surgical needs of our population, to put in hours that require work in the face of fatigue. Job sharing, back-up systems (which themselves only obligate providers to more times committed to being available for duty), use of advanced practice providers or other practice extenders, and other strategies notwithstanding, there don't appear to be straightforward or adequately resourced opportunities to change this equation.

All this of course begs the question, if we are there to serve the public and its needs with skill and compassion, where is the right "balance" between service and continuity of care versus provider fatigue? When does the care of the caregiver take priority if that person is to render care worthy of our calling? This is all the more pertinent in the modern era, given the emergence of data that correlates empathy on the part of the provider (perhaps one of the first casualties of excessive fatigue) with patient experience, compliance with a care plan, and outcomes.

The data presented in this chapter highlights the fact that surgeons and surgical trainees recognize the effects of fatigue on their functions, but also believe functioning in the face of fatigue is necessary to their role. Knowing one's limits through experience gained in a supervised and supported setting, developing systems that attempt to manage issues such as call frequency and intensity and post-call workload, and building communities of practice that allow flexibility in our responses to the unpredictable nuances of urgent patient care may all have their place in mitigating fatigue's effects. That all being recognized, unless someone finds a few thousand extra providers, deployed strategically based on demographic need, it appears that for most surgeons, and for the foreseeable future, my erstwhile ER mentor may have summarized things well: this is what we signed up for.

CHAPTER 2

Patient Handoffs

Can't Colleagues Assume Care Capably?

Fatigue can be a beast. Not always, but sometimes. I've done things I can't remember doing, like the verbal order I just told you about. That's a little dangerous. But I've got to be honest with you. I think the danger from handoffs is greater than fatigue-related errors from people working lots of hours. (PGY5-M)

Midway through a complex and lengthy vascular operation observed from the foot of the table, the attending surgeon exclaimed loudly to his third-year assistant that Voltaire was right: perfect *is* the enemy of good. He then described how choice and technique must be informed by frequent and prudent assessments of relative risks and rewards. Gains from painstakingly careful—but inevitably slow—dissections or suturing can be more than offset by greater blood loss, continued administration of general anesthetics and fluids, and a myriad of other operative risks. The pursuit of perfection for one segment of an operation may induce problems in others and yield a net loss if not catastrophe. In this and many other moments during the fieldwork, the weighing of relative risks and rewards emerged as central to surgical work and culture.

In that light, it is no surprise that surgeons overwhelmingly view efforts to curtail fatigue as but one factor in a larger risk-reward calculus. Shorter shifts, fewer total weekly work hours, and mandatory time away from the hospital reduce fatigue, as many surgeons acknowledge, but those changes also introduce other risk factors. Chief among those is a loss in what is uniformly called the continuity of care for patients. Continuity is lost when information about patients is transferred from one caregiver (or team) to another during what is called a patient handoff (also called a hand-over, check-out, or sign-out). Prominent surgeons (e.g., Fischer, Healy, and Britt 2009, 136) have criticized limits on resident shifts largely by stressing that such restrictions undermine what they call "the fundamental principle of continuity of care." They pose the matter this way: Does a patient receive better care from a fatigued surgeon who knows them well and was present at the operation, or a fresh one who knows little about them and was not present for their operation? This is the fatigue-versus-familiarity tradeoff, and it is key to understanding why surgeons struggle with work-hour reforms.

This tradeoff has long been present in the 24/7/365 world of acute healthcare. More than forty years ago, Zerubavel's groundbreaking *Patterns of Time in Hospital Life* showed that both physicians and hospitals viewed changes of personnel and the transferring of responsibility for a patient's care from one physician to another as a "necessary evil" (1979, 42–49). In the past, discontinuities in patient care were minimized by having few shift changes, by fostering temporally flexible and long work schedules among physicians, and by emphasizing the importance of medical records. Zerubavel argued that records were a "major facilitator" and an "effective mechanism" of functional interchangeability, the ability of one physician to smoothly substitute for another (45–46). In addition, he argued that "the belief that medical responsibility is not mechanically transferrable from one physician to another also *precludes temporally rigid work schedules* which are based on fixed leaving times" (49, emphasis added). For him, temporally flexible work schedules and patient charts permitted functional interchangeability among the physicians and residents he observed. However, temporal flexibility is now ceding to rigidity, whereby clocks—not the ebb and flow of patient care needs—increasingly guide professional engagement among residents.

Two elements of the reforms are central to understanding the fatigue-versus-familiarity tradeoff. First, they require residents to leave the hospital *sooner* and *more fully* than in the past. By sooner, we mean that shift lengths, call schedules, and overall work weeks have contracted, which imply that any given resident is in the hospital less and thus must relinquish and thereby transfer care more often to another person or team. By more fully, we mean that residents are not routinely supposed to return to the hospital to help out with care if a need arises once they leave. Nor are they to routinely field phone calls and check patient records remotely if concerns or questions arise about a patient. When they leave the hospital, residents are now more nearly off duty and unavailable than ever before.

A second important element of the reforms is the widespread adoption of approaches to covering patients at night that had in the past been uncommon. Many programs adopted what is called night float, which involves a team of residents who start work in the evening (often at 5 or 6 p.m.) and then leave in the morning (often at 6 or 7 a.m.). They maintain that schedule for five days (often Sunday through Thursday) and then work part of a day on a different schedule. Residents are commonly assigned to night float for stretches of at least a month, during which time they are not attached to a particular surgical service. Instead, they cover patients on all of the surgical services, thereby engaging in what is called cross coverage. Another format for night coverage of patients is a more purely call-based form of cross coverage. In this format, a small number of residents who worked a day shift stay for the night, providing coverage for all patients, not just those assigned to the service on which they worked during the day. Night float and cross coverage mean that residents care for a wider range of patients at night, many of whom are completely unfamiliar. In the past, residents were not split into distinct day and night staff; most commonly, a resident on each service would work during the day, night, and then a portion of the following day. In that way, someone who was present on the service during the day would still be in the hospital at night should complications arise. Hour restrictions mean that few residents are now permitted to stay at night after working during the day, thus sharpening the discontinuity between day and night staff.

Our aim here is to explore these issues in some detail. What about continuity of care and the familiarity that it supposedly permits are so important in the minds of surgeons? Why and how do restrictions on hours worked—all, of course, in the name of fatigue mitigation—hamper continuity of care? Do patient charts permit one surgeon to step in for another? In our view, these are critical issues, as they shed light on whether surgical work hinges more on *individuals* than an *organization*. In short, does surgical work demand that a particular surgeon be intimately and continuously involved in a patient's care? Or can several surgeons safely and effectively care for a patient, thus allowing them to play more *team-based* rather than *individual* roles in pursuing continuity of care?

Information on these issues was obtained in several main ways. The fieldwork offered many opportunities to observe the comings and goings of surgeons, acute care challenges that would often span many hours, and the construction and use of both patient charts and so-called "op notes" (the document that summarizes an operation). At the fieldwork site, nine follow-up interviews, three with residents and six with attendings, were conducted to draw out and clarify observations. Those interviews focused on handoff issues and allowed for extensive probes about the construction, use, and value of patient records. The three waves of multi-center studies offered a chance to pose survey and interview questions that yielded most of the information used here. We begin by highlighting the results of twelve survey items asked over three waves. We then elaborate and clarify those patterns by drawing on two main interview questions. A first was quite general, asking surgeons whether they believed that the reforms had any bearing, good or bad, on patient care. That question often sparked comments about continuity, fatigue, and trade-offs between the two. A second was the question about fatigue, drawn on in the last chapter, which asked surgeons whether long shifts diminished their cognitive or physical capacities. Responses to that question often had a "yes—but" format, wherein fatigue was acknowledged but described as a relative risk alongside discontinuities in care. Together, the responses provide key insights into the fatigue-versus-familiarity tradeoff, a primary reason surgeons struggle with the reforms.

A Survey-Based Overview

Table 2.1 contains results from twelve questions, with four collected during the first wave, seven during the second, and one during the third. Questions are broken out by wave and numbered to ease the discussion. As in the last chapter, cells in the table contain results for the percent of residents and attendings who "agree or strongly agree," along with the significance of the difference between the figures for the two groups. The table is best grasped by first looking at the column of results for faculty. We then compare the two groups.

Three patterns stand out when looking at results for faculty. First, there is little overall support for the notion that the reforms improved patient care. Items 1, 5, 6, and 7 draw little support, with no more than 10 percent of attendings in agreement that the reforms either improved care or reduced the likelihood of errors in patient care. Second, attendings believe that the reforms decreased the continuity of patient care (item 2 at 90 percent) and introduced new challenges with respect to information transfer and communication (item 8 at 78 percent), familiarity with patients (item 9 at 82 percent), and the doctor-patient relationship (item 10 at 70 percent). A substantial 61 percent of attendings believe that night float (item 3) diminishes the quality of patient care. And third, all three waves probed whether a lack of familiarity with a patient is a more important cause of errors than fatigue (items 4, 11, and 12). Attendings side with a lack of familiarity, as the percentages range

TABLE 2.1. Beliefs about Duty-Hour Restrictions, Continuity of Care, and Quality of Care among General Surgery Faculty and Residents

Item	Data Collection Wave / Exact Question Wording	% Agree or Strongly Agree	
		Residents	Faculty
	WAVE 1 QUESTIONS	N = 112	N = 145
1	The shift to the eighty-hour rules improved the quality of care provided to surgical patients.	32	8*
2	The shift to the eighty-hour rules decreased the continuity of care provided to surgical patients.	71	90*
3	The night float system diminishes the quality of patient care.	43	61*
4	Lack of familiarity with a patient is a more important cause of errors than fatigue.	76	92*
	WAVE 2 QUESTIONS	N = 305	N = 286
5	The eighty-hour rules improve the overall quality of patient care.	29	6*
6	Studies demonstrate that the eighty-hour rules enhance patient safety and outcomes.	17	7*
7	The eighty-hour rules decrease the overall likelihood of errors in patient care.	36	10*
8	The eighty-hour rules compromise patient care due to problems with information transfer and communication.	35	78*
9	The eighty-hour rules diminish residents' familiarity with patients.	39	82*
10	Frequent transfers of patient-care responsibility strain the doctor-patient relationship.	39	70*
11	Lack of familiarity with a patient is a more important cause of errors than fatigue.	68	72
	WAVE 3 QUESTION	N = 286	N = 279
12	Lack of familiarity with a patient is a more important cause of errors than fatigue.	78	89*

Notes. An asterisk (*) next to the second percentage for a pair of contrasts indicates a significant difference in the percentages at the .05 level; a plus sign (+) indicates significance at the .10 level (from Pearson's chi-square tests).

from a low of 72 percent in the second wave to 92 and 89 in waves one and three, respectively. Fatigue matters, as we described in the previous chapter, but familiarity and the continuity it implies are seen as more consequential.

Comparisons between attendings and residents show clear and often sizable gaps, as all but one item (11) indicates a significant difference, and the average difference is 22 percentage points. In many cases, the results for residents nonetheless align with attendings. Fewer than 36 percent of residents, for example, believe that the reforms improved care or reduced the likelihood of errors in patient care (items 1, 5, 6, and 7). They also agree, overall, that the reforms decreased the continuity of patient care (item 2 at 71 percent) and that a lack of familiarity is more important than fatigue when it comes to errors (items 4, 11, and 12 at between 68 and 78 percent). Gaps are most notable on item 3, which is about night float, and items 8 through 10, which deal with information, communication, and doctor-patient relationships. For all four items, faculty largely agree, but residents disagree. All four target resident behavior, not just the reforms in a more general way, and our sense from discussions after the survey administration is that some saw these questions as impugning them, not the broader culture and social organization of residency.

Analyses of the role of faculty and resident gender are found in Table 2.2. The results for attending surgeons are clear and consistent: gender plays little to no role in shaping their views. Given the relatively small sample sizes of female attendings, especially in the smaller first wave, we pay attention to gaps, not just indications of statistical significance, to guide that conclusion. The average gap is less than 4 percentage points, whereas the largest is 10. Among residents, the evidence shows a generally similar pattern with a few exceptions. Here, three items differ significantly (items 1, 2, and 9), all showing that females see more merit (item 1) and fewer problems (items 2 and 9) with the reforms than their male peers. Among residents, the average percentage-point gap by gender is 10, with the two largest gaps—27 and 30 points—occurring with items 1 and 2, both from the earliest wave of data collection. Early evidence of an occasionally sizable gender gap has given way, over time, to views that are largely similar.

We also considered potential differences between those in academic and community programs and those with more or less experience. As with the analysis of fatigue in the previous chapter, differences were not common, and gaps that were significant in a statistical sense were not large or meaningful. For example, for item 12, more experienced attendings (those with 11 or more years of experience) were 8 percentage points more likely to agree (90 vs. 82 percent) than their less experienced peers, but a difference of that magnitude hardly constitutes a sharp dividing line between colleagues. Similarly, and on the same item, 87 percent residents with three or more years of experience agreed compared with 74 percent of those in their first and second years. Again, while the difference is significant in a statistical sense, the primary finding remains the same: strong majorities of both groups claim that a lack of familiarity is a more important cause of errors than fatigue. We now unpack these general patterns with the qualitative evidence.

TABLE 2.2. Beliefs about Duty-Hour Restrictions, Continuity of Care, and Quality of Care among General Surgery Faculty and Residents by Gender

| | | % Agree or Strongly Agree | | | |
| | | Attendings | | Residents | |
Item	Data CollectionWave / Brief Question Wording	Men	Women	Men	Women
	WAVE 1 QUESTIONS	N = 125	N=18	N = 79	N=29
1	The eighty-hour rules improved the quality of care	10	0	25	52*
2	The eighty-hour rules decreased the continuity of care	90	94	78	48*
3	The night float system diminishes the quality of care	62	61	44	32
4	Lack of familiarity is more important for errors than fatigue	92	94	80	69
	WAVE 2 QUESTIONS	N = 231	N=51	N = 206	N=97
5	The eighty-hour rules improve the overall quality of care	6	4	73	69
6	Studies demonstrate that the eighty-hour rules enhance safety and outcomes	7	6	15	20
7	The eighty-hour rules decrease errors in patient care	10	12	34	39
8	The eighty-hour rules compromise care due to problems with information transfer and communication	79	75	34	36
9	The eighty-hour rules diminish residents' familiarity with patients	82	82	43	30*
10	Frequent transfers of patients strain the doctor-patient relationship	71	61	62	58
11	Lack of familiarity is more important for errors than fatigue	73	69	65	75
	WAVE 3 QUESTION	N = 203	N=73	N = 177	N=107
12	Lack of familiarity is a more important cause of errors than fatigue	88	95	79	78

Notes. An asterisk (*) next to the second percentage for a pair of contrasts indicates a significant difference in the percentages at the .05 level; a plus sign (+) indicates significance at the .10 level (from Pearson's chi-square tests).

Fatigue versus Familiarity

A contrast between tired caretakers who know their patients and fresh ones who do not was drawn repeatedly during the field observations and interviews, often by residents as well as attendings. Unless fatigue was extreme, the vast majority argued that patients receive more benefits from caregiver familiarity than harm from caregiver fatigue. Knowing what has happened to patients—especially via *direct* experience with their care on the ward and in the operating room—was viewed as critical, even if the caregiver was diminished by fatigue. Consider the following comment by a resident near the end of her second year of training:

> *Do you feel that there is a link between the eighty-hour rules and care, to either help or enhance it or to maybe degrade or erode the quality of patient care?* Absolutely. It totally degrades patient care. *How so?* I've actually not seen benefits. What I have seen is harmful. I don't care how tired I am. I know my patients better than anybody. I physically examine them every day. I admitted them. I wrote their H & P [history and physical]. I've seen all their labs. I've seen all their images. You can't have a night float system that comes in and knows that. And to care properly, you need to be there on rounds. I'm seeing every patient and writing every note—night float isn't. Therefore, I feel like even after I've been awake for thirty-six hours or however long, I can still make better judgement calls on my patients because I know them better than the on-call team. (PGY2-F)

Direct involvement in the day-to-day aspects of care, and participating in rounds, where patients are often discussed in detail and plans are formulated, are key to "judgment calls" made by residents. Those judgments affect the care they provide, the perceived seriousness and meaning of changes in a patient's condition, and whether and when they consult an attending about a patient. All of those bear on the care patients receive.

Attending surgeons were quick to note the importance of knowing details about a patient's condition and what happened during an operation. The fatigue-versus-familiarity tradeoff is clearly evident in the words of the following attending surgeon:

> *In your experience, is there an important change in your cognitive or physical performance as shift length increases?* I definitely think that there's a change. The hit to performance might be significant at twenty-four hours or even eighteen. But what you have to weigh are the consequences of changing at that time. Discontinuities could be harmful if you're in the middle of a case that's been really technically difficult and there's been many aspects about that case that are unique and you don't have time to communicate that. Or you're about to make a key decision about taking back a patient [to the operating room] that hinges on a lot of information that's unique to being in the operating room and no one else has that information. In situations like that, even if the performance hit for fatigue is high, the consequences of not having that person there are even higher. So sure, I believe fatigue decreases performance, but there's no fixed time at which the risk-benefit tradeoff is more favorable to changing surgeons. (A-M)

The statement includes a common claim, namely that both fatigue and familiarity matter, but that the costs of fatigue must be weighed against the importance of familiarity. That assessment depends heavily on contextual factors, not simply on the fact that someone has worked a particular number of hours. Among surgeons, it is simplistic and wrong to conclude that fatigue inevitably or even regularly offsets potential benefits from continued care by a particular surgeon. For them, a judgment needs to be made rather than a fixed rule followed.

Why View Changes of Personnel as Problematic?

As the fieldwork and interviews unfolded, it became clear that shift changes and handoffs were widely viewed as a weak link in the provision of safe, high-quality patient care. Moreover, the importance of direct experience was pointed to time and again, suggesting that being present during critical moments in a patient's care—as opposed to hearing or reading about what transpired—provided a surgeon with a distinct advantage. Both ideas are evident in the comments drawn on thus far. What has not been clear, however, are the main lines of reasoning that support each conclusion. Handoffs are problematic, say surgeons, for three main reasons: first, it is easy to inadvertently omit important issues during a handoff; second, there is too much information to convey everything that might be important, even if everything of value comes to mind during a handoff; and third, some concerns are difficult to explain, verbalize, and hence share. Moreover, surgeons argue that patient records are a poor substitute for direct experience and good oral exchanges during handoffs because they tend to be incomplete and out of date.

The handoffs that took place during the fieldwork were substantially similar in format to those described in the interviews. Each surgical service maintained a spreadsheet file containing basic information about every patient on the service, where each patient was a row in a grid that fit easily on a single side of a sheet of paper. The service list contained columns for each patient's name, medical record number, date of admission, attending surgeon, diagnosis or procedure that was performed, and, very briefly, pending matters such as studies or procedures or a plan for the patient. Handoffs typically involve an oral exchange—in person or over the phone—between one resident and another whereby they "run the list." To run the list when handing over a service from day to night, the day resident would highlight pending studies, needed procedures, patients that particularly concerned them, and things that needed to be followed up during the night. When the night float team went off duty in the morning, handoffs to day residents noted any patient who had changed location or status, study results that had been pending but were now available, any interventions performed, and information about new patients that had been admitted during the night. In some cases, both residents had a printout of the service's patient list in hand at the time of the handoff on which the incoming resident could, and often would, jot a few notes. In other cases, one or both parties lacked the list and would simply talk and listen during the handoff.

Many described how it was easy to forget to mention something important and impossible to deliberately and fully cover everything that might prove to be important. For example, trauma services frequently have a lot of patients, some of whom stay for months.

> Some services have an incredible volume. You know, on trauma, if they have thirty patients on the floor, there's no way I'm going to remember every single thing about every single patient. Especially since some of the patients have been there for three or four months. (PGY2-F)

A chief resident, in commenting on the problem of covering all known issues, remarked that "no matter how long or detailed your checkout, you are more than likely going to miss some things" (PGY5-M). The problem of forgetting to note something important was excused to some extent by the prevailing view that it is impossible to convey everything.

> *You mentioned earlier that it was harder to care for patients when you're on call at night. Could you say more about that? What's the challenge?* The challenge is that you don't know the day-to-day things. You can be on call at night twelve days into this particular patient's stay. You've had twelve days of notes—you're not really going to sit and read through twelve days of notes to find out what the residents and the attending have said every day and how you've gotten to the point that you've gotten to. That can be challenging. Just not feeling like you know the day-to-day about a patient that you do on your own service. Again, the hope is that's communicated to you when you're on call. However, there's just not enough time to go through the nitty gritty details on every little thing—"well this happened day three, and then this happened day five, and that's why we're here on day twelve." You never know the whole story. (PGY1-F)

Residents need to make educated guesses about which issues are worth noting because the time involved in reviewing every potentially relevant detail of a patient's history and condition would be too great. Patients, they say, are like a book, and a handoff can at best be an executive summary. In addition, many believe that the small number of issues that are most likely to be relevant in a subsequent shift may be obscured or forgotten if too many details are reviewed. But which pieces of information are relevant and which are extraneous can be difficult to know in advance, and of course depend upon medical knowledge and experience.

The difficulties described thus far largely involve failing to mention something that one knows to be important either because it was forgotten or because a complex patient could not be described fully. Two additional issues pose especially thorny challenges to effective handoffs. A first is that some important observations or understandings of a patient's condition are simply difficult to convey effectively to another surgeon. Consider the words of the following resident:

> Even if you get a fantastic checkout from somebody, it's never everything you know if you've been taking care of a patient. Sometimes it's just a gestalt, not details that you can verbalize. I've taken care of patients in the ICU who were very sick. You get to know them so well that just by a small change in their vital signs— which nobody else would notice because they're still within the normal range— you know that something's happening. You've seen how small variations like that made bad things happen. So, I know that I need to start working down this pathway to head off whatever's about to happen. But, you can't necessarily explain or verbalize that to people. It's a sense you get from knowing a patient well. (PGY2-F)

That "sense you get from knowing a patient well" can be difficult to explain or verbalize, a comment often made in connection to operations and the twists and turns they can involve. In her comment, the resident notes how changes in objective information that might be "in the normal range" can nonetheless provide critical clues to emerging problems for a particular patient. Familiarity gained through direct involvement is the bedrock of such intuitions and insights. Surgeons especially highlighted the challenge of conveying findings from neurological or physical exams, which have a subjective component.

> *Could you give me an example of something that's hard to hand off well?* Yeah, there are a lot of things, such as just the amount of tenderness on an abdominal exam. The appreciation for the change in that amount of tenderness is impossible, I think, to tell another doctor how much tenderness they experienced. The only way to do that would be to take the in-coming doctor around with you and examine the patients together. But there's usually not enough time built into the system to allow that sort of evaluation to occur. Even if you had them with you, they would lack the trajectory— what the patient was like two days ago, three days ago versus today. (A-M)

Another attending summarized this problem in the following way:

> In general surgery, in particular, there are some things that are not measurable
> that you now need to pass off, like physical exams or neurological status. It may
> be different at six o'clock in the morning than six o'clock in the afternoon, but if
> you have different people evaluating those things, you may end up with differ-
> ent interpretations. You can try to document it, but some things are intangibles.
> It's more of a feel thing. So it's a tradeoff. (A-M)

These and other comments indicate that some situations present formidable communication challenges. During the fieldwork, surgeons would occasionally remark that a patient "doesn't look right" or that "something seems
wrong." For the most part, those comments, like the quotes presented above,
are intuitions that can be difficult to articulate and share. Another example
involves largely subjective assessments of changes in abdominal tenderness,
which can determine whether and when an operation might be performed. An
awareness of these communication challenges leaves surgeons uneasy about
handoffs and the ability of teams to provide care that equals what is provided
by individuals through continuity of care. As one attending summarized it,
"no matter how perfect your system of information transfer is, there is always
voltage lost across those transfers" (A-M).

A second thorny challenge to effective handoffs springs from the character
of medical records. If oral exchanges during handoffs are hampered by for-
getfulness or brevity, one could imagine how incoming surgeons could dig
through records to fill out their understanding of patients. Zerubavel (1979,
45–46), after all, argued that medical records facilitate and permit one doctor to substitute for another. However, the fieldwork and interviews strongly
suggest that medical records are often incomplete, difficult to comprehend,
or dated. That statement includes progress notes, operative notes, and lab and
imaging results.

Progress notes, which detail patient conditions, orders, and outline the
plan for a patient on a daily basis, are often of limited value because of when
they are written, by whom, and the frequency with which they are updated.
Consider, for example, the following observations:

> *Why is an oral exchange so important? Why can't an in-coming surgeon learn enough*
> *by simply reading the chart and examining the patient?* Most of the notes are writ-
> ten by residents between five and seven in the morning. So notes mostly rehash
> the events from the day before and suppose a potential plan for the day—most of
> the time before the resident has talked to an attending. If events occur and docu-

mentation follows in a chart, you understand the process of the day. However, it doesn't necessarily occur that there will be future notes from that day from that particular team. That doesn't mean that a plan has not been considered or implemented without further documentation in the chart. A CT scan might have been performed, or blood cultures may have been drawn. And although that may be reflected in the orders of the chart or in the labs of the chart, it may not be reflected in the notes of the chart. *Do caretakers just need to be more conscientious about documenting things in patient charts?* Sure, and in some respects that's absolutely true. But in order to get anything done, you have to make choices, and one choice most of us make is to be less compulsive about recording everything. (PGY4-M)

Many factors thus serve to diminish the value of the patient chart, making oral exchanges between surgeons critical.

Attending surgeons made similar comments but also drew out additional challenges when it comes to making significant use of progress and operative notes. What emerges as a strong theme in faculty comments is a relative lack of direct input into or oversight of progress notes, leaving residents, not infrequently inexperienced ones, as the main authors. In this connection, consider the following comment by an attending:

Now since patients have fairly extensive medical records, why isn't it relatively easy to pass off care to another surgeon? Several things, I think, make it hard for us to do that with consistency. One is a simple thing—entries can be badly written, so much so that they make no sense. And we also have a high degree of variability in the degree to which, particularly at the faculty level, good charting is done. There are some faculty that rarely write a note in the chart, others that write nicely detailed notes on a daily basis, with the most common practice probably in between— where maybe a critical concept will be appended to a resident's note. But not infrequently, you'll be rounding and you'll see a resident note, written by an intern, so somebody with relatively little experience. And you'll see at the end, "patient seen and examined and concur with the above" and a name stamp. That's documentation suitable for billing purposes, but it's not meaningful, and says nothing about the cognitive process involved. Some of our consulting services, I've noticed, will go days without an attending-level person writing in the chart. So no thought process is recorded by an attending. But I think for those reasons, the chart, despite the importance of the written medical record, is often very much an incomplete document, especially at the senior-most thought process level. (A-M)

Much of the reasoning that guides patient care is thus not in the patient chart, a document largely produced and maintained by those with the least experience and medical knowledge.

A similar problem besets operative notes, which are often composed by residents once an operation ends. In a clear majority of cases observed in the OR, the attending had left the room to talk with the patient's family as the operative-note dictation was being delivered by a resident, and in no case was a dictation provided by a resident obviously monitored by an attending who remained in the OR. Like progress notes, operative notes are limited by their authorship. But another issue is that surgeons are strongly disinclined to document fully their concerns or worries. Operative notes thus become minimalist documents that are unlikely to alert others to likely postoperative complications.

> *Let's imagine that X [his faculty partner] leaves town and you'll take care of his patients. Can you do that well by just looking at the patient charts and seeing the patients?* Impossible. No way! *Why?* Well, I think the things that are important to us in a checkout are oftentimes not in the chart, not in the medical record. Just to give you an example, let's say X has a Nissen up there [a baby on the ward who had a Nissen fundoplication, a surgical procedure to treat gastroesophageal reflux disease]. And we always manage it the same way every single time. He may not put in his dictation that he had a bleeder from a short gastric vessel. He got control of it, but he's a little worried about it. So, if he was going to leave town, he would tell me, "keep that baby on a monitor. Get a CBC tonight or in the morning. Because I was a little worried about the short gastric." But he wouldn't have put that in his dictation. He wouldn't say, "I'm worried about a bleeding short gastric vessel." Never. No way. *Why is that? It seems like critical information.* Medical-legal concerns are surely part of it, but I think it's just a surgeon's worry—and you don't put that in an op note. But I would convey that to whoever was getting the primary phone calls on that baby, or to my partner if I was leaving town. (A-M)

Another attending provides additional insight into the medical-legal concern:

> If you articulated every fear about a major operation, your op notes would be almost unreadable, and you'd be airing things that not everybody needs to know. With a trusted partner, it would be fine. But, if a lawyer reads that—and they can—it might not be fine. And so people don't say, "I was a little nervous about whether

I'd really controlled the bleeding." They say, "at the time of closure there was no active bleeding." But that obscures a concern. (A-M)

A "surgeon's worries" are thus routinely omitted from the documentation that summarizes the operation. While legal concerns surely motivate that omission, another part is cultural tradition—that one simply does not provide much detail in the op note. In another interview, an attending said that legal concerns were real, but that he thought it would be a mistake to pinpoint them as the main reason the notes contain few details. In his view, it was purely a cultural pattern: "We've long had a system in which op notes aren't very helpful— so why bother to do them in a long and elaborate way?" (A-M)

This approach to documentation leaves other surgeons unable to piece together quickly from the medical records alone what happened during an operation and what might surface as a postoperative complication. Those who lack first-hand information must run through many plausible possibilities rather than quickly homing in on what is most likely given the way an operation unfolded. That takes precious time and can be extraordinarily expensive if an incoming surgeon enacts a "full court press" in response to worsening patient conditions. In many cases, delays of this sort make little or no difference, but in others they mean the difference between easy and difficult, life and death. Nipping problems in the bud requires effective and timely oral communication during handoffs because patient records are often insufficient.

The Curious Weakness of Patient Records and Handoffs

Surgeons see many reasons why patient records and handoffs can and do fail to provide a solid foundation for team coverage of patients. Those concerns are offered as a primary rationale for their struggles with reforms that require more frequent handoffs and greater reliance on patient records. Individually provided continuity of care is touted as the gold standard; team-based approximations are widely seen as falling short. It is difficult, however, not to suspect that the social organization and culture of surgery combine to undermine the capacity of surgeons to more easily transfer care from one surgeon to another. One issue has already been noted, namely a lack of compulsion when it comes to creating and maintaining detailed and accurate progress notes for patients. Two additional patterns are noteworthy: first, the conditions under which handoffs take place; and second, the extent of oversight and training.

In practice, handoffs tend to be hasty events that rarely offer the opportunity to thoughtfully review and confirm understandings about patient conditions and plans. During the fieldwork, thirty-seven handoffs were observed, thirty of which were from day to night teams. The process of running the list for a service with, say, twenty patients most commonly took less than five minutes—giving each patient about fifteen seconds of attention—and never longer than fifteen minutes. Rarely, however, was each patient discussed, as just a few dominated each discussion. The haste with which handoffs take place is said to flow from time constraints, but it is also part of a culture that absolutely abhors belaboring anything that could be construed as obvious. Consider the following comment:

> Time constraints are a big part of signouts. The people making that call to get signout in the morning, the morning team, they're coming in early and have a lot to do. They want the most important information condensed into the least amount of time as possible. They don't want to hear about every blood pressure and every worry and every this and that. They want the meat, now, and that's it! What do I need to know or do? What disasters have occurred? And you tell them in the briefest, most concise manner possible. Alternatively, the signout from the day to the night team tends to be a little more lengthy because the day team has "the plan," if you will. And they can spend more time communicating that plan to the night float team. Ideally, you just get the meat! (PGY4-M)

The extreme brevity of morning handoffs, often done by phone as residents drive to the hospital, was "observed" (i.e., one end of the conversation was listened to—except for a few on speaker phone) to focus on "the meat"—the bare minimum that needed to be shared. Incoming day residents and chiefs have to see patients and round before at least some of them head off to the operating room for cases that start at 7:30 a.m. In some transitions, there is no handoff, or only what might be called a second-hand handoff. Trauma cases or lengthy procedures in the OR can delay some residents to the point where a new team takes over and receives only delayed, if any, news about the patients for whom they assume responsibility. In addition, restrictions on call schedules mean that some residents must leave by noon after a night on call and therefore hand off their patients for the balance of the afternoon. Those patients will, in turn, be handed off again early in the evening. More links in a chain increase the risk of information loss and distortions, per the often-mentioned telephone game played by children.

Handoffs are also done away from patients and often in moments filled with distraction. In no case did any observed handoffs involve joint rounding on patients with incoming and outgoing residents. Rather, handoffs were always conducted by running the list, either face-to-face or over the phone. And while most night float or call arrangements have a scheduled start time of, say, 6:00 p.m. for the night team, few programs, including the one observed, dedicate and then protect time for handoffs or provide overlapping shift time to facilitate a slower and more deliberate pace for handoffs. By dint of scheduling, handoffs tend to be rushed and brief. Consider the following comment by a mid-level resident:

> Signouts are a problem. At six o'clock the day residents and the intern all sit down with the incoming night float residents and run the list—we go through the patients and report what was done, what the issues are, who needs attention, or if there's any outstanding consults or whatever. Being the night float guy for a month recently, I really saw how people just blow through the list. If the night float came in any earlier they'd be over eighty hours. Same for the day teams staying later. So, if you came in any earlier to get a better signout or had an hour of overlap, everyone would be over their hours. So, it's just not a very effective system. Ideally, we'd sit down, take thirty minutes, run through the list, but it's oftentimes just a couple of minutes for more than forty patients. (PGY3-M)

A lack of protected time devoted to handoffs surely nudges residents in the direction of "blowing through the list" and providing, per a previous comment, "just the meat."

What is not sufficiently clear from the comments thus far, however, is just how chaotic handoff time can be due to the funnel-like change in staffing. Many patients managed by many day residents are handed off to just a few nighttime residents. Interns staying for night float in the program that was observed received handoffs from no less than five surgical services, meaning that the handoff time is one in which many contacts are made by multiple residents to a small night crew. Observations of handoffs confirm that dubbing them as hectic is no overstatement. During handoffs, residents are working through screens of on-line patient information, taking phone calls, talking with one or more residents sitting next to them, and managing multiple messages via their beepers. The rushed and distracting format of handoffs in practice clearly suggests they fall well short of an ideal context for the exchange of information and responsibility for patients.

A second dimension of the practice of handoffs is equally remarkable: a prevailing silence and detachment on the part of attending surgeons. Just as attendings do little to ensure that progress and operative notes are complete and accurate documents that might help a new surgeon step in and manage

a case, they do next to nothing in the way of teaching, evaluation, or oversight when it comes to handoffs. During the fieldwork, no observed handoff
involved a faculty member as a participant or observer, and residents said
that was typical.

> *I can't recall a single instance of attendings being around when the day teams check
> out to night float. Have I missed that?* No, I don't think so—they aren't around for
> that. *So no attending's ever observed you checking out and then said something like,
> "I liked most of what you did, but there are two things you could do better."* No, no, no!
> *Okay, that's emphatic. Have you ever heard of such a thing being done?* No, not at all.
> I guess I could be checking out wrong every day and I'd have no idea! (PGY2-M)

Of course, if disasters occur during the night, and attendings learn that important information was not passed along, displeasure gets passed down the hierarchy. But whether handoffs in general are done well—or even how they are
conducted—is not on faculty radar screens. One attending surgeon's comments during the fieldwork are telling, in part because he was regarded as an
exemplary educator by residents:

> *Is it your sense that checkouts from day teams to night float are pretty good?* I have no
> idea. None! We don't observe it and we don't know how it occurs. Should we do
> better with that? Sure. I don't even know how the residents do checkout. There may
> be a system, but we didn't teach it to them, and we don't model it. We don't listen
> to our interns checking out to other interns, or to anyone, for that matter. In fact,
> I don't think I've ever done that, and I don't think anyone on the service has ever
> done that. *Can you think of situations when something fell through the cracks—that the
> signout to night float wasn't good for one reason or another?* Oh god yes! I can give you
> multiple examples, some scary. Just on this service, I'd say things important enough
> to worry about fall through the cracks at least once a week, maybe more. (A-M)

There are three central issues here: first, faculty have no tradition of observing or evaluating resident handoffs; second, a model for the content and format of handoffs is not taught to residents by faculty; and third, handoffs are
thought to fall short fairly often. These issues in the fieldwork site were fully
consistent with what was learned in the interviews.

These patterns create a tension that is difficult to reconcile: deep concerns
about handoffs and thin documentation, and yet little real effort to improve,
let alone ensure, a level of quality in handoffs and documentation that would
permit one surgeon to more easily and confidently stand in for another. Fear

and nonchalance are strange bedfellows. Whatever may prompt that pattern, there is little doubt that surgical culture and practice serve as impediments for the full emergence of team-based surgical care. Handoffs have recently become a topic of educational attention, but it is not yet clear that an educational policy initiative will—or can—substantially alter the practices and problems highlighted here.

What about Fresh Eyes?

As surgeons understand it, fatigue and familiarity rise and fall together: staffing arrangements that increase familiarity also induce fatigue. Policies aimed at curbing fatigue run an ironic risk, say surgeons, of making patients less safe because they are less familiar to their doctors. But is familiarity always an advantage? It is easy to imagine how a capable surgeon who is not familiar with a case—what we are calling fresh eyes—might bring a valuable perspective. Ruts or dead ends, after all, may be easier to escape if one has not made an investment in the thought processes that led there. No less than the Institute of Medicine has advanced the idea that handoffs can and should represent an opportunity to draw on the value of fresh eyes (Ulmer, Wolman, and Johns 2008). Can fresh eyes—and the new look at a case or situation that they imply—be advantageous?

Evidence about the value of fresh eyes emerged indirectly as surgeons spoke about the fatigue-versus-familiarity tradeoff and the stay-or-go decisions that are the subject of the next chapter. Two main insights about the value of fresh eyes emerged: a first challenged the notion that a fresh-eye perspective made any sense given the way night shifts are staffed; a second suggested that while care for chronic health problems can and does benefit at least occasionally from fresh eyes, acute conditions—the mainstay of surgical work—rarely benefit from fresh eyes. Responses to fresh-eye questions often bordered on exasperation, as though the question stemmed from inexcusable ignorance about the flow of work and the way night staffing is structured in residency programs. Consider first a senior resident's response, which followed a discussion about continuity of care:

> *I wonder what you think of the argument that there might be times or situations where a fresh pair of eyes and a clear head that hasn't been thinking about a case might bring new insights to patient care?* I think if you had the same amount of staffing at night, that would be wonderful and maybe possible. But what you end up with is one small team, in our institution, that's covering seven services

at night. Seven services! A fresh pair of eyes is a wonderful, great idea, but it's totally unrealistic, absurd. You are stretched so much at night that the patient might not ever see that fresh pair of eyes, and something bad might happen to them. *So it's a conceptual possibility, but the thin staffing that you have doesn't allow it?* Right. There's really no time—you can't bring fresh anything to patients on seven services! (PGY4-M)

Quite clearly, the sense here is that any potential fresh-eye advantage will not be realized because night teams are small and overburdened. Faculty comments also pointed to staffing challenges and the bare-bones agenda of night teams—to, in short, put out fires and then hand patients over in the morning.

You've been very clear in saying that there's a loss of familiarity with a patient and the patient's course when the primary caregiver leaves the hospital. But I wonder if there are situations where a fresh pair of eyes and perhaps a new perspective may counter that loss of familiarity, maybe with a net positive effect. I think on the face of it, prima facie, that's a good question. However, the agenda of those people to whom the handoff is given is not to provide a fresh set of eyes. They're not thinking through the case very hard at all—they're firefighters taking care of it for the time they're assigned to care for the patient and then they go home. On night float, you're putting out fires—you're not actively participating in the care plan and thinking through the patient's course. And you're praying that you don't get called about that patient! So no news is good news! Your aim, pure and simple, is to hand the patient back intact, the status quo, to the service in the morning. The number of residents in-house at night is so limited that they can't rethink cases or be fresh eyes. (A-M)

Night float was routinely described as a way of biding time until the "real" care team—those faculty and residents who staff services during the day—returned. These comments suggest that temporal and staffing discontinuities between day and night are linked to different levels of involvement and responsibility. Day teams are clearly primary and for night teams, "no news is good news" because their aim is to simply get through the night.

Staffing levels were the primary reason night residents were unlikely to rethink cases with a fresh perspective. A second factor, mentioned mostly by faculty, was the distinction between chronic and acute care. One put this as the difference between formulating an effective plan—often difficult with chronic conditions—and executing a plan—doing things in an organized and efficient way when facing an acute care need. Surgeons, of course, deal with both chronic and acute issues, and one linked them to fresh eyes:

Do you think there are different types of cases that would benefit from those two approaches—fresh eyes versus continuity? I do. I'm a vascular surgeon. We have patients who have chronic disease states and acute disease states. And sometimes, as someone who's caring for a patient with a chronic disease—let's say a lower extremity wound—we think we've done all we can do for their wound. And we've been seeing it in the clinic or hospital over the course of time. We go to sign out to our partner, one of the other attending surgeons, and he looks at the wound and says, "Hey! What are you doing? I'd do this, this, this, and this." So that's a good example of where a fresh set of eyes for a patient with a chronic problem is very beneficial. I've seen that happen countless times, both with my partners and me. . . . Where I think that's not beneficial is where you decide you have to intervene acutely, if you decide you are going to the operating room to fix an acute problem. Someone comes in with a cold limb and they don't have any blood flow down there. You are not going to have a long and involved discussion about what you are going to do. You are going to use your best judgment to re-vascularize that extremity. That's the difference for me—is it a chronic problem, where fresh eyes are a great thing, or an acute problem, where you don't need extra cooks, but just need to deal with the issue. (A-M)

As in this comment, the fieldwork offered many instances in which chronic conditions became fodder for discussion and consultations among attending surgeons. Patients who kept rebounding to clinic, or those in the hospital who did not appear to be improving as expected, often prompted surgeons to seek out fresh eyes and hopefully a new perspective. In acute situations that demand quick thinking and action, adding "extra cooks" only occurred in the face of relative inexperience with a particular condition or technique.

Surgeons thus see some potential merit in fresh eyes, but believe that it is practically impossible for a fresh-eye advantage to occur with any regularity at night, when a skeletal staff is saddled with many patients and distracted by traumas, consults, and emergency surgery. To read the medical records and rethink a case requires altogether too much time given other demands. It is also at odds with the prevailing view of surgeons that night staff serve largely to "hold the fort" and "manage fires." Day and night staff are simply not equivalent and do not function as such.

Reflection: I'll Be by at Eight O'clock

One of the many challenges of providing care for complex patients is handling the relays of information on which that care hinges. Particularly with patients in intensive care settings and complicated illnesses affecting multiple organ systems, the involvement of multiple specialists has become commonplace. In addition, given that the estimated half-life of medical knowledge has shortened from a century one hundred years ago to current estimates of eighteen months, relying on an increasing array of consultants for their focused expertise has become somewhat normative. Needless to say, as patient needs and the teams managing their care become more complex, coordination of care amongst those teams becomes critical.

I was in my second year of training, caring for a complex patient in the intensive care unit after she sustained injuries that put her on a ventilator. In that era there were relatively few of the individuals we would now call intensivists in the profession, and her ventilator management was being overseen by a pulmonary (lung) specialist. She had reached a point in her recovery where it appeared she was ready to be taken off the ventilator. We were trying to decide the best way to coordinate that, and as was common practice, decided to "rest" her on full mechanical breathing settings for a night (when staffing was always a bit thinner), and extubate her (remove the breathing tube) in the morning. It was agreed that I would remove the tube on my early morning rounds, and the pulmonary physician would come by within an hour thereafter, specifically by 8 a.m., to check on her progress. He would reinsert the tube should she not prove able, despite our best assessments, to stay off the machine at that point in her recovery. So far, so good.

I came by the next morning and removed the breathing tube at the agreed upon time. The patient was at that point reasonably comfortable and stable, and I went about my morning workflow with other duties as planned. I can't remember all the details now, but remember circling back to see the patient sometime after 8 a.m., only to find that she was tiring out, clearly failing her trial of being off the machine, and that the pulmonary specialist hadn't made it by at the specified time. We were able to reach the specialist, who had been caught up in some unexpected other duties that morning; he came shortly thereafter, and we were able to get the breathing tube replaced and the situation stabilized. The patient became stronger, was later in her course successfully removed from the ventilator, and eventually discharged from the hospital.

As he and I debriefed afterwards, he a very respected, competent, and fully trained provider, and I still a relatively junior trainee, we realized that our patient had had a "near miss" in her course for the simple reason that our transfer of responsibility, despite best efforts, left her vulnerable between our respective and agreed upon roles. I walked away from the experience thankful for the outcome, and frightened at what might have been.

The issue of handoffs has become a critical one in current medical parlance. Estimates suggest that the number of such transfers of responsibility has increased by 40 percent or more with the advent of duty-hour restrictions and their attendant requirements for transfer of care responsibility from one physician or team to another. Much has been learned in the process. The use of standardized templates, face to face communication with closed loop or "say back" strategies, senior supervision, and other mechanisms have all been used to improve and attempt to assure the quality of information exchange. Unfortunately, amidst the time pressures and manpower adjustments involved in day versus night workflow models, and as illustrated by some of the quotes shared in this chapter, the system can and sometimes does fall short.

Apart from information exchange, there are perhaps a couple other reasons that handoffs in care are points of significant risk in patient management. One of these is the ubiquitous downsizing of the care team during nights and weekends. While it is recognized that the volume of nonemergent activity diminishes in a hospital after hours, and that staffing needs on many fronts change accordingly at night or on a weekend, the load of work of the inpatients generally does not change all that much. Particularly in the current era where only the most ill or socially compromised patients are kept in a hospitalized setting, the care of inpatients diminishes only modestly after "normal" working hours, and urgent and emergent problems if anything may increase. Thus, there is a necessary funneling effect, as the chapter outlines, in the handoff saga. At the epicenter of the vortex, the patient and the multitasking caregiver can easily become affected by a prioritization mindset that involves regular decisions over what must be done now versus what can or even should wait until morning or 'morrow. This theme will get more attention in the next chapter as seen through the lens of an individual resident making decisions about whether to stay and do something themselves at the end of a shift, or hand off to the incoming team.

The other issue impacting the handoff equation, besides adjustments in team and support staff size, is that of ownership. This issue will also be developed further in subsequent chapters. For the present discussion regarding handoffs of care, suffice to say that surgeons have long prided themselves on this issue, and sometimes even speak somewhat disdainfully of other specialty areas they see as "shift workers." I remember stories from my training years of attendings canceling planned vacations because a particular patient had a complication and they were not willing to abandon them by transferring their care to a perhaps less-invested colleague at a critical point in their course. I distinctly remember as a chief (final year) resident going in to operate one night on a patient one of my fellow chief residents had previously operated on and been responsible for. Our program director came in to help me with the case as the responsible faculty member, but did so complaining not about his duty, but the lack of ownership my resident colleague had shown in not coming in to do the case on his weekend off. The message was clear: you are responsible for the patient once you have operated, and if that interferes with the rest of your life, that is what a professional does.

How does one preserve such a sense of duty in the midst of duty-hour restrictions, generational shifts, and the avalanche of data coming out about physician wellness, burnout, and compassion fatigue? How does one model that in a sustainable fashion in a training paradigm, meaning culturally and not just in regard to call schedules? Can team strategies and communication competencies replace intrepid individualism in a modernized care model that allows quality care in a more fluid and complex work environment than prior generations have had to manage? Are surgeons trained with a mindset to protect against fatigue through shared care models going to be less likely to invest their careers in rural and other underserved areas, where such protection may not be sustainable in the face of demographic need and workforce challenges? These are real questions with which we must continue to grapple, and no doubt part of the solution will be in the area of systems and structures that help ensure accurate and timely information exchange focused on the patients' needs. At the same time, our societal enamorment with system-based and technical solutions still requires a personal ethic in order to be effective. As T. S. Eliot is once purported to have said, modernity has become preoccupied with identifying systems "so perfect we will no longer have to be good." Such systems not only remain elusive in our day; they always will.

Handoffs or ownership? Systems or personal ethic? Our experience would say we need both/and, not either/or.

CHAPTER 3

Stay-or-Go Decisions by Residents
Why Not Leave When a Shift is Over or
Hour Limits Are Reached?

I hope the reason why most of us go into medicine is to treat patients and be there for them. And sometimes, I feel we get wrapped up in the hours thing, where we decide we can't do something because of the hours. But we can't be more concerned about hours than patients! (PGY2-M)

"That sounds hopelessly pie in the sky," she said, gruffly. "None of these researchers seem to understand—or want to understand—our day-to-day, the things we actually do every day. You'll learn more if you stop reading and just watch what happens at the end of the day. Then you'll be able to separate baloney from what really happens and what might be possible." And such was the frank advice I was given by a chief resident early in the fieldwork after asking for her thoughts about a journal article I had read about a "new professionalism." Since she was not familiar with the piece, I summarized it as we walked back from morning clinics. Van Eaton, Horvath, and Pellegrini (2005) had argued that traditional conceptions and enactments of "patient ownership" by residents could and should be replaced by new understandings and practices based on the principles of teamwork. Traditional patient ownership was highly individualistic, with residents knowing everything about their patients and doing everything for them. That practice, implored Van Eaton and his colleagues, must give way to shared responsibilities and team ownership nurtured by clear guidelines as to what residents would be expected to know and do for their patients and those they cross-cover along with instruction in how to conduct handoffs and hence transfer information, responsibility, and care across shifts. As Van Eaton and his colleagues acknowledged, these changes would transform residencies.

The chief resident's conclusion that it was "pie in the sky" began to come into focus as the fieldwork progressed. As described in the last chapter, residents have generally not been taught how to conduct handoffs, as recommended by Van Eaton and his colleagues, although this is more recently a point of emphasis for the ACGME. They also have little clear guidance as to how to handle the many issues that can and do surface at the end of the day. Given the substantial but uneven flow and timing of patient-care needs, some activities will not be wrapped up before the shift change, which then poses the stay-or-go decisions explored in this chapter. What allows a resident to leave—the go decision—at the end of a day shift? And what might delay a timely exit—the stay decision—when she is scheduled to leave? If residents often delay departures, then they must be able to trim hours after one or more long days if they are to abide by the eighty-hour weekly limit, which is an *average* over four weeks.

Evidence suggests that adherence to the eighty-hour average is uneven, that some falsify time records, and that delays in departing at the end of a shift in specialties like surgery are routine (Carpenter et al. 2006; Landrigan et al. 2006; Szymczak et al. 2010; Tabrizian et al. 2011; Arora, Farnan, and Humphrey 2012; Drolet et al. 2013; Bryne, Loo, and Giang 2015). The efforts of residents to subtract—to come in late, leave early, or take a day off—have been overlooked by research on the reforms. Our analysis explores how residents understand and experience both delayed departures and efforts to subtract hours on a subsequent day if they have added hours to one or more previous days.

Data are drawn from the fieldwork and the second and third waves of the multi-center data. In the second-wave interviews, residents and attendings were presented with three distinct clinical scenarios. In each, a resident had worked a regular day shift and was about ready to check out to a night resident or team when he or she was presented with (1) an urgent need on the part of one of his or her patients for a chest tube, (2) a request on the part of a patient and his or her family for a conference about the patient's care, and (3) newly arrived consultant recommendations that meant one of the resident's patients would need to have work done in the evening (e.g., studies and labs) or care would be delayed the following day. Importantly, each issue surfaces at the cusp of a shift transition, and they vary in urgency and include both procedures and counseling.

For each scenario, residents and faculty were asked what they thought a typical resident in their program would do, what they felt ideally should be done, and the reasoning that guided their views. Each scenario closely parallels one developed by Van Eaton and his colleagues (2005, 233) to illustrate traditional behavior and the new professionalism. In their view, events of this sort used to prompt residents to abort their departures to complete the late-arriving duties; a new professionalism, on the other hand, meant only that a departure would be delayed until the night team could be brought up to speed to take over. Residents, in particular, readily recognized the scenarios—saying that they happen all the time—and addressed them at length. Most also added what *they* would do, even though that was not asked in the question, and elaborated on their decision-making when facing these clinical scenarios.

Evidence is also drawn from the third wave of multi-center data. In that wave, we drew on what we had learned from the field observations and the wave-two interviews to craft and administer fourteen questionnaire items. Residents were asked to estimate the weekly frequencies of delays at the end of a day shift due to particular circumstances and to assess the ease of trimming hours on subsequent days to offset extra hours on previous days. In the wave-three interviews, we also explored whether delayed departures were common, what prompted them, why residents stayed, and their experiences with efforts to balance long hours by trimming hours on one or more subsequent days. These general questions were not tethered to specific clinical scenarios. We begin with an overview of the survey results before exploring the qualitative evidence.

A Survey-Based Overview of Delayed Departures and Efforts to Trim Hours

Table 3.1 shows the sources and approximate weekly frequency of delays as residents come to the end of a weekday's duty period. Unfortunately, the meaning and salience of some of the specific questions will remain a bit murky at this point, as descriptions of things like "dumping" (item 10) are best presented when we review the qualitative evidence. Our recommendation for readers is to note the broad contours of the results, move to the qualitative material, and then circle back to the table once dumping and other issues have been grasped. Note that the category of "three or more times" was used because residents claimed in a pre-test that it was difficult for them to remember exactly how often common events of this sort occur. For them, "three or more times" per week becomes "often," which is sufficient for our purposes.

TABLE 3.1. Frequency and Sources of End-of-Shift Delays: General Surgery Residents

Item	"The approximate weekly frequency with which you delay your departure at the end of a weekday's duty period because of the following issues—responses are 0, 1, 2, and 3 or more times per week."	Percentage Distribution				
		Approximate Weekly Frequency (from 0 to 3 times)				
		None (0)	Once (1)	Twice (2)	Three or more times (3)	Mean
1	To meet or communicate with patients or their families.	7	44	39	10	1.5
2	To teach or give instruction.	16	50	29	5	1.2
3	To round with an attending.	15	39	33	13	1.4
4	To complete a procedure in the operating room.	3	33	49	15	1.8
5	To complete a bedside procedure.	14	51	28	7	1.3
6	To complete work available night staff might not have the skill to accomplish.	42	37	18	3	.8
7	To complete work night staff might not have the information to do easily or well.	16	41	34	8	1.3
8	To complete work night staff might not have the time to accomplish.	20	42	28	10	1.3
9	To complete work you view as valuable for your education.	11	41	39	10	1.5
10	To avoid the perception of dumping on others work you might have finished.	6	26	47	23	1.9
11	To continue care for a patient who is very ill, complex, and difficult to hand off.	8	41	42	9	1.5
12	Because there is simply too much work to finish during a day's "official" duty period.	23	30	32	15	1.4
13	Because of poor management of the team's overall workload.	46	43	9	2	.7

Notes: N = 291 residents (wave 3 data). Mean calculations use 3 as the value for the open-ended upper category of "3 or more." They are thus truncated estimates of the overall mean.

Perhaps the most important result is that delayed departures are astonishingly ubiquitous: only two of 291 residents reported zeros for all thirteen items. Moreover, only two of the thirteen items (6 and 13) have a statistical mode of zero, indicating "no delays" was the most common response provided by residents. Even for those two items, delays occur *at least once a week* (58 percent are at that level for item 6 and 54 percent for item 13). Statistical modes were

TABLE 3.2. Mean Levels and Sources of End-of-Shift Delays: General Surgery Residents by Gender

Item	"The approximate weekly frequency with which you delay your departure at the end of a weekday's duty period because of the following issues—responses are 0, 1, 2, and 3 or more times per week."	Mean Weekly Frequency	
		Men	Women
1	To meet or communicate with patients or their families.	1.6	1.5
2	To teach or give instruction.	1.3	1.2
3	To round with an attending.	1.4	1.5
4	To complete a procedure in the operating room.	1.7	1.8
5	To complete a bedside procedure.	1.3	1.3
6	To complete work available night staff might not have the skill to accomplish.	.9	.8
7	To complete work night staff might not have the information to do easily or well.	1.2	1.6*
8	To complete work night staff might not have the time to accomplish.	1.1	1.6*
9	To complete work you view as valuable for your education.	1.4	1.6*
10	To avoid the perception of dumping on others work you might have finished.	1.8	1.9
11	To continue care for a patient who is very ill, complex, and difficult to hand off.	1.4	1.7*
12	Because there is simply too much work to finish during a day's "official" duty period.	1.3	1.5+
13	Because of poor management of the team's overall workload.	.6	.7

Notes: N = 291 residents (wave 3 data). Mean calculations use 3 as the value for the open-ended upper category of "3 or more." They are thus truncated estimates of the overall mean. The statistical significance of mean differences is assessed with two-tailed independent-samples t tests. An asterisk (*) next to the second mean indicates a significant mean difference at the .05 level; a plus sign (+) indicates significance at the .10 level.

at least one for all other items, which means it was at least a weekly source of delay. Four items (4 and 10–12) have modes of two, indicating that delays typically occurred twice a week because of a procedure in the operating room (item 4), concerns about dumping (item 10), care for complex patients (item 11), and workloads (item 12). The highest mean—1.9, or nearly twice a week—stems from concerns about dumping (item 10), an issue we draw out later in the chapter.

We also explored the role of program type, experience, and gender. Program type did not affect the patterns, but about half of the items (1–4, 6, and 11) have means that differ significantly by resident seniority. In all cases, the frequency of delays increases with seniority. Gender patterns are shown in Table 3.2. Five items differ significantly for men and women (items 7, 8, 9, 11, and 12), and in all cases indicate that women delay their departures more than their male peers.

TABLE 3.3. Program Characteristics, Resident Attributes, and Resident Difficulties in Trimming Work-Hours

Row	Characteristic	Level or Type	% Disagree or Strongly Disagree that Trimming Hours is Easy	Number of Residents	Significance (P) of the % Difference
	PROGRAM CHARACTERISTICS				
1	Academic Program	Yes	58%	155	.920
2		No	59%	133	
3	Number of Categorical Residents	< 20	68%	75	
4		20–35	59%	118	.050
5		> 35	50%	95	
6	Advanced Practice Clinicians on Services	< 70%	56%	155	.290
7		> 70%	62%	133	
	RESIDENT ATTRIBUTES				
8	Postgraduate Year	1	65%	66	
9		2	57%	56	
10		3	59%	56	.153
11		4	65%	52	
12		≥ 5	45%	56	
13	Gender	Men	54%	177	.056
14		Women	66%	108	

Notes. The overall distribution of the difficulties-in-trimming variable ("It is easy to balance out extra hours one day by cutting hours on a subsequent day") is as follows: strongly disagree = 21% (59); disagree = 38% (109); neutral = 13% (37); agree = 26% (74); strongly agree = 3% (9). Significance was determined by Pearson's chi-square tests.

Overall, then, the effect of gender is clear: most typically, patterns of delayed departures do not differ for men and women, but when they do, women are delayed more often than men.

Table 3.3 indicates how program characteristics and resident attributes are related to the ease of trimming hours. For ease of presentation and interpretation, those who disagreed or strongly disagreed (59 percent) that it was easy to balance out extra hours one day by cutting hours on a subsequent day were grouped and contrasted against the smaller percentage of residents who agreed (26 percent), strongly agreed (3 percent), or were neutral (13 percent). In the interviews, explored below, it became clear that for many, "neutral" was a way of saying "it depends," so we included those responses in the broader agreement category.

In terms of associations with program and resident attributes, we considered the program type (academic versus community), the number of categorical residents in the program, and resident experience and gender. Two of these factors—the number of categorical residents in the program and gender—are significantly associated with the ease of trimming hours. Residents in smaller programs find it more difficult than those in larger programs to balance out extra hours one day by cutting hours on a subsequent day. Women are 12 percentage points more likely than their male peers to perceive it to be difficult to trim hours. Overall, resident perceptions of the ease of trimming hours after one or more long workdays are largely similar, suggesting that residents face a common issue, not one that differs substantially across programs or by resident characteristics. We now draw out the meaning of these behaviors and the cultural and organizational factors that constrain and channel them.

Available and Able? Deep Concerns about Night Staff

Residents do not draw on clear guidelines when they face stay-or-go decisions at the end of a shift, and instead emphasize discretion. Most adopt a flexible interpretation whereby the rules are viewed as more nearly advisory than mandatory. Most typically, the assessments that shaped stay-or-go decisions centered on whether night staff were likely to be both *available* and *able* to handle patient-care needs. That assessment required residents to size up the night crew and the tasks to be transferred and determine whether it was prudent to hand off the work. It is important to recognize that day and night staffing are not equivalent. Residents described how small night teams covered all floor patients as well as consults, traumas, and urgent and emergent procedures. Capable and conscientious night teams might get tied up or have to prioritize activities; it was thus impossible to *bank* on night teams getting to passed-off issues immediately, if at all. One resident's comments are typical: if there is an acute issue like the need to place a chest tube, then staying is the right decision.

> (*chest-tube scenario*): Stay and put in the chest tube. *Okay. Is that what should be done too?* Absolutely. *Why not pass that off to night float?* If I'm caring for that patient and I've been with that patient all day long and something is acutely changing and I'm standing there, then I'm going to fix it. We won't just sign out to the night float person and say, "Hey, this guy's got a pretty bad pneumothorax. His

sats [oxygen level] are coming down. You really should go put it in right now!" That's not feasible. If you're a night float person who's getting called to the OR, if traumas are coming in—there are so many things that can start happening at 5 p.m.! It's not the best thing to do for the patient to expect to go from a four-man team on the service to a skimpy night team that covers everything and dump something urgent on them. So put the chest tube in! (PGY3-F)

Because night crews are small and easily overwhelmed, the near-universal refrain in response to the chest-tube scenario was that the day staff should stay and place it themselves. Van Eaton and his colleagues envisioned the day team conferring with night staff to make sure that the chest tube was on its way to being placed before they left. In practice, residents see that as a risky delay in care and an undue burden on night staff.

The third scenario about late-arriving recommendations from a consultant suggested that work would need to be done at night or a patient's care would be delayed the next day. Unlike the chest-tube scenario, following up on the recommendations does not pose an urgent issue where time is of the essence. Nearly all residents said that this work, in moderation, can and should be passed to night teams. But even with this non-urgent work, residents said that it was imperative to be prudent about how much work was being passed along to the night team.

(consultant recommendations scenario): I think that's typically something that's handed off to the night team and we should do that. I think that's the purpose of having the hour restrictions—to have someone there who can take care of those functions so that care isn't delayed. But we need to be careful because the night team is smaller than the day team. . . . I've gotten too much work checked out to me when I was on night float and I sometimes wouldn't finish the daytime work until one o'clock in the morning. It can be a bother to patients—to wake them up in the middle of the night to recheck physical exams and to discuss signing things with them. We have to get a feel for how much we're handing off, and be responsible to not hand off too much on a busy service. (PGY4-F)

Being responsible implies an awareness of how much is being handed off and what that might mean for the night residents and their patients.

Underlying the comments about thin night staffing is a perceived imperative to provide timely and efficient care. Timely care, which means that a patient receives needed care without delay, emerged as an issue in many observed situations and in the interviews. Delays required to hand off care can become sources of concern for residents and costly for patients.

(*chest-tube scenario*): Place the tube and then leave. . . . If it's something that's urgent and needs to be done, here at our institution, we take care of it. *Why not check it out to night float?* It might not be done in a timely fashion. If it's fairly urgent, the person who is receiving checkout has to leave and go do it, then they miss the rest of checkout. If it's urgent and they stay for checkout, the patient could decompensate, and that would be bad. (PGY4-M)

Also evident here, and common in resident comments, is the idea that handing the procedure off to an incoming resident could hamper their ability to receive needed information about the patients they will care for at night. The timely care imperative was an often mentioned and undoubtedly substantial reason behind the reluctance of residents to pass work to the night team.

Perceptions of efficiency also loomed large. Residents described how it would often take longer to track down a night-team resident and sign out something like the placement of a chest tube—let alone a family conference—than to do it themselves. Finding night staff and informing them sufficiently was widely viewed as an inefficient use of time.

(*family-conference scenario*): I think the typical resident would go ahead and have the family conference. . . . *So what would be, just briefly, the downside to checking out a conference like that?* It's inefficient and it's unprofessional. It's inefficient because the surgery resident who's never met the patient or the family has to go and establish rapport and try to answer all the questions they might have. It's going to take two or three times the time it would take the daytime resident to do that conference. One has been following the patient, the other's never seen them. Horribly inefficient and unprofessional. (PGY4-M)

In general, if a day resident can do something more quickly than a night resident, then the tendency is to believe that he or she should delay the departure and do that work. A first concern about night staff is thus that they might not be *available* to do things in a timely way—if at all—because the team is small and demands can pile up quickly and unexpectedly.

A second concern about night float is whether they will be *able* to complete various patient-care activities even if they are available. Three main considerations were paramount: experience mismatches, case knowledge, and the specificity of relationships and trust. In most training programs, care at night on the wards is in the hands of junior residents and interns, with more experienced residents assigned to manage consults, trauma, ICU patients, and emergency surgery. Responsibilities can of course be shared, and more senior residents might be able to chip in, but relatively inexperienced residents nonetheless provide the vast majority of care for regular inpatients at night. A concern about experience mismatches appeared for each of the three scenarios.

> (*chest-tube scenario*): It's all going to depend on who's there covering you. *What's your thinking there—can you explain that a bit?* Sure. So if this happens and there is someone in house who is of your same level of experience, who is free—I guess that's an important part of it. I think most residents probably would just stay and do it, and I think that's probably the right thing. I think that if you needed to be somewhere and you had someone of the same level you can hand it off, that's okay. Obviously, if you have an intern who is the person you're signing out to, you're going to be staying and doing that chest tube. (PGY4-F)

A day resident who confronts a stay-or-go decision thus needs to assess the experience of the night resident who would likely be involved: is he or she up to the task?

Case knowledge is a second and central concern about passing work to night teams. Residents were quick to stress that daytime residents are aware of the fluid plans and discussions within the team and with patients and families that might not be documented in patient records. Consider a resident's observations about family conferences, which were widely seen as extremely difficult for a resident to conduct well if he or she had not been directly involved in the patient's care:

> (*family-conference scenario*): There are huge advantages to staying for a conference even if you're supposed to be going home. It starts with not having to look down at the H & P or the progress notes while you're talking to the family. It's really weird to talk to someone and have to keep flipping through screens of the medical records. If I've been involved in the decision making of the care that's been delivered to that patient, then I have the opportunity to explain accurately why things were done. I'm able to communicate what transpired in the order in which it transpired. A lot of times family members want to know, "What happened that my family member needs an operation tomorrow?" We don't document in the medical record a lot of the whys. It could be that a previous operation didn't go well or it could be that we made the decision at the beginning we'd give him forty-eight hours. We might not write that in any notes. The person who's aware of those decisions gets an opportunity to speak about why those decisions were made—instead of somebody else having to guess or presume. That's horrible. (PGY2-M)

Although comments about the importance of case knowledge were most prevalent when it came to the family conference, they also surfaced when residents
mulled other scenarios.

A final concern about the ability of night teams to manage care involves
beliefs about the specificity of relationships and trust. Many argued that the
relationships and trust a resident forges with a patient and a family, even over
just a day or two, cannot be transferred to someone else at night. A surprising
number of residents in different programs used the same expression—"they
aren't generic"—to describe relationships with families and patients. The
importance of established relationships and trust were seen as especially critical to the family-conference scenario and impossible to transfer to a nighttime resident:

> (*family-conference scenario*): I think it's very reasonable to stay. So we do that and
> we should do it. *Why?* I think we don't check out those types of conversations
> because the night team does not have the relationship with the patient and the
> family that the primary team does. It puts the cross-covering residents in a diffi-
> cult situation. You can't really be the cross-covering person that doesn't know
> the patient, doesn't know the family, and come in and start talking about how
> you're going to have this life changing operation. I think that's very off-putting
> to patients and family members. They don't have that personal relationship and
> personal history and level of trust. . . . I guess this is a very roundabout way of
> saying we can't really check out trust. (PGY4-F)

A key issue here is discomfort: a conference with an unfamiliar night resident
might be off-putting to the patient and family and feel unprofessional for the
resident. In sum, concerns about whether night staff will be *available* and *able*
to manage work passed from day staff inclines residents to delay departures
at the end of a shift.

Cultural Concerns: Patient Ownership, Dumping, and Inefficiency

Without doubt, residents have strong concerns about night staffing, but it
would be a mistake to conclude that the social organization of care alone
shapes stay-or-go decisions. At many points during the fieldwork and in the
interviews, it became clear that residents faced a cultural obligation to continue to care for one or more patients past the end of their shift even when
concerns about the availability and ability of night staff were not particularly
pronounced. Obligations stemmed from three main sources: the continued

prominence of individual patient ownership and an aversion if not a fear of attributions of dumping and inefficiency. Although each can be seen as re-lated to—if not interlocked with—concerns about night staff and the social organization of care, they are distinct components of stay-or-go decisions that are more nearly cultural in character.

Consider first the traditional notion of patient ownership. In the proposal for a new professionalism advanced by Van Eaton and his colleagues, patients would be the collective concern of a team as opposed to being "owned" by any given resident. To own a patient in the classic sense, a resident would immerse herself in their care, knowing everything about them and doing everything she could for them. Responsibility for the well-being of the patient, by and large, was assumed by the resident—the patient became "her" patient even though everyone knew ultimate authority and responsibility was held by an attending surgeon. The problem with that approach is that it runs counter to the idea that care can and should be provided by teams.

Resident comments in the interviews and behavior observed during the fieldwork point to the continued salience of traditional patient ownership in shaping stay-or-go decisions. Many comments about the clinical scenarios mixed worries about the availability and ability of night staff with brief declara-tions about patient ownership. An intern, for example, exhorted "if they're my patient, I want to take care of them!" (PGY1-M), echoing the words of a chief in a different program: "it's about taking ownership of your patients—and some-times you have to sacrifice going home to finish things" (PGY5-F). Expressions including "*my* patient" and "ownership" lace the speech of residents. Consider the comments of the following resident:

> (*chest-tube scenario*): They would stay to put the tube in. *Why not check it out so you can leave?* I think I probably speak for just about everyone in our program. You feel like it's your responsibility, especially if it's your patient on your service. We don't, in general, like to check things out. . . . Sometimes you have to for whatever reason, but in general, we like to take responsibility for our patients and take care of them, have them set up for the night so hopefully nothing will come up with them. *Now is that because you think it's the right thing to do or is it because the night folks might get slammed or not be as capable?* We are slammed at night, but it's more that it's your patient, it's your responsibility, it's the right thing to do. (PGY4-M)

The comment is a characteristic expression of traditional patient ownership and its emphasis on individual responsibility. Residents assigned to a spe-cific service own those patients, and are thereby individually responsible for their care.

Most commonly, residents were not as strident as the one quoted above, offering a mixture of rationales for stay decisions. For example, the previous section ("Available and Able?") led off with an excerpt from a resident who emphasized thin night staffing. Shortly after making that statement, she noted how patient ownership also played a role in her thinking:

> (*chest-tube scenario*): *So your main concern is that you don't know if night float is going to be slammed, so it's just prudent to do it yourself so you know it gets done?* Yeah, I think so. And it's your patient. You're the one who's been caring for that patient. Night float has a ton of patients. They've spent very little time with any of them. They don't know the day-to-day, hour-to-hour things that have happened to your patient. So if it's your patient and there is something urgently going wrong, I would never advocate just leaving. (PGY3-F)

This comment is typical in mixing the notion of "it's your patient" with other rationales for staying. The pull of traditional patient ownership is no doubt key to many delayed departures.

A second influence on stay-or-go decisions is a deep aversion to what is widely known as dumping. To dump is to pass work along to others, mostly but not exclusively across a time threshold (day-to-night or night-to-day), that is interpreted by the receiving resident as work that *could* and *should* have been accomplished by the originating resident. Those who dump fail to do their "own" work. Of course, not all work that is passed off constitutes dumping, as some situations leave little choice but to hand work off to others. But even those situations *can* be interpreted as dumping if the resident passing off the work has a reputation for dumping. To determine if dumping occurred requires a hasty assessment—based on precious little information—of the tasks (could they have been done?), the quantity of tasks (is the amount of work excessive?), the shift (was it extremely busy?), and the person (does he or she do this often?). Unless a resident has an unassailable reputation, the tasks are an unambiguous instance of work that simply had to be passed along, or the shift was clearly frenetic, he or she inevitably runs some risk of being tagged as a dumper when work is passed off. Dumping is believed to stem from character flaws, a poor work ethic, inefficiencies due to inadequate medical knowledge or procedural skill (i.e., a resident is slow because he has to think too much about what he is doing), or an inability to organize one's work effectively. All are serious, potentially career-ending problems.

The new professionalism clashes with the anti-dumping culture. The problem residents face is that *any* work that is passed off *can* be viewed as dumping, whether it should be or not. Since incoming residents were not present for the shift, they cannot accurately assess whether various tasks could or should have been completed, but they routinely do so anyway. The only way to protect oneself from a dumping allegation is to rarely, if ever, pass work to others, and to minimize how much is transferred. Team-based notions of "sharing the workload" are thus difficult to implement given the continued salience of an anti-dumping, do-your-own-work culture. Consider, for example, the following commentary that emerged after a clinical scenario was discussed in an interview:

> You need to think about how much you're checking out and what it involves. Having a few things, checking on labs, those sort of things, checking on results or making sure something occurs is okay, but needing to put in a chest tube, that's different. If I get a call about low blood pressure and their urine output's been dropping off, well you don't check that sort of stuff out. . . . To me there's a big difference between asking them [night staff] to make sure a fire doesn't flare up again versus, hey, here's some crap in your lap—when he has three other services checking out all doing the same thing. Never dump—ever! My view is that there should be no fires going on when you hand off. Things should be under control and the new person's job is to keep them under control and address new fires, not to be handed multiple, acute issues. (PGY3-M)

Both *what* is checked out and *how much* is checked out are singled out as especially important. A fire, a developing fire, or even too many small and normally legitimate tasks that might overwhelm the small night staff are seen as things to handle himself. Various efforts in the fieldwork and interviews to pinpoint what could be checked out without risking attributions of dumping brought little clarity to the matter. Like Justice Potter Stewart's classic shibboleth about pornography—"I know it when I see it"—dumping defies crisp delineation because it depends on a shifting mix of many different contextual and historical factors. The only certain way to avoid an allegation of dumping is to pass little to no work across shifts.

Concerns about inefficiencies in managing a day's workload represent a third strand of culture that fosters delayed departures. Residents and attendings spoke of the developmental importance of learning to anticipate, organize, and dispatch long to-do lists in a satisfactory but timely fashion. Those abilities are hallmarks of an efficient resident. Residents believe that those who are tagged as inefficient risk negative evaluations and formal remediation. Remediation can, and often does, mean that a resident must repeat one or more rotations or, worse, an entire year in the program (Yaghoubian et al. 2012). Attributions—correct or not—of inefficiency are thus feared by residents (see also Hafferty and Tilburt 2015). Consider how the following resident links stay-or-go decisions to concerns about inefficiency:

> Whenever you're handing stuff off that means there is work that wasn't done. That doesn't necessarily mean you are inefficient—there just could have been a pile of work to do. However, there is a feeling of "I didn't get it done. That was inefficient. I should've had it finished!" You don't want to hand it off. I know I've felt that way many times. I don't want to be the one resident who, every night, is handing off three or four things, when someone else is like, "Nope—nothing to hand off! All my patients are tucked in!" (PGY3-F)

A desire to project an image of being efficient and hardworking can set in motion a pattern of delayed departures. Staying to complete work draws less attention than passing it off.

Residents who dump disrespect other residents and are not seen as team players. The aversion to dumping is buttressed by the organization of night care—thin staffing, a lack of familiarity with patients, and skill mismatches—and a form of team comradery.

> The day team, definitely, you want to be a good resident. You want to make the night as easy as possible for the night team. . . . It's definitely a pride thing. It's a we're-all-in-this-together thing. We're a team. You don't want to leave your teammates up the river without a paddle! (PGY5-F)

An intern added, "we try to work as a team—let's not start everybody off for the night on a bad note by dumping" (PGY1-M). In stark contrast to the new professionalism envisioned and advocated by Van Eaton and his colleagues (2005), good team members do their own work and pass little or no work to night residents.

Trimming to Offset Extra Hours?

Our evidence strongly suggests that residents often add hours to their days by delaying scheduled departures. But do they subtract or trim hours on subsequent days to stay within their eighty-hour weekly limit? The single strongest cultural pattern in our data is that residents often failed to link addition and subtraction: an overly long day, or even a string of such days, did not routinely trigger thoughts about trimming hours on subsequent days in order to balance hours and remain within the eighty-hour average work week.

For many, each day was conceptualized as separate and independent, which meant that what happened on one day had no bearing on what would happen on a subsequent day. The following comment was typical:

> Well, it sounds like on a regular basis, you find it pretty easy to add hours to your official workday. Is it practically possible for you to then subtract on a subsequent day? No. Never! That's pretty emphatic. So, you can't come in later or leave earlier? Yes. 100 percent. Subtraction is impossible. There is no one to cover if you're not there a lot of the times. Residents are stretched so thin as it is to cover all the services, to cover all the work that needs to be done, that if you have to stay late one day it doesn't mean that there is going to be less work the next day. So, I've never left early because I've been there longer the day before. . . . I've never seen anyone subtract. I don't think it's ever even a thought that anyone has had to say, "I was here late yesterday, so can I go home early today?" That just isn't part of it—you forget about it and the next day's just the next day. (PGY2-M)

Importantly, the resident offers a rationale for why an effort to trim hours would be difficult—"residents are stretched so thin"—but then adds at the end that the idea of balancing addition with subtraction does not even surface. The most common way of expressing this idea was to cast days as "separate," as in the following pair of comments: "Each day is separate—you start at five thirty in the morning and it really doesn't matter what happened the day before" (PGY2-F) and "the next day is just the next day" (PGY5-M). This approach to hours upends the questionnaire item about the *ease* of trimming hours by suggesting that some do not even entertain the *possibility* of trimming.

A second cultural pattern links efforts to trim hours with undesirable attributions. In a first version of this attribution, those who sought to subtract hours risked being viewed as weak or lazy. Consider a few examples of this way of thinking:

> There's a certain level of responsibility we have, and you don't want to feel like you're the quote unquote weak one if you stayed late and then ask to come in late the next day. You don't want to be seen as a slacker or the kind of person that wants or needs to take time off or anything like that. It's very hard to take time off. No one ever really comments about it either—you just have the feeling that you should be there. (PGY2-M)

A notable aspect of the statement is the notion of a prevailing silence wherein "no one ever really comments about it." Another resident drew out much the same idea in a more spirited manner:

Every single hour that every one of us puts in is absolutely necessary. There is too much work for the number of people who do it! A few months ago, somebody said, "I'm over my hours—I'm not going to come in until later." That person is lazy! That person let their team down! That person let their patients down! I think they did, too. I think that the culture in surgery looks down on almost anyone who would do that. (PGY2-F)

In both cases, efforts to trim hours are linked to unwanted attributions, as no resident wants to be viewed as a slacker, weak, lazy, or the sort of person who lets their patients and team down. Another form of this cultural pattern involves concerns about how a request for time off might invite questions about efficiency. Consider the following comment, which opens with the recurring notion that every day is separate, a "new thing":

If you stay late on one or more days, can you make up for that time on subsequent days by trimming hours? No. Eat it and forget about it. *Why is that?* Every day is just a new thing with its own demands. But really, you never want to report that you're going over hours. If you're over hours, you have to tell someone why you're over hours— it means an email or conversation with upper levels. They could ask, "Why aren't you being efficient enough? Other people in your group can take care of this—why can't you?" And you're like, "Well, I think they're doing what I'm doing, but they're not doing it openly or being honest." You never want that conversation. (PGY3-M)

The tendency for residents to remain silent about work-hour challenges makes it difficult for those who wish to speak up, as doing so draws attention and poses a risk.

Together, these concerns about unwanted attributions—laziness, weakness, and inefficiency—combine to dissuade residents from trimming hours. But it is important to recognize that they are decidedly secondary to the issue with which we opened: for many, the idea of trimming is not even on their radar screens, as one day is simply seen as separate from the next, a "new thing" to manage. One resident, in commenting on the possibility of trimming hours, emphasized that for him "this is hypothetical—I don't even try to make time up. I don't and won't" (PGY4-M). In that way, there is a form of daily "work hours amnesia" that forestalls thoughts about trimming hours on subsequent days after one or more long workdays.

The social organization of work and time also make it difficult to trim hours after one or more long workdays. Most weekdays unfold with a set of inter-dependent activities that need to take place during particular hours.

Residents, especially interns and junior residents, arrive very early in order to pre-round on patients and update medical records. More senior residents and chiefs tend to arrive a bit later, but are then constrained by the need to round and get patient-care tasks identified and assigned before heading off to check on the status of early OR cases and prepare to operate. Many spoke about how days and activities have a rigid temporal order that does not bend to the needs of residents to trim hours. The rigidity of days and tasks becomes an impediment to trimming hours:

> In theory, you can subtract, but it's hard to do. Surgery starts at seven fifteen in the morning. If you don't have all your patients seen, your floor work in motion, and have some interns running around doing that, your day is not going to go well. You're going to be behind. I've seen a few people do that—come in late—but I think the results are always disastrous. You see them struggling all day trying to catch up because they felt like they needed the ten hours off between shifts. My inclination is not to do that. (PGY4-F)

Several residents spoke about how a delayed arrival created a challenging day, which then served to reinforce the notion that "coming in late is really hard" (PGY4-M) and that residents should treat each day as separate.

> I had one chief last year who had me and the mid-level come in late because we were over hours. I hated that because I didn't know anything about what was going on with the patients on the service! While the chief thought it was a nice thing to help with our hours, we ended up playing catch up for most of the day and not knowing anything about the patients. It ended up being more detrimental! (PGY2-F)

While trimming via late arrivals was widely seen as difficult and impractical, most residents noted that trimming via an early departure was more promising and sometimes possible. In every discussion of early departures, residents emphasized how the service workload and staffing were critical in thwarting or facilitating departures. Consider the following comment:

> If the service is busy, no one is keeping a log where they say, "You stayed late on Monday, so we better get you out on Wednesday." No way—never happens. You eat it and never mention it. If a service is busy enough to require you to stay late on one day, then it's likely to be like that pretty much every day—or it could become that way even if there seems to be a slow afternoon. But if it's not a busy

service, if there's nothing going on on a given afternoon or a bunch of cases get cancelled for whatever reason, on the rare day that happens, if you've been late and you're not on call or whatever, someone might say, "Hey—I've got this. You get out of here!" We try to get each other's backs that way, but it's not really something you can plan for or expect. (PGY5-M)

If a service is busy, then residents tended to believe that long hours were likely to be a communal problem: "if one member of a team is over hours, pretty much all of them are" (PGY2-F). Trimming hours in that case would add to the burden shouldered by other residents. If emergent consults or cases surface, "it gets dicey if some get to go home—you can end up being slammed and short-staffed in a hurry!" (PGY1-M).

It is important to note that the possibility of subtraction does not imply that it is frequent, substantial, or predictable.

You don't really subtract very much at all. If it's a really slow day, you can subtract, if you're lucky. Let's say you have four people on the team and only one OR is going. You only have a couple of patients on the floor. Some of you might be able to go home early, but the most you would get would be about an hour. It's not a lot of time! (PGY2-F)

Another resident remarked, "Sure, if we can get people out early, we'll take advantage of it—but it doesn't happen that often, and you can't count on it" (PGY5-M). In one estimate, "even on slow services, early departures happen maybe a few times a year" (PGY2-F). Residents spoke of these opportunities as prized and memorable, but they were nonetheless not substantial or predictable enough to routinely balance out days in which work hours were added. Given that efforts to trim risk attributions of laziness, weakness, and inefficiency, the risk-to-reward balance tilts dramatically toward risk. It is thus not surprising that residents do not routinely look to trim hours and instead consider each day as separate.

Sustaining Long Hours: Supervision and Mixed Messages

The fieldwork and interviews suggested that violations of the work-hour rules by residents are common: they work too many hours, stay later than they should after a night on call, give themselves too little rest between shifts, and take fewer than one day off each week. Efforts to trim hours appear to be more often a theoretical possibility than a regular accomplishment. One chief summarized her view of the rules:

> Honestly, from my personal experience and what I have now seen in two different surgery programs, I would say that the rules are an idea but not a reality. Some residents come in thinking they are real, but as you get more senior as a surgery resident, you pay less and less attention to the rules. Most people disregard or dismiss the number limits. You go to work. You do what you need to do for your patients and your own education. If you stay within the rules, that's fabulous, but if you don't you don't really talk to anyone about it, and you don't report blowing your hours. I speak for the majority—I'm sure of that. (PGY5-F)

A pattern of work-hour violations is entirely consistent with broader evidence (Carpenter et al. 2006; Landrigan et al. 2006; Szymczak et al. 2010; Tabrizian et al. 2011; Arora, Farnan, and Humphrey 2012; Drolet et al. 2013; Bryne, Loo, and Giang 2015). Survey evidence identifies surgery residents as the least compliant of all specialties with the work-hour rules: 67.8 percent reported that they did not comply "with all duty-hour regulations" and 62.1 percent admitted falsely reporting their hours to appear to comply with the regulations (Drolet et al. 2013).

We have focused thus far on aspects of culture and social organization that nudge residents to work too much. We now add to that analysis by considering the character of resident supervision, which is unlike supervision in most workplaces, and the role of mixed messages. Interns and junior residents are most directly supervised by more experienced residents, usually the senior or chief resident on the service. All residents are supervised indirectly, and at times directly, by the attendings on the service to which they are assigned. Any patient-care work performed by a resident is done under the medical and legal authority of the patient's attending, with whom the proverbial buck stops. Attendings also provide end-of-rotation assessments that are drawn upon during periodic and annual reviews of residents.

The fieldwork observations made clear that attendings are in regular and substantial contact with residents in person, by phone, and sometimes through emails and texts. They often work shoulder-to-shoulder as they provide patient care and perform operations. They nearly always do that in clinics, when they jointly round on hospitalized patients, and in the OR. But that contact is not constant, which means that the workdays of attendings commonly intersect rather than overlap with those of residents. For example, attendings rarely know when residents arrive or leave, or even what they might be doing during most moments of a day. An attending might work with a senior or chief resident much of the day in the OR, but she would not know much about the other residents, or what that senior or chief did before or after their time together in the OR. Attendings thus have incomplete information about the hours and schedules of the residents with whom they work.

In the fieldwork program, and all of those with which we are familiar, resident work hours are self-reported and retrospective, leaving plenty of room for misrepresentation. Hours are regularly reported to a residency coordinator and questions about compliance with the rules are posed on a survey administered by the ACGME early each year (January through April). Work hours are also commonly reported to the chief or senior resident on a service. Those reported to the senior, chief, or coordinator are not anonymous or confidential: residents can and do get asked to account for the hours they submit, especially if they exceed limitations. Information about work-hour compliance provided to the ACGME is reported back to programs in a way that preserves resident anonymity. At the fieldwork site, and in all other programs we know, there is no monitoring of reported versus actual hours, and no apparent staff or attending interest in doing so. In short, a resident's work hours are what they say they are.

These practices and policies provide a context in which residents believe they *can* violate the rules without putting their programs at risk of official sanctions. The trick, they say, is really no trick at all: report compliant hours to both the program and the ACGME and forget about tracking actual hours. Consider how one resident put it:

> Our residents are committed to patient care. So the vast majority of us will just end up violating our hours, but we lie about them so that we are compliant. There's such a stringent oversight of all the hours now, even if you are over by an hour, or the computer average is 80.2. That's ridiculous. But we get called about that by our program coordinator if we submit hours that are noncompliant. I'll be honest—I submit, every week, 6 a.m. to 3 p.m. on days I'm not on call or off. As far as the computer is concerned, that's what I do. But of course that's bullshit. I put that down but work whatever hours I think are right. I don't even keep track of my actual hours. *So it's only when people are honest and report working too much that things become dicey?* Right. Lie and things are great! I should say that us staying, at least in our program, isn't an institutionally imposed thing, where the administration or attending force us to stay. We take it upon ourselves to stay and do that because we feel responsible for the patients. It's nothing that's imposed on us—it's our choice. (PGY5-M)

When residents say that they "are committed to patient care," "feel responsible for the patients," and violate the rules because they choose to embrace that commitment and responsibility, they affirm and sustain traditional surgical values—to be discussed more fully in the next chapter—that many attendings hold dear. To do so, however, they must lie by submitting false time logs, a practice that was described repeatedly during the interviews. However, not all residents under-report their hours, or do so consistently; nor do all provide the same hours-worked data to their program coordinators and the ACGME. Trouble does surface for some programs.

Supervision and reporting practices thus set the stage for work-hour subterfuge. Mixed messages from faculty and senior residents join with the cultural and organizational issues described earlier in the chapter to further nudge residents toward long-hour practices that violate the rules. Despite official and often dramatic proclamations about the need for work-hour compliance, faculty routinely speak and act in ways that encourage long hours. At least on the surface, there are many instances of mixed and confusing messages as to whether residents should strictly abide by, flexibly interpret, or disregard the rules. Consider, for example, the following comment by a program director:

> The duty hours create a situation where many times we talk out of both sides of our mouth. I know this happens to me regularly in the program director role. I'll get up and I'll say, "Commit yourselves to your patient's care. Be there! Be conscientious! Look at and know the details! Don't go home until you've checked the potassium—or whatever! And if you don't do that, I will!" But then in the next sentence I'm saying, "You've got to be duty-hour compliant! You know it's your responsibility to police this. We can't take care of this for everybody. Make sure you're accurate when you turn in your hours. It kills me if you turn in on your ACGME anonymous survey that you worked over eighty hours three times in the past month when you're not turning it in on the forms I see." So it's a very mixed message. It's this is what we want and idealize, but this is the limits of the world we live in. So I think the eighty-hour rules have created that sort of schizophrenic mind-set. (A-M)

The surgeon clearly believes that behaviors consistent with traditional obligations are in tension with those required to comply with the reforms. Nearly identical—and similarly contradictory—comments were voiced by the program director during the fieldwork and in interviews with attendings.

Mixed messages may be more apparent than real. In the fieldwork and in several interviews, I had opportunities to discuss mixed-message statements by program directors, attendings, and senior residents. Residents quickly emphasized on each occasion that the messages were clear, not mixed. Correct or not, residents firmly believed that what faculty and senior residents said about committing themselves to patient care was *authentic*—that it was what they really thought, cared about, and hoped to see in residents. What faculty and senior residents said about limiting work hours, in contrast, was thought to be thoroughly *insincere*—that it was what "they have to say" because of pressure from the ACGME. Through interpretations of that sort, "mixed messages" become straightforward marching orders.

Faculty deeds, not just their words, also play a role in helping to sustain long-hour practices that challenge the reforms. In the fieldwork, it was common to see or hear about faculty staying late, well past the day-to-night shift change, or coming back at night to care for patients. We detailed some of those patterns in the earlier chapter on fatigue, arguing that the practice patterns of faculty help sustain the belief that "real life" surgery requires exposure to, and mastery of, working while fatigued. When faculty stayed late or came back at night, it was obvious to all that their obligations were unbounded by the time limits that at least officially constrain the clinical activities of residents. Consider an attending's description of the dilemma residents face when they see faculty stay to care for patients:

> I think a big problem for residents is that they model how attendings behave. So if we've been up all night with a resident and they're going home, they see the attending is not going home, and that hurts their potential professionalism. The program director and the residency coordinator are beating up on them to go home so they stay within the duty-hour regulations, yet they see the attending, who has also been working all night, staying to take care of the patient. So, they make a choice, "Do I lie about my hours and stay and take care of the patient, or do I abandon the patient and go home?" That's a struggle for the residents. (A-F)

Seeing faculty behave in this way undoubtedly helps to sustain long hours among residents and thereby undermine the reforms. One resident described her reaction to the occasional situation in which an attending demanded that she leave because she had reached her work hour limits: "Quite frankly, it makes me and other residents feel like jerks when we have to leave a critical patient, our own patient, and hand them off—that's terrible!" (PGY3-F).

Messages that encourage long hours also come from senior residents and chiefs. Senior residents and, especially, the chief resident on a service assume supervisory and teaching responsibilities for junior residents and are evaluated

on their performance by their attending surgeons. That responsibility encourages senior residents to press their underlings to do what must be done, even
if they would rather not, in order to stay in the good graces of their attendings and to meet patient-care needs. Some senior residents described how
they contributed to a mixed-message environment:

> In our program, we're supposed to be out by 7 p.m. But we do our very best to tell
> our junior residents that 7 p.m. is not a time you need to leave, even though that's
> what our program director and faculty say. You don't need to leave the hospital
> at seven! What we say, as often as we must, is that you leave when your work is
> done. And so I think there are some mixed signals. (PGY5-M)

The comment is characteristic in that at least some senior residents were willing and able to counter messages about work-hour practices conveyed by program directors and their attendings.

Reflection: It's Different Here

Eighty percent of current general surgery residency graduates go into post-
residency fellowship programs after completing their residency. Typically, this
means moving to another location and culture for one or two years of additional training that qualify the graduate for subspecialization in an area of their
choice. In these new settings, the graduates encounter a new culture as well as
new work relationships.

Several years ago now, one of our program's graduates matriculated into
a trauma/critical care fellowship at a prominent institution. The fellowship
was accredited by the ACGME, and therefore subject to duty hour requirements parallel to those that govern residency training. A couple months into
the fellowship, our graduate called me. "Dr. Mellinger, it's different here" were
his opening words after we exchanged greetings. When I asked how so, he
proceeded to remind me of the conversations we had had about duty hours
during his residency years, encouraging compliance for all the reasons summarized in this volume, not least the ACGME mandate. The graduate proceeded to tell me that in one of his early months in the fellowship, he had
logged well over one hundred hours of work per week, due to a colleague
being away and there being no added personnel to cover the workload for
some critically ill patients. At the end of the month, he was summoned to the

department chair's office. As my former resident walked into the room, the chairman slid a piece of paper with the resident's duty hour report across the table in his direction and said, "I see there has been some mistake on your duty-hour reporting." The message was clear: do the work, lie about it, and don't repeat this scenario by reporting a violation again. That is how we play the game here.

Scenarios like this one can breed a certain sense of gravitas if not self-righteousness from nearly every perspective. For folks in regulatory roles who either never have, or no longer do work in the front lines of health care delivery, it is perhaps easy to pontificate on the excesses and perceived dangers of the historical "all in" training paradigm which the very term resident implies. For the program director, there is a sense of having to be the ultimate steward answering to a complex set of masters. Included in this are residents expecting an advocate and educational prioritizer, faculty ultimately responsible for patient outcomes with their own nonregulated duty hour pressures and challenges with burn out, and accreditation authorities without whose blessing the whole program can be jeopardized. For the resident, the playing field is perhaps even more complex, with competing interests around patient care, maximizing the educational experience upon which their subsequent career will depend, helping the program maintain accreditation, and maintaining the trust of colleagues with whom they share a complex, unpredictable, and high-stakes work environment.

In the midst of such challenges and tensions, and with the cost of our American system being at such a premium compared to the rest of the world, one would think that the human resource margin to make adjustments when needed—including day to day in real time to allow duty-hour compliance—would be built into the system. Unfortunately, and particularly so in major urban settings with heavy service loads of high-acuity indigent care such as my former resident found himself in, such is not typically the case. It seems the costs of our system hinge more on other factors than personnel and staffing needs. These include our first world temptations and indulgences (obesity and tobacco are the two biggest drivers of national health expenditure), the costs of developing and maintaining cutting edge pharmacologic agents and technologies, and the liability management necessities of our system, including the defensive medicine that is bred therefrom. C. Everett Koop once quipped that Americans wanted three things in their health care system: state-of-the-art care, immediately available, at an affordable price. His response was that we could pick any two of the three.

It is of course too easy to blame regulators, administrators, the medical profession itself, and "system issues" for the challenges of trying to balance continuity of care, quality, learning, and safety, with the latter including the alertness and health of the caregiver. In such discussions, flexibility is often highlighted as part of the potential answer. The image that comes to mind is that of an NFL quarterback who approaches the line of scrimmage, and seeing a defensive alignment that makes the preconceived plan ineffective, changes the plan in real time to allow effectiveness. Such an image has an appeal for the duty-hour restricted resident; if you had a rough night, go home early today or come in later tomorrow. The difference is that the quarterback still has eleven players to work with, and what is at stake is a game, not the lives of others. Cut the quarterback's team say down from eleven to seven, keep the defense fully staffed, and you start to get a picture of what day-to-day adjustments might look like as a reliable tool in addressing work hour compliance challenges.

Accordingly, real-time adjustments in resident manpower prove to be practically ineffective in managing duty-hour pressures, despite the theoretic attractiveness of such a strategy. The reasons for this are complex, but include the limited manpower margin and variable workload that are part of the health care delivery equation. While larger programs and institutions who have built some added flexibility into their workload coverage capabilities through advanced practice providers may do better than others, the latter solution is itself complex, as will be discussed in a subsequent chapter. For the majority of programs, and especially on services with higher emergency loads such as trauma and acute care services where my former resident landed for his fellowship, using tomorrow as a promissory note to right today's debts is not a reliable strategy, because, as it were, "each day has enough trouble of its own."

CHAPTER 4

Professionalism, Old and New

Time and Morality in Surgical Training and Practice

I think that the eighty-hour rules were created by someone with no knowledge of surgery or the training process. Or, if they did have knowledge of it, they have a complete disregard for it because the culture is what makes you a surgeon. (PGY5-M)

Studies of the educational consequences of the duty-hour restrictions have largely focused on case volume and mix, time for didactic instruction, and in-service and board exams (e.g., Fletcher et al. 2005; Durkin et al. 2008; Kairys et al. 2008; Vaughn et al. 2008; Bennett et al. 2017). Although important, those processes and outcomes bear primarily upon the *technical* dimension of residency training and overlook the *cultural* dimension, which focuses on how doctors-in-training learn, understand, and discharge professional obligations. The Institute of Medicine affirmed the importance of culture by noting that one of "three cardinal educational principles" that underlie residency training is "to reinforce professionalism and its obligations" (Ulmer, Wolman, and Johns 2008). Bosk's (1979, 190) classic study of a surgical residency program likewise led him to the conclusion that it was "above all things an ethical training."

Many comments in the previous chapters were accompanied by passionate statements about professional obligations. Thus far, we have only tangentially touched on those beliefs, focusing instead on how surgeons understand and respond to fatigue, the problems of transferring information and responsibility during patient handoffs, and the challenges of delaying departures and trimming hours. Our aim in this chapter is to explore more fully whether and how surgeons perceive a conflict between professional values and the reforms, an issue that has received little attention in previous research. An analysis of this sort necessarily probes beliefs, which some medical researchers disregard and dismiss as mere opinion (e.g., Philibert et al. 2013, 476), even though beliefs are often the bedrock of behavior.

Our evidence comes from the survey and interviews from the second wave and from the fieldwork. The interviews and survey questions asked residents and attending surgeons to comment on how surgical professionalism is understood and enacted and whether they believed the reforms aligned with surgical professionalism. In addition, many questions in the interviews, ostensibly about other issues, sparked commentaries about professionalism, making it one of the most dominant and recurring themes in the interviews as a whole. For attendings, this topic produced extensive and passionate commentaries, far exceeding those offered by residents. The reason for that can best be understood by their perspective and experience with pre-reform residencies. Their perspective derives from being post-residency surgeons able to reflect on the meaning and importance of their residency experiences and, importantly, how things have changed. Residents, immersed in training, lack the perspective afforded by time and direct experience with pre-reform residencies. In the chapter, we thus draw less on the comments of residents and more on those offered by attendings.

Time and Professional Obligation Prior to the Reforms

The meaning and significance of present-day matters often come into focus only when contrasted against the past. Since our interviews and fieldwork began after the work-hour restrictions were put into place, we lean upon Bosk's (1979) trenchant field study of a general surgery program to outline several salient issues and set a baseline. Bosk's study, conducted in the 1970s, points to patterns and ways of thinking that dovetail with how attendings describe the past and how they interpret and evaluate present-day beliefs and behavior. For our purposes, three of Bosk's ideas form an essential backdrop: first, his distinction between the technical and judgmental errors that residents commit and those that are deemed normative; second, how normative errors were minimized; and third, why normative errors received outsized attention.

Residents are expected to make technical and judgmental errors. Errors of that sort include mistakes during surgery itself—such as inadvertently puncturing an artery, suturing incorrectly, or requesting the wrong type of suture—and during pre- and postoperative encounters with patients—such as mistaking one surgical problem for another or failing to anticipate or manage properly the emergence of a postoperative wound infection. These failures of knowledge and technique are never welcomed by attendings or more senior residents, but they are understood as inevitable as less-experienced residents acquire medical knowledge and learn to perform procedures. Once made, a given technical or judgmental error must be reported, not hidden, and should surface again only rarely, if ever, for any given resident. In short, "learn and move on" is the credo, and only those who continue to make the same mistakes—whose learning curves come to be seen as too flat—or who fail to report and deal with them promptly—who come to be seen as dishonest—draw the strong ire of senior residents and attendings. Just as children cannot learn to walk without incurring bumps and bruises, even the most capable and conscientious resident is expected to make these sorts of forgivable mistakes in the process of becoming a competent surgeon.

In stark contrast, normative errors are neither expected nor easily forgiven. As Bosk (1979, 51) aptly describes it, a normative error is a failure in "assuming a role" whereas a technical or judgmental error is a failure "in a role." Failing to assume the role of surgeon means that a resident has not been sufficiently diligent or conscientious—"lazy, negligent, or dishonest" in Bosk's (53) language—in what they say and do. A normative error means that a resident has failed to "act like a surgeon," a failure viewed in moral terms and thought to stem from deep and possibly permanent character flaws, not shortcomings in knowledge or skill common to the inexperienced. Most commonly, normative errors involve a resident's failure to know nearly everything about a patient's past medical history and current condition, changes in the patient's condition, the results of any studies or labs that have been performed, the observations or recommendations provided by consulting services, and critically, failing to keep more senior residents and attending surgeons abreast of any important issues or changes. Shortcomings in these areas violate the "no surprises rule," wherein residents have an obligation to always be on top of things so that their attending surgeons are not blindsided by new developments. As extensions of the eyes and ears of attending surgeons, even interns are assumed to have the ability to avoid normative errors through force of character, not knowledge or technique. Those who committed too many normative errors were called "minor surgeons" and "morally bankrupt" and risked expulsion from the residency program (57, 61).

Residents sought to avoid all errors, but they dreaded real or alleged normative errors. Like now, residents at the time of Bosk's study in the 1970s had to eat and sleep, interact to some extent with friends and families, pay bills and manage other mundane aspects of everyday life, read and study about basic science and surgery, help educate and supervise medical students assigned to their surgical service, and provide quite a bit of clinical care. But those involvements were never to get in the way of them knowing everything about their patients and keeping their attendings fully—but of course not excessively— abreast of whatever might turn out to be important. Bosk's comments are worth noting at some length:

> Undoubtedly, trying to meet such multifocal demands [i.e., eating, sleeping, families, patient care, and so forth] explains to some degree why normative error occurs. Attendings, however, never allow such factors to excuse normative error. For them, there is no "good" excuse for a normative error because *no other system of relevance is ever allowed ascendancy over the basic doctor-patient dyad and because normative errors are always interpreted as evidence that the houseofficer placed some other concern above patient care.* (57, emphasis added)

Residents, for example, could not say "I don't know what happened—it was my night off," because any effort to deny responsibility or excuse ignorance "communicates to attendings a disinterest in clinical care" (76). Without doubt, the pervasive and deep fear of normative error was a cornerstone of the all-consuming character of surgical residencies.

But why were normative errors so salient and intolerable? And why, despite the obvious need for residents to master so much knowledge and technique, would Bosk conclude that "my claim is that postgraduate training of surgeons *is above all things an ethical training*" (190, emphasis added)? Why subordinate technical performance to what amounts to moral performance—the commission or avoidance of normative errors? For Bosk, the answer was that technical and judgmental matters are often unclear, meaning that "honest errors" occur because knowledge and its application are not—and will never be—perfect. In contrast, surgeons expect what Bosk calls "perfect compliance with the norms of clinical responsibility" (181). Surgeons are to "help as best he [or she] can," to be "available when the occasion demands," to offer "sacrifices of time and energy," and to "do everything possible" (169–70). Surgical outcomes are of course always uncertain, but clinical conduct need not be, and that conduct forms the basis of a surgeon's moral claim that he or she did the best they could. In addition, technique and judgment are largely invisible and difficult for colleagues to assess, whereas the discharging of clinical responsibilities is often highly visible and hence easily assessed. For the most part, Bosk argues that "negligence is defined in terms of clinical norms—moral values—and not technical standards" (181).

A Moral Shift? The Loss of Patient Ownership and the Rise of Shift Mentalities

Duty-hour restrictions are widely thought to collide with the clinical norms described in Bosk's analysis. A first and primary conflict centers on what is often described as a moral shift, the sense that the traditional understanding of what a surgeon *owes* a patient has been challenged by the reforms. Attendings worry that this shift is not limited to residencies but rather will affect how surgery is practiced in the future. For the most part, this concern surfaces via ubiquitous references to two overlapping ideas, patient ownership and shift mentalities, and how the former has waned and the latter has risen due to the work-hour reforms.

Patient ownership centers on the responsibilities surgeons assume for their patients. Analytically isolating the most common components of traditional conceptions and enactments of patient ownership can best be done by presenting and then reviewing several comments by attending surgeons. Consider a first statement, rife with the passion that is common when faculty talk about these issues:

> *Let me ask about professionalism, which you already addressed a bit. Many argue that it involves something more than medical knowledge or surgical technique, but exactly what it involves seems a bit unclear.* I do agree with that. *All right. Could you give me some examples of the kinds of things you believe are most important about surgical professionalism?* Well, I think that what distinguishes us as professionals from others is that we accept when we sign on for this line of work an obligation to our patient to be there for them, to provide them with the highest quality of care, both from an intellectual or cognitive or technical standpoint, but also from an oversight standpoint. And that means attention to detail, responsiveness, and quite frankly, it incorporates at some level a certain degree of willingness to be exploited, to sacrifice one's time, and to be available to one's patients. That's patient ownership as I've always known it, and I don't think my take is unusual. I just think that the willingness to put yourself out there, to be exploited without even regarding it as exploitation, to simply say that this is a measure of my obligation to the patients that I am responsible for, and I'm going to take care of this. I think that philosophy is what really distinguishes us. (A-M)

Patient ownership is widely understood as a moral boundary that distinguishes surgeons from those who do other forms of work. It goes well beyond typical notions of customer or client care or loyalty to represent a devotion to do everything one can in terms of developing and then applying one's mind and procedural capacities, engaging in appropriate supervision of patient care, and sacrificing one's time to provide the best patient care one can. The idea that one is to willingly submit to being "exploited without even regarding it as exploitation" subordinates self-interest and extolls the virtue of "putting patients first," an expression that is often invoked when surgeons describe traditional patient ownership.

Those who focus on the shift—and leave according to the hands of the clock rather than when patient-care needs have been met—are widely described as having a shift mentality. Shift mentalities dramatically clash with traditional patient ownership, which requires that one strive to "sacrifice one's time and to be available to one's patients." Consider, for example, how the following surgeon links the "mentality of shift work" to a loss of individual responsibility commonly associated with traditional patient ownership:

So you've commented a good bit about handoffs. Is there anything else that's been affected by the eighty-hour rules? I think some of our ultimate professional ideals have been cast to the wayside with this eighty-hour work week. It's completely overturned how we have traditionally thought about patient care: that there's one person that's ultimately responsible and it doesn't matter what time of the day or what day of the week it is if something needs to be done. It totally changes the system of the surgeon being ultimately responsible for their patient. We've gone from there's somebody who has to own up for whatever course of action occurs in a patient's treatment to this mentality of shift work where you go from one doctor to another to another. If something happens, well, it's the fault of the whole system. I think we're engendering this thought process in our trainees where they no longer feel ultimate responsibility and they never develop real patient ownership so that they're willing to go the extra mile that we have traditionally gone. We're telling young doctors that it's okay if they go home and their patient is going to be alright—well, maybe. I just think the people that have changed the system don't realize what we have ingrained in our culture for one hundred years about ultimate responsibility and making us humble doctors that want to do the best we can for our patients to saying, "Well, it's okay for me to go home now because I might be tired." I think that will spill over into their practice when they get out on their own to a tremendous extent. At this point, they're no longer trained the way we'd want them to be trained, and many think that there are other objectives that are more important than their patient's well-being. I just think that could bring the whole thing to a crashing disaster at some point. (A-M)

This surgeon describes patient ownership as an "ultimate professional ideal," an emphatic but common claim that is highly individualistic in character. Traditional patient ownership means a *particular* surgeon assumes responsibility and therefore must essentially disregard time and "own up" for patient well-being. Typical of comments of this sort, the surgeon derides the practice of patients going from "one doctor to another to another" and the tendency to fault "the whole system" if something goes awry. Fears about the consequences of a loss of patient ownership were often dramatized with expressions like "a crashing disaster."

In the minds of attendings, the rise of shift mentalities has two main drawbacks. First, shift mentalities induce discontinuities because the care of a patient will transfer from one surgeon to another. Handoffs, as argued earlier, are widely viewed as weak and dangerous links in the chain of care. This concern leads to comments, like that given above, about patients going from "one doctor to another to another" and the risks that is thought to entail. Traditional patient ownership and continuity are seen as protective. Second, shift mentalities are commonly associated with a mental switch that turns off when shifts end. Several surgeons described how they find it helpful to think about patients when they are at home and ostensibly off duty. That patient-on-the-mind practice is thought to help surgeons craft care plans in ways that are impossible when an out-of-sight, out-of-mind shift mentality is embraced. Consider the following comment, which highlights this situation:

> Shift mentalities destroy professionalism. What happens with the residents is that they say, "This is just a job. I'm coming to work for ten hours and then I'm done, I'm getting the hell out of here." As opposed to, professionalism means that this is your lifestyle even when you're not on the job. And even when you're at home, you're still thinking about your patients, you're still worried about them. The shift mentality is terrible because it actually trains you to not be a professional surgeon. Because it's, basically, "I'm responsible, I'm in the hospital, I'm out of there, it's not my responsibility, someone else will take care of it." That is not what we're trained to be as surgeons. You have a high index of suspicion, something bothers you, you can't sleep, you get up and you go take care of it right away, as opposed to taking care of it tomorrow morning which might be too late. That's the difference between having a dead and a live patient. (A-M)

Even at home, surgeons are implored to think about their patients. Those who embrace the traditional role of surgeon do so without regard to the clock.

Comments about patient ownership are often abstract, as in those provided thus far. Many, however, also described more concretely what behaviors were compatible with traditional patient ownership. A first and typical comment is as follows:

> *So you've described your concerns about handoff issues—about a loss of information and a lack of familiarity with patients. Are those your main concerns about the eighty-hour rules?* I would say yes. The other thing that I do notice and will add to that is, in general, I notice among the residents a lack of ownership of the patient, particularly at night, but I mean even to some degree during the day in the sense that this patient is my responsibility up until I sign out at six o'clock. And then conversely on the other end, at night, they're baby-sitting, they're putting out fires but nothing more. *Now when you say a lack of ownership, could you give me an example of what situation you might see and then say, "That's evidence of a lack of ownership?"* Really easy. Patient X needed this study result followed up on, say it's a radiologic study or something like that. The study was done by four thirty, they sign out at six o'clock, but the intern just signs it out to the person who is coming on at night, where they still had time to check it themselves. The response in that situation is, "Well, I just left it for the night guy to check on." I think most of us and even some of our senior residents right now, would have checked on all of those things because they feel they're obligated to because it's their patient. That's actually the standard of care in medicine in general: you order a test, you follow up the result. (A-M)

A lack of ownership implies a failure to assume responsibility for patient care. At night, patient ownership reaches a nadir, as residents are often overwhelmed and just "baby sit" patients and "put out fires" until day residents return. In the day, a lack of ownership is evident when a resident leaves unfinished aspects of patient care that could have been completed. They are, in effect, checking out early, and pushing work to the night staff that they could and should have done. That is of course what was described earlier as dumping. Actions of that sort are widely seen as evidence of shift mentalities and a lack of patient ownership.

Residents also recognize and comment on these issues. For example, one handoff session observed during the fieldwork included a chief, an intern, and a third-year resident. An intern from the vascular/transplant service provided in-person checkout just a few minutes before 6 p.m., the change-over time when night float became responsible for patients. During the handoff, the intern emphasized that a "just ordered" abdominal CT for a patient should be checked and the attending called that evening with the results. After finishing the other handoffs, the night-float intern checked online and learned that the scan had been completed several hours earlier. "I can't believe it," she said, loudly and indignantly, and the other two night-float residents quickly agreed, turning to me and saying, "it's so bad to do that." As the chief and I walked to the radiology reading room to confer with the night radiology resident about the results, I asked her a simple question: Why get upset?

> It's not just the dump or the lie, the chief says, even though they matter. It's that everybody will know less and that's asking for trouble. The service's intern would have known exactly what the attending wanted from the study, what the broader concerns were, and how wired he was about the results. Those interests would have been communicated to those doing and then interpreting the study. Now those people are gone and we've got one person staffing the whole room (the large radiology reading room was empty but for one night resident), and he knows nothing whatsoever about the study. Who knows what else is on his plate right now. The attending's notes about the study won't be available for another day, so the night resident will have to read it again and that's of course what he says and not what the attending said. It's all more work for us and it risks problems where it should have been taken care of by the intern on the service. (fieldnotes)

Interviews produced similar comments by residents, such as the following:

> I also think ownership of patients is important. It's something that I think is changing with the shift work mentality that's emerging. *Could you expand on that? What might you see when you watched a resident who was taking ownership versus one who wasn't?* I think a resident that has ownership of patient care follows up on studies even if they know someone else is supposed to follow up on it. They trust the other resident or intern, but they want to know for themselves. Also, for example, when it comes time to hand off to the next team to say, "Oh, there's this CT scan pending. You can follow up on that," instead of being more proactive about getting things done and wanting to do it themselves. *So, ownership means maintaining control or responsibility rather than passing it off to somebody else?* Yes. *And you think that the eighty-hour rules have increased a shift-work approach where there's less ownership?* Oh yeah. Absolutely. It's because we're supposed to leave, so some do but others don't. (PGY4-F)

In the fieldwork event, the ownership issue was presented largely as a practical matter that caused more work and potential trouble for the night-float residents. In the interview comment, having ownership means that one *wants* to know the result of a study and *wants to check it themselves* rather than passing it off to someone else. The shift, in that sense, does not end until questions posed have been answered. In both cases, shift mentalities mean that involvements are driven by the clock, not the tasks at hand, an approach that flies in the face of the temporally unbounded character of traditional patient ownership.

Like their attending surgeons, residents also recognize that covering many unfamiliar patients at night or on the weekend is not ideal. Not surprisingly, residents are far less likely than attendings to say that they merely "baby sit" or "put out fires" at night, as those are interpreted as pejorative expressions. However, they suggest a difference in how they approach care, as in the following comment:

> I think there are some times when one person is on the service, and they're post call or whatever, and then they're leaving and then they're trading out the patients to someone else. I'm not going to say a drop off, but sometimes someone who's been taking care of the patient day in and day out is obviously going to have more interest than somebody who's just covering. I think we do a good job of covering for each other and carrying that out, but I do feel like there is a little bit of a loss there. I don't think it's even necessarily detrimental at all times to patients. It's just that that interest level isn't there as much because it's somebody new to you. (PGY4-M)

The "interest level" noted here is complex. In part, it is driven by the fact that handoffs rarely leave night residents feeling confident that they know enough about patient conditions and care plans to be as involved as the day-team residents. Thin knowledge and the possibility of being swamped by emergencies combine to dampen interest, perhaps unknowingly, even among the most diligent residents. Additionally, direct involvement in a patient's care—such as being the resident who participated in her operation—surely sparks interest in the patient's care and well-being. That is a widely held explanation for why more senior residents seem to embrace patient ownership more fully than junior residents, as the following resident notes:

> I think there's less ownership of the patients than there might have been in the past, especially from a junior resident's standpoint. It's more like, "This is where I go for work, these are my patients during the day, but I don't have to cover them

at night and someone else takes care of them." And whether that's a value or a piece of professionalism that we're not teaching, I don't really know how I would classify it. But I think that more of that becomes apparent with time in the program. As people progress, they begin to have more of that ownership, and it begins to be their own decision. Not that they are required to stay until the patient is taken care of and tucked in, but rather that that's their patient. There's more of a direct correlation with, "I operated on this patient now and I take more ownership." It's now my patient and I'm more their physician rather than just the person covering for them on the floor. Not everybody's like that, but many are. (PGY4-F)

Direct involvement, however, is not sufficient to ensure that level of interest, as this and other residents are quick to say that "not everybody's like that."

Rampant Normative Error?

The reforms are widely thought to have unleashed a torrent of normative errors, the failure to sufficiently immerse oneself in, and know everything about, a patient's past and present conditions. They provide a new, unassailable justification and hence defang normative errors because residents can claim that they were unaware of various details about a patient's condition or care because they were *required* to be off-duty and away from the hospital. Bosk's claim that there was no good excuse for a normative error no longer holds. Resident compliance with the work-hour rules undermines their ability to be nearly omnipresent and all-knowing. This change makes it difficult for attendings to know what they can expect of residents and whether they are exhibiting sufficient diligence and conscientiousness. Surgeons did not use the expression normative error to describe these concerns, but Bosk's concept is apt and helpful because it explains why attendings utterly lament residents' loss of familiarity with patients.

Comments about normative errors were pegged primarily to knowledge during rounds. Rounds have many purposes and are conducted at different times of the day with different mixes of medical students, interns, residents, chief residents, and attending surgeons. Those in which a chief resident is present or, more importantly, an attending, are occasions to probe, develop, and assess general medical knowledge and familiarity with a particular patient's past medical history, present condition, and care plan. On some occasions, the interactions are casual, but on others an aggressive "pimping" can occur, wherein a chief resident or an attending challenges underlings' knowledge and reasoning. In

Bosk's (1979) fieldwork, rounds were a common way to detect normative errors. An extract from his analysis illustrates this process:

> Questions follow in rapid succession: What are the blood counts? What did the latest chest film show? When is the barium swallow scheduled? Such questions are an attempt to establish if a subordinate knows what is going on with the patient. If a subordinate knows the facts of a case, questioning can move on to questions of treatment; but if a subordinate does not know what is going on with a patient, then the reason for this must be established. Here, there is only one acceptable defense: "The lab has not completed the test yet." *Any other excuse such as "it's not my patient" or "I was off last night" indicate to an attending that a subordinate is not putting forth minimal effort to meet the requirements of his role.* (97, emphasis added)

In the fieldwork and interviews, faculty often complained about residents' lack of familiarity with patients. Consider the following comment and how it contrasts with Bosk's account:

> During rounds, if there's a test, study, lab values—whatever—there's no hesitation to say, "I don't know. I just don't know what it says." "I don't know" is a pretty common response now. There's no way I would have just said, "I don't know," unless I had a really good reason. "Tell me about his H & P." "I don't know." It's a work ethic problem. You've got to be willing to work hard—it's a tough job. There's no two ways around it. That's one of the biggest problems with the eighty-hour work week. Before the work-hour restrictions, if somebody didn't know things during rounds, well, it's because they didn't care. So it reflected on them in a very bad and important way. But now, it's routine that they don't know the answers. If you were the minority and you didn't know the answer, you were going to be in trouble—there were going to be consequences. But if the majority doesn't know the answer, then what are you going to do? (A-M)

This comment reveals several common beliefs among faculty. The increased frequency of "I don't know" normative errors is thought to stem from a mix of three sources: first, an erosion of a work ethic, either due to the work-hour restrictions or, for some, broader generational changes; second, the loss of clear-cut standards as to what residents are to know, what excuses will be tolerated, and what consequences will follow normative error; and three, limitations on familiarity and knowledge implied by the need for residents to work less and be away from the hospital more often. The surgeon's comment, above, points to all but the third source.

The idea that familiarity and knowledge are at least sometimes victims of the reforms tends to be woven into comments in a complex way. It is not uncommon, for example, for surgeons to acknowledge that the reforms diminish familiarity, but that does not prevent work ethics, for example, from also being salient. A structural issue—less time at the hospital—is routinely recast as a personal or generational deficiency—a flawed work ethic. Consider how the following surgeon mixes concerns about time constraints, work ethics, and sanctions for poor performance:

> There are things that I expect that are just sort of maintenance in terms of taking care of patients. We should inventory our patients' medication profiles every day to make sure they're getting what we think they're getting, what we want them to get and not getting anything else. I say to my residents, "Have we looked at the meds today?" I get dumbfounded, cross-eyed looks. No one has done this, so we stop and we do it. Well, in part they can't do that because they don't have time to do it. These aren't stupid or ill-willed people, but I do think that there's an ethic or compulsiveness that's lacking. When I was a resident, you wouldn't think to not have information at hand. Roundsmanship was all about having every single fact nailed down so that, God forbid, if the chief resident or attending should ask you a question, you knew everything there was to know. That ethic has been lost. And the consequences were different. I mean, we would get yelled at, we would just get verbally abused in the hallway in front of the entire team. That's not necessarily the greatest way to live but it conveyed a message. Not that I would want to do that—I would not. But the underlying information base and that model of care is still what I'm looking for, but I can't get it out of my residents in this environment. (A-M)

The attending recognizes time constraints, saying that "they don't have time" to inventory the medication profiles. As is common, however, time constraints clearly recede as an explanatory factor, giving way to a loss of a work ethic and the social control provided by the threat, if not the delivery, of verbal abuse.

Morbidity and mortality conferences were a second key setting in which normative errors emerged. The tradition in these conferences, which were both observed during the fieldwork and often mentioned in the interviews, is to have the more senior residents on a surgical service present cases of complications or deaths. The presentations offer opportunities for procedural and patient-care issues to be discussed, but they also provide another forum in which attendings interrogate residents to assess their familiarity with cases and their broader medical knowledge. Because chiefs and other senior residents are less often in the hospital because of the reforms, many believe that there has been a marked increase in "I wasn't there" and "I don't know" types of responses during these conferences, a point made by the following surgeon:

> Let me give you another example of how the eighty-hour rules matter. Again very subtle, but the psychology is changing. Do you attend morbidity and mortality conferences? *Yes, I do.* Okay, how often do you now hear, by the fact that I'm stating it, I hear it frequently, so-and-so stands up to present a complication or a death. And someone asks, "Well, what happened at this point?" And the resident says, "Well, I wasn't there myself, but from what I understand, on-and-on." And we accept that. Interestingly, our reaction is "Oh, okay, you weren't there. Oh, gee, I guess it's okay you don't know much about the patient even though you're the chief." We've become numb to that as well. That wasn't a common refrain years ago. We've changed the rules of the game and that's the difference. (A-M)

Similar expressions of disappointment if not exasperation on the part of attending surgeons were heard during the fieldwork. Attendings offered two reasons for their disappointment: the low value of second-hand evidence and a sense of diminished responsibility. With respect to evidence, if most of what is presented is not based on actual experience, then the presentation is considered a waste of time because it is seen as conjecture, not description. Second, presentations of that sort indicate that what it traditionally meant to be a senior resident, let alone the chief resident on a service, has shifted away from the standard that they "know and monitor everything." While interns and junior residents were traditionally expected to exhibit patient ownership, more senior residents and, especially, the chief resident on a service were also expected to embrace ownership of the service. In the past, the expression "a resident-run service" meant that residents had near-complete responsibility for a service. That level of independence and responsibility, say attendings, has waned, and one indicator of that change is diminished case familiarity during morbidity and mortality conference presentations.

Survey Results and Signs of Dissent

What we have done thus far is to present the key aspects of the most typical way surgeons understand professional obligations and why they believe they are in tension with the reforms. Here, we provide survey evidence to show the prevalence of various convictions and to probe dissent from prevailing views. The twelve wave-two survey items presented in Table 4.1 were crafted

TABLE 4.1. Work Hour Reforms, Professionalism, and Conflicts

| | | | % Agree or Strongly Agree | | | | |
| | | | Gender | | Experience (Years) | | |
Item	Question	Total	Men	Women	<8	8–19	>19
1	Surgeons should be responsible for the continuum of care for their patients.	96	96	94	97	96	94
2	Professionalism requires that one subordinate self-interests to the interests of patients.	79	80	73	77	80	82
3	Surgeons must accept inconvenience if it is required to meet patient needs.	97	97	96	97	97	97
4	The eighty-hour rules imply that residents' schedules take precedence over patients' needs for care.	69	70	63	64	72	74
5	The eighty-hour rules encourage an unprofessional "shift mentality."	85	86	82	84	86	87
6	The eighty-hour rules are fully compatible with the practice of "doing what is best for patients."	17	18	16	21	13	19
7	The eighty-hour rules diminish residents' familiarity with patients.	82	82	82	84	83	79
8	Ideals such as "continuity of care" and "putting patients' interests first" are not static or immutable—they should change with the times.	27	27	29	31	34	18*
9	"Doing what is best for patients" is more nearly a guideline than an obligation.	10	12	4	9	16	7
10	An orientation to "work-life balance" conflicts with the idea that surgeons should subordinate self-interest to the interests of patients.	34	38	16*	25	35	45*
11	Family life and non-work obligations often conflict with professional obligations.	79	80	75	77	78	84
12	You have to take care of yourself before you can care for others.	51	49	59	57	52	44
	Sample Sizes	286	231	51	100	88	86

Notes. An asterisk indicates differences by gender or years of experience are significant at the P < .05 level, as determined by a chi-square test statistic. Samples sizes for the group analyses differ slightly from the overall total due to non-response with respect to gender (four cases) and experience (twelve cases).

by drawing on what we had learned from the fieldwork and from statements from surgical societies about central professional values and obligations. The table indicates the exact questions that were posed to attending surgeons. In addition to providing overall results, we break the results out for men and women and for those with differing levels of experience as attending surgeons. Since there are no obvious dividing lines for experience, we (roughly) split the distribution into thirds, thereby distinguishing those with fewer than eight years, between eight and nineteen years, and those with twenty or more years of experience. The point of the contrasts is simple but intuitively plausible: do women or younger surgeons have distinctive understandings of surgical professionalism and how it squares with the reforms? We follow our discussion of the survey results with an overview of recurring themes of dissent evident in the interviews.

We begin by reviewing the overall results presented in the "total" column that is to the right of each question. The first three items explore professionalism and closely mirror what is commonly expressed by surgical societies. Nearly all surgeons agree that they should be responsible for the continuum of care for their patients (item 1 at 96 percent) and that they must accept inconvenience if it is needed to meet patient needs (item 3 at 97 percent). In this context, inconvenience is interpreted largely as needing to come in early, stay late, or return to the hospital. To a lesser but still substantial extent, surgeons believe that professionalism means "putting patients first" by subordinating their own self-interests (item 2 at 79 percent). Items 4 through 7 probe ways the reforms might conflict with professionalism. Large majorities believe that the reforms diminish familiarity with patients (item 7 at 82 percent) and encourage an unprofessional shift mentality (item 5 at 85 percent); few believe that the reforms fully support the practice of doing what is best for patients (item 6 at 17 percent). The results suggest widely held views and conflicts between the reforms and professionalism.

The final five questions (8–12) explore elements of change. For example, a few surgeons, in informal conversations and during the fieldwork, suggested that core professional values should change over time, and that professional values impose guidelines for behavior, not obligations. Item 8 suggests that about 27 percent of attendings agree that traditional ideals regarding "putting patients first" and "continuity of care" should change with the times. That minority view reflects a theme found in the interviews. It is also the first question that shows a statistically significant gap across levels of experience. While most believe that professional obligations often conflict with their family and nonwork obligations (item 11 at 79 percent), they are less likely to say that orientations to "work-life balance" conflict with the tradition of subordinating self-interests (item 10 at 34 percent). This latter issue prompts the only statistically significant difference by gender, and it produces a second and final divergence across experience levels. In our interviews, this view tends to blend with another, namely the need to take care of yourself before you can care for others (item 12).

Before turning to the interviews to further draw out forms of dissent, it is worth emphasizing a prevailing pattern: the results suggest shared views, not those that diverge often or sharply by gender or experience. Of the twelve items considered, gender mattered for one, experience for two. In a similar way, the dissenting views that we now turn to are not exclusively or even primarily championed by one or another sub-group of surgeons.

Dissent takes two main forms. In a first, a minority of surgeons discussed how a substantial gap has emerged between *ideal* culture—the strong emphasis on continuity, patient ownership, and sacrifice discussed earlier—and *real* culture—the actual beliefs and behaviors of surgeons in practice environments. In a second, another minority described how the ideal culture was admirable but nonetheless too much of a burden because of changes in broader culture and the practice of medicine. Consider first the distinction between ideal and real culture. One way this was expressed featured observations about the increasingly collaborative character of medical care, such as the following:

> I think that there is in the surgical tradition this very individualistic idea that one surgeon for one patient throughout their period of care is the model. Frankly, I think it's a model that will retire. In fact, surgeons actively collaborate with a number of different groups, including medical intensivists and anesthesiologists, and yet this idea that we're somehow the captain of the ship continues to exist. I think that's an ideal that isn't the reality. The reality is that we collaborate in both the inpatient and outpatient settings pretty actively. But it's one of those things where old-fashioned patient ownership is your spoken value versus your real value. (A-M)

Surgeons who spoke about collaboration eclipsing traditional patient ownership consistently voiced concerns about the quality of team-based care. With team care, surgeons worried that responsibility and oversight were less consistent and present; critical aspects of care could be uncoordinated or overlooked. The surgeon quoted above, for example, argued that even in teams, "somebody needs to say that I'm responsible." Another noted how "our safe systems aren't that mature—we still rely on provider vigilance and if you undermine that or the sense of ownership, it's problematic" (A-F).

Observations about a gap between practice and ideal versions of patient ownership and continuity were more common than reflections on the rise of collaboration. These comments were matter-of-fact, suggesting that actual practice had simply moved away from strict patient ownership and continuity over time. Consider this comment, drawn from a broader discussion of the need to work while fatigued:

> It used to be that if I operated on somebody and I finished my case at five in the afternoon and I was not on call, I would still get called for any complications that the patient might have had at night. Now, we've changed to where if I operated, and I'm not on call that night, I'll sign out to my new or old partner. They have the sign out and assume responsibility at 5 p.m. If my patient has to go to the operating room that night, they'll go with them, not me. They'll take calls about them too. We have adapted. We are changing. (A-M)

Coverage of this sort certainly falls short of traditional patient ownership and continuity, but that shortcoming was not emphasized or even noted. In this case, the comment was a prelude to the observation that schedules that might seem to reduce the need to work while fatigued—like the transition in care that relieved one surgeon at 5 p.m.—did little more than shift the burden of fatigue onto a partner. That point, not the waning of patient ownership or continuity, was the intended focus of the comment. Comments that included an awareness of the loss of patient ownership tended to take the following form:

> I think there are differences in how people view ownership and continuity of care. Some of my partners and other surgeons in the area still think that you yourself always have to be the person who's available. I don't believe that. I would say that many surgeons don't believe that literally. Many of us actually do have a pretty good balance between work and non-work life. It's possible to have time away where you're not being called in the middle of the night because you have call coverage with other people. It's possible, I believe, to do that in a way that provides very good patient care but doesn't subject an individual to being available every minute of every day to the point that they have no personal time. We provide continuity, but it's sometimes through a partner who knows enough to care properly. They'll be available and responsive, not me. (A-F)

While many faculty tout the virtues of ownership and continuity, few appear to realize how often they fall short of those ideals due to frequent travel for professional and personal reasons. During the fieldwork, for example, it quickly became evident that attendings were often away from the hospital, leaving patient care in the hands of residents and partners on their service. Even the partners noted in the comment above, who appear to revere traditional ownership and continuity, almost certainly suspend both to travel. One attending, during an interview, acknowledged the frequency with which he and his colleagues were away from the hospital, and how it was then difficult to say that something that approximates surgical shift-work—with its lack of continuity and patient ownership—should be denigrated.

> I'm very close with a colleague who works for Kaiser Permanente, and they have gone to a pure shift mentality. They have a day team and a night team and they absolutely love it. They're all very family focused or leisure-time focused. And they really feel like they have the best of all worlds in the sense that they practice surgery very intensely when they are on, when they're responsible, and that they have done all they can to try and maximize the quality of the change-over of shifts and information and whatnot. Some of the biggest critics of shifts and shift-type places like Kaiser are the high-end academic surgeons. And it cracks me up because most of these guys are out of town at least as many days as these Kaiser doctors are off. Somehow or another, they think they're providing old-fashioned continuity and ownership and all of that. I had this debate with the former chairman of surgery at [prestigious private university program], and he was very critical of the Kaiser model. I was like, "Come on! You're out of town ten days a month with somebody covering your practice. How is that different? How is that continuity or ownership?" (A-M)

Of course, ideal and actual behavior rarely align perfectly, and the point here is to merely note that it is not at all uncommon for surgeons who esteem patient ownership and continuity to leave their patients in the care of others. The culture of ownership and continuity clearly has ideal and real variations.

A second and less common form of dissent suggested that the ideal culture of ownership and continuity was admirable but too burdensome due to broader social changes. A typical comment of this sort was short and emphasized diminishing reimbursement for surgical care:

> I think that patient ownership is on the rocks. If reimbursement continues to take a significant hit, I think it will probably be the first thing you see go. People

are going to say, "Screw it—I'm not going to be captain of the ship anymore! I'm captain until five o'clock and then someone else is captain!" Because right now, part of the surgeon's reimbursement helps pay for availability and continuity and that kind of professionalism. (A-M)

Other comments tended to blend issues, weaving together the too-burdensome argument into a broader perspective on family, culture, and the practice of medicine. Consider this emotionally charged comment by a young surgeon who had recently become a father:

> It's true that one patient being taken care of by a physician from beginning to end is an incredible ideal. But at the same time, we need to consider the well-being of generations of general surgeons who have fought that battle to the loss of their relationships with their families, children, friends, and everything else around them. We've also shifted away from men-as-breadwinners and women-as-homemakers. We don't live in that world anymore. The cost to self isn't bolstered by any social factors that make it worthwhile. We're paid less, we work harder, the demands are higher, the legal risks are higher. There's no more sense that a doctor is actually attempting to strive for the highest good for the patient. I just don't see how the ideal of ownership can hold together anymore. Times have changed! (A-M)

The comment ties into something not clearly present in other quotes—namely, the idea that "taking care of yourself" is a worthwhile goal and that surgical work can be personally debilitating. It also goes beyond a narrow focus on reimbursement to touch on broader changes in medicine and society. As with others, this surgeon went on to say that any sort of team-based approach to ownership and care was also fraught with problems related to coordination and responsibility. But the glimmer of something less onerous was nonetheless powerful in his mind, despite what seemed to be significant pitfalls.

Reflection: Of Bulldogs and Bleeding

During my fourth year of residency, I had one of the more intense experiences I encountered. I was the only resident on a cardiothoracic surgery service. There were up to forty patients on the service at a time, often a half-dozen of them in the intensive care unit, and it was my job to see them every day, alongside my other duties. The goal was to get there before the attendings, get everyone seen, write my notes and get the key orders in, all before getting to the operating room for the first case that would start around seven thirty. I had enough experience at this point to have some sense of how to manage that workload, and I had the benefit of some private nurses hired by the surgeons to help manage their patients who became my allies in getting things done as I tracked in and out of the OR through the day. One day we had a patient who was particularly challenging and not doing well. One of the attendings, as we discussed the plan to try to get this person through their illness, taught me something I can't say I have never failed at, but which I never forgot. He said that when a patient got that sick, your only choice was to "dig your teeth into them like a bulldog, and don't let go until they got well." He was saying that the issue was not just one of cognition or craft; it was an issue of commitment.

During another rotation working with urologists, I had helped one of the faculty do a prostatectomy. Bleeding is the bane of many operations, and can be a particular problem with prostatectomy patients. The night after the surgery, the patient developed significant bleeding, and I worked hard that night replacing blood products, keeping his urinary catheter patent, and managing underlying issues that could have been contributory. The attending surgeon left that in my care, and the next day when he came in and things had stabilized, said to the patient in front of me, "You were trying to check out last night, and this young doctor didn't let you. We should both thank him."

Both those experiences taught me elements of ownership. In the first instance, I was being taught that one's commitment to a patient became even more critical as the patient became sicker. In the second instance, I experienced something of the reward of being the one who didn't leave and saw the outcome through, without which the technical feat of the surgery may have been a therapeutic failure. I was learning that commitment, and commitment specifically to the less glamorous aspects of caring for someone that involved being there as dictated by the need, was part of the ethos of being a physician and a surgeon.

There is a sense in which this chapter is the most fundamental of what is being shared in this volume, at least in what it has exposed. The questions around what it means to care for someone else, to commit to that, and to define one's professional and even in some sense one's personal identity around that commitment is in many ways the most fundamental question that the duty-hour restrictions have begged. This is because the concept of commitment and ownership for the care of another, to put their welfare first, underlies all the other questions about fatigue and its boundaries, handoffs and shared-care models, staying or going and when to do either, and adjusting day-to-day work as part of a larger spectrum of professional obligation. To use the language of my mentors, can a bulldog ever tag team with another bulldog, or does that mean to "let go" and thereby modulate the level of commitment my mentor was calling me to? Is it possible to "check out" and still have honored one's commitment to prevent one's patient from doing so?

What strikes me powerfully in reading the quotes shared in this chapter are these questions of professional identity and its formation. There is no question that those who have conceived of duty-hour restrictions have done so to promote patient care by competent and adequately rested, unimpaired professionals who have committed to the competencies that are expected to allow both care by the professional, and care of the professional through whom that care is rendered. That being acknowledged and affirmed, one also senses in the quotes a deep concern that the professional lens may not be able to be in focus, at least in the eyes of those viewing care through it, if it is aimed at the guardrails on the gurney rather than the patient lying on it. This is the more fundamental question of duty-hour reform; this is the ultimate question of unintended consequences.

I once was privileged to hear a panel of nonmedical individuals who had enjoyed outstanding success in their chosen fields describe their leveraging years—the years when they laid the foundation for their performance in their subsequent career path. One was a violinist and a concertmaster, one a national-championship-winning athletic coach, and one a business entrepreneur who had resurrected a failing iconic transportation business. All three were adamant that they would not have been where they were in their success if someone had limited their investment during their developing years to eighty hours of work per week. Their sense of who they were in the services they provided to society was forged in a crucible that stretched and challenged them in ways that more reasonable structures might have limited. It was clear they would have done it again.

That being said, the costs of medical training are not without their consequence. One surgery residency of national prominence in the era in which I trained used to boast of its 100 percent divorce rate for residents who entered it married, as though that somehow proved the commitment of the program to excellence. With resident and even student burnout rates reported in the 40 to 60 percent range, there is no question that the costs can be too high, and we now know that outcomes for patients are indeed affected by compassion fatigue and burnout in the caregiver. Parallel discussions come up when resident attrition is discussed—general surgery having one of the highest of all specialties both historically and currently. Are we training the "Navy SEALs of medicine," and attrition is a necessary byproduct, or are we stunting a generation of caregivers so that they won't be able to run the marathon of a surgical career, and at a time when the workforce needs them?

Obviously these are easier questions to ask than to answer. What can be said without vacillation is that the forge in which professional identity is made is complex, and commitment must remain a dominant theme therein. Perhaps it can even be the centering bubble of the leveler, as it were: commitment to one's patient, including the commitment to being well to care for them. The devil, as usual, will be in the details.

CHAPTER 5

Less for You, More for Me?

Changing Workloads for Attendings and Advanced Practice Providers

The cost of having residents work less is that attendings work more. Quite simply, I become the continuity link—I'm always on call for the service. And there's something ironic to me about a system that says that twenty-five year olds are more prone to fatigue and therefore require more time off than fifty-year-old faculty members! (A-M)

There are more and more surgeons over the last ten to fifteen years who are failing their boards right out of residency. I strongly believe that's because of the duty-hour restrictions. Residents aren't getting enough experience. . . . Now we're throwing in a potential solution—more and more extenders—that further limits their exposure to cases and patients. (A-M)

The reforms altered the division of labor in residency programs. Even though the reforms appear to often fall short of their stated limits, it is widely believed that residents perform less clinical work and engage in less supervision of other residents and medical students than in the past. Stahlfeld, Robinson, and Burton (2008, 358) voiced a common sentiment that "by limiting work hours, more people are required to do the same volume of work." A study conducted prior to the enactment of the reforms suggested that faculty anticipated that a portion of what residents had traditionally managed would become their responsibility (Winslow, Bowman, and Klingensmith 2004); one conducted shortly after the reforms were adopted suggested that substantial majorities of surgical faculty believed that the reforms had, in fact, increased their work hours and negatively affected them (Winslow, Berger, and Klingensmith 2004). Little else is known about the character of faculty experiences or whether early reactions have persisted or changed over time, as research has focused overwhelmingly on residents.

The reforms did, however, further accelerate a movement to add staff who could assume some of the work previously managed by residents. Many residency programs hired staff variously called mid-level providers, non-physician providers, physician extenders, or advanced practice providers (APPs), the term we adopt here. Most advanced practice providers are either nurse practitioners (NPs) or physician assistants (PAs). The primary reason academic medical centers give for hiring more advanced practice providers is to help comply with the ACGME duty-hour restrictions (Moote et al. 2011, 456). This process, however, began in the 1970s, well in advance of reforms in the state of New York in 1989 and those implemented nationally in 2003. By 2009, 79 percent of general surgery programs had at least one advanced practice provider, with a median of 3.5 in programs that employ at least one (Pezzi et al. 2009). They are, at this point, common in all programs, although not on all surgery services.

Tasks handled by advanced practice providers differ across surgical programs and services. Duties include, in many but not all programs and services, taking histories and doing physical examinations, seeing consults, seeing patients in the emergency room, first assisting in the operating room, performing bedside procedures, providing inpatient floor work, rounding, chart documentation, discharge summaries, and follow-up plans (Stahlfeld, Robinson, and Burton 2008; Jones and Cawley 2009; Pezzi et al. 2009; Kahn et al. 2015). In many programs, advanced practice providers perform those duties only during the day, but some programs have them cover nights (Buch et al. 2008), with some reporting 24/7 coverage (Rejtar, Ranstrom, and Allcox 2017). There are thus no set shifts they work or standardized duties performed, leading Buch et al. (2008, 52) to highlight the "immeasurable differences" in what advanced practice providers do across programs and services.

Two broad patterns regarding advanced practice providers are established. First, they reduce resident workloads, help them comply with duty-hour restrictions, and are desired by residents. For example, a multi-center study of surgical residents and their ICU rotations reported that 80 percent believed that advanced practice providers reduced resident workloads (Kahn et al. 2015). Likewise, 73 percent of academic medical centers report that advanced practice providers help them comply with duty-hour restrictions (Moote et al. 2011). An analysis of ACGME data from site visits and surveys with nearly half of all surgery residency programs shows that residents in 37 percent of programs identified an increase in advanced practice providers as an "opportunity for improvement" (Caniano and Hamstra 2016, 211). Second, advanced practice providers enhance care and administrative outcomes by helping to reduce length-of-stay, re-admissions, and post-discharge emergency room visits (Christmas et al. 2005; Robles et al. 2011; Berger and D'Cunha 2012). Rejtar, Ranstrom, and Allcox (2017) also report that advanced practice providers reduced the incidence of unplanned patient transfers to the ICU from the general surgery service in a children's hospital.

The educational impact of advanced practice providers is less established. For some, the fact that advanced practice providers often handle a portion of routine paperwork tasks, thus freeing residents to be in the operating room or to engage in other educationally oriented activities, is enough to declare them an educational asset (Perry, Detmer, and Redmond 1981; Thourani and Miller 2006; Pezzi et al. 2009). Others point to a more direct educational role, suggesting that they provide clinical instruction for residents that adds to what they learn from attendings, nurses, and other staff (Buch et al. 2008; Kahn et al. 2015).

The story, however, might be more complex. For example, in a multi-center study of ICU rotations, fewer than half of general surgery residents claimed that advanced practice providers positively affected their experience, with 31 percent noting that they were a "detriment" and 21 percent reporting "no effect" (Kahn et al. 2015). A single-site study (Resnick et al. 2006, 163) found confused lines of communication among surgical team members, especially among interns and PGY3s (50 and 80 percent in agreement, respectively), and that 59 percent of residents did not understand the role of the advanced practice providers on the surgical services. Other studies hint at the possibility that attendings might come to rely upon, prefer, and trust advanced practice providers more than residents (Bahouth, Esposito-Herr, and Babineau 2007; Hayman et al. 2012), that they might disturb the team hierarchy and usurp patient care experiences (Todd et al. 2004; Foley et al. 2008; Stahlfeld, Robinson, and Burton 2008; Kahn et al. 2015), and that nurses might call them for patient-care issues and thus bypass residents (Kahn et al. 2015). These possibilities have not yet been explored carefully, but surely merit attention.

In this chapter, we draw primarily upon survey and interview evidence from all three waves of the data to explore the changing workloads of faculty and the promise and problems of shifting work to advanced practice providers. We begin by examining perceptions of faculty workloads, activities, and responsibilities and whether they have been altered by the reforms. The first- and second-wave interviews included both survey items and interview questions about those issues, and the topic also surfaced frequently during other portions of the interviews. Quite a few residents, in both the interviews and fieldwork, commented on faculty workloads. But residents make such comments as outsiders looking in, suggesting that faculty views and experiences are best understood by letting their voices dominate the discussion. Our analysis draws upon self-reports, not objective measures of workloads, hours spent at work, or the frequency with which attendings on call return to the hospital at night or on weekends. It is possible that self-reports are shaped to some extent by status-incongruent demands—the often mentioned need, for example, for faculty to perform lowly "intern work" or to "become chief residents again." Those new pressures are explored as well.

We then shift to a consideration of the promise and problems of advanced practice providers in residency programs, drawing primarily upon the third wave of data collection. We focus on the views and experiences of attending surgeons, not residents or advanced practice providers. Attendings have a long-term perspective on resident education and in many cases considerable experience working with advanced practice providers, often in more than one healthcare setting. Their perspective, of course, is not the only one of value, but it is a particularly important one and a worthy starting point for the analysis.

We aim to make three contributions in this chapter. First, empirical attention to the reforms has focused almost exclusively on residents, not on others who staff or contribute to the overall operation of residency programs. Although resident experiences are central, they are not the entire story, and it remains possible—as Kellogg (2011) claimed—that one source of resistance to the reforms on the part of attendings is the perception if not the reality that they have assumed additional work and responsibilities. Second, our analysis adds to previous chapters in pointing to a radical upending of many traditional patterns and practices described in classic studies of residency programs such as Bosk's (1979) *Forgive and Remember*. The reforms served to dramatically accelerate changes already underway. And third, the educational effects of advanced practice providers have remained remarkably unexamined, despite the substantial and rising presence of such staff in residency programs. As we will show, they offer much that is promising, but they pose challenges as well.

A Survey-Based Overview of Faculty Work Experiences

Table 5.1 presents results relevant to the issue of faculty workloads and responsibilities from fifteen survey items scattered across the first two waves of data collection. In most instances, exact question wording shifted at least slightly across waves, which means that only two item pairs (2 and 3; 9 and

TABLE 5.1. Resident Work-Hour Reforms and Faculty Work Experiences by Gender and Experience

Item (Wave)	Question: "The eighty-hour rules . . ."	% Agree or Strongly Agree				
		Overall	Men	Women	Age 32–48 or Experience 1–10 years	Age > 48 or Experience >10 years
1 (1)	increase the overall time I am on call.	37	37	39	32	42
2 (1)	increase the number of times I have been called back to the hospital.	42	38	69*	48	35
3 (2)	same as above—wave 2.	19	17	26	14	22
4 (2)	increase the likelihood that residents contact me when I'm away from the hospital.	21	18	31*	26	16*
5 (1)	increase my workload at the hospital.	69	64	94*	77	58*
6 (2)	increase the amount of time I spend at the hospital.	44	40	61*	44	45
7 (1)	require that I perform work previously handled by residents.	73	72	89	83	62*
8 (2)	increase the frequency with which I perform duties previously handled by residents.	70	69	73	69	71
9 (1)	increase the stress I feel from my work.	61	57	78	64	54
10 (2)	same as above—wave 2.	39	38	43	35	42
11 (1)	decrease the satisfaction I derive from my academic position.	55	53	65	63	44*
12 (2)	make academic medicine less appealing.	35	36	33	36	35
13 (1)	decrease faculty expectations and standards for residents.	75	73	83	83	65*
14 (1)	decrease the time I have available to teach residents.	67	65	82	70	62
15 (2)	decrease the satisfaction I derive from working with residents.	37	34	47	38	35
	Wave 1 Sample Sizes	*146*	*124*	*18*	*74*	*64*
	Wave 2 Sample Sizes	*286*	*231*	*51*	*135*	*139*

Notes. An asterisk indicates statistical significance at the P < .05 level (chi-square). Subgroup Ns may differ from overall Ns due to a small amount of missing data. Age and experience groups were used for the wave 1 and wave 2 analyses, respectively.

10) are identical over time. The table contains overall results and those broken out by gender and by either age or years of experience, both of which were roughly split at the median. The first wave included age, the second experience, but both allow for a reasonable exploration of the possibility that younger faculty early in their careers experience the reforms differently than their older and more established colleagues. In addition, we explore gender, as we have done in previous chapters, given the plausibility of the idea that it might well shape experiences.

Consider first the overall results. The first four items bear on call experiences, and include how much the attending is on call and how often they are contacted and return when they are away from the hospital. The pattern here suggests a modest increase in activity, but also the possibility that an early increase has diminished over time, as evident in the drop from 42 to 19 percent of faculty (items 2 and 3) who say they have seen an increase in the number of times they have been called back to the hospital. Items 5 through 10 provide clear evidence that substantial percentages of faculty believe the reforms have influenced their work. Roughly 70 percent of faculty believe that the reforms increased their workloads and that they now do work previously carried out by residents (items 5, 7, and 8). The reforms increased the stress attendings feel from their work, but that early majority view (61 percent, item 9) has diminished to a minority view (39 percent, item 10). Items 11 through 15 point to challenges for academic medicine. Faculty believe that their standards and expectations for residents have diminished (75 percent, item 13) as has time for teaching (67 percent, item 14). There is also evidence of a decreased appeal and satisfaction in academic medicine.

Differences by gender, age, and experience are found for fewer than a third of the items. The gender differences, while only occasionally significant, show rather consistently that women believe more strongly than their male peers that the reforms have increased their work and responsibilities. For example, 64 percent of men—but a nearly unanimous 94 percent of women—felt the reforms had increased their workloads (item 5). Age and experience show a similar pattern, where younger and less experienced faculty more strongly link the reforms to their own workloads and experiences. That pattern holds for every statistically significant difference (items 4, 5, 7, 11, and 13). In sum, concerns about the workplace implications of the reforms are not being driven wholly, or even largely, by older male surgeons. We now unpack these patterns more fully with the qualitative evidence.

Clinical Care Workloads for Faculty

Surgical residencies traditionally involved a division of labor whereby residents carried out many of the day-to-day aspects of patient care. Bosk's (1979) description of a surgical residency program, for example, suggested that residents carried a heavy clinical load, whereas faculty popped in and out and provided more nearly supervision, often remote, than direct clinical care. The work patterns of attendings had already changed markedly prior to the reforms, thus only vaguely resembling the patterns in Bosk's analysis. The widespread sense among attendings is that the reforms further increased their clinical workloads. The increase includes, for example, paperwork related to clinic visits, paperwork for pre- and postoperative hospitalized patients, postoperative checks and dressing changes, the ordering and evaluation of tests or studies, and various bedside procedures like central and peripheral lines. Greater involvement in things of that sort is viewed as an increased clinical workload.

Consider a few comments on the issue of direct involvement in paperwork and patient care. A first is by a critical care and trauma surgeon who claims there is "no question" that his workload increased as a result of the reforms:

> *Do you think that your activities and responsibilities have changed because of the eighty-hour rules?* No question. They have. Absolutely. *How so?* Gone are the days when you just call up the resident and say, "Take are of this." You're writing a lot of notes. We're doing a lot of direct care. I'm putting in lines and stuff when the residents are too busy and not available. There's a lot more hands-on clinical care. I'm dictating. Some of my clinics I run on my own, and I have to see all the patients, dictate all the notes, etc., and the same with my partners. That's just the way it is. *And you think that's directly attributable to the rules—that residents aren't available in your clinic or for other things?* Yes. They're definitely not available, particularly on the weekends. There are just not as many people around. For the kind of work I do, which is critical care and trauma, notes aren't always written on the patients. They're not all seen. Before that would have been a real problem— I would've seen much anger had I done that! (A-M)

Echoing a common sentiment, this surgeon specifically highlights more involvement in writing notes, engaging in direct patient care, doing more dictations, and seeing clinic patients without as much—if any—resident support. A key aspect of many comments is a strong contrast with the past that often mixes indignation with resignation. The idea, for example, that residents would not complete notes on patients—or even see them all—would have been "a real problem," but is now just "the way it is." Another comment underscores newfound involvement by attendings in a mundane but nonetheless important aspect of direct patient care—dressing changes—and how that breaks with tradition:

> *Do you think that your activities and responsibilities have changed because of the eighty-hour rules?* What I'm doing now, my attendings would never have done, ever. *Like what?* For example, I find myself doing dressing changes on patients. I don't think any of my attendings at [residency program] changed a dressing since they graduated from their residency. And I'm doing it on just about every patient here. That's because of the hours. They have to prioritize and, you know, they'll take care of it later in the day and triage what's more important. Granted, if the patient's dressing is not addressed, they have stool in their wound, they've got a wound infection. I've had this just in the past two weeks. And so I as the attending am actually doing intern work, which I never would have thought I would have to do when I was an attending. Never! (A-M)

Attendings expressed both surprise and disappointment that they were now routinely doing such forms of "intern work." Tasks routinely called intern work—the province of the least skilled and experienced members of the residency—seem for some starkly inconsistent with the status of surgical attending. Such work, however, is essential, and a common refrain among attendings is that they shoulder that work if they must: "The bottom line is if there is not a resident to do it, then ultimately that responsibility ends up on my plate. It has to be done." (A-M)

Two other issues that bear on shifting clinical workloads involve the character of on-call work for attendings and communication patterns. Because nights are now commonly managed by night-float residents who have less familiarity with patients, face multiple demands on their time, and may be less senior than in the past, attendings claim that their on-call nights demand more time and attention. Notice how this mirrors what was described in the chapter on residents' stay-or-go decisions. In short, both day residents and faculty assess the *availability* and *ability* of night staff when determining whether to stay to complete patient-care tasks (residents) or to stay in the hospital or return if at home when on call (faculty). Consider the following comment about nighttime call activities and involvements:

> *Do you think that what you do and your responsibilities have changed in some respects because of the eighty-hour rules?* Yeah. I would say absolutely—no ques-

tion. *Can you expand on that?* In the past, I had the ability to stay at home more during a call night when I felt I had a resident in house watching my patient that was turning sour that was appropriately doing the things that needed to happen. Now, on call, I'm in the hospital more. I'm doing my own central lines, or teaching the junior residents how to do them because they have never done one. I'm putting in a-lines [arterial lines]. I'm floating Swans [Swan-Ganz catheterization]. I'm doing the stuff myself a lot more than what I used to. . . . You just can't rely on residents as much, and need to be much, much more directly involved. (A-F)

In this account, nights on call are quite active because resident teams are not sufficiently *able* to insert a-lines or Swan-Ganz catheters, largely because the residents available are less experienced. The end result is less sleep and more direct faculty involvement in clinical care. A second comment on this issue highlights more fully the *availability* of night staff and how direct involvements have increased:

Do you think your activities and responsibilities have shifted in some way because of the eighty-hour rules? Oh yeah. I'm working like I did as a resident again. With the night-float system, the resident that's covering the pediatric surgery service at night is covering four other services at the same time. So they're carrying five beepers. They're rarely ever available. I'm in the ER admitting kids with a butt abscess at two o'clock in the morning because there's no resident available because he's scrubbed on the emergency general service, doing something else. . . . The ER calls us directly now because if they call the pediatric surgery night float person they won't even get an answer the majority of the time. If they get an answer, it's going to be three or four hours before the night float guy can get down there. So we just tell them, "look, call us." . . . It really gets tough. I worked twenty-eight hours straight here, not too long ago, in the ER. I had no resident. (A-M)

Even without the reforms, there is little doubt that the attending would have become involved in at least some of the activities he described in the quote and in his longer comment (such as performing an appendectomy). But there is also little doubt that a loss of resident assistance with initial consultations in the ER, conducting histories and physicals, writing admission orders, and scheduling procedures implies more direct faculty involvement and longer workdays.

Hinted at in this comment as well is the possibility of new, more direct and numerous communication channels. As many attendings described it, one effect of the reforms has been to upset the communication hierarchy. In the past, although perhaps in an ideal fashion only partially realized, communication to and from attendings was quite constrained. Chief residents managed surgical services, communicated with the less senior residents and interns, and served as the primary—if not exclusive—point of contact with attendings. Nurses and other staff would communicate with residents who then communicated with their chiefs who, in turn, decided if and when to communicate with relevant attendings. The attending quoted above suggests this latter pattern has waned in that the ER was now instructed to directly contact attendings, not residents. Another attending expanded on these communication challenges:

> *Do you think that your activities and responsibilities are different because of the eighty-hour rules?* I certainly don't work any less since the eighty-hour work rules came in! I take more phone calls from nurses, from nurse practitioners, from the cross-covering residents who just aren't quite sure what to do. So I take more phone calls to sort out things that the original team would know because I round with them. . . . There are more people that I have to communicate with even during working hours rather than being able to talk to a single senior resident who then passes it down his chain of command. . . . There's a fragmentation and multiplication of communication. (A-M)

As this attending frames the issue, the fragmentation and multiplication of communication is brought about in two main ways: first, by a loss of information during handoffs to cross-covering teams; and second, by the loss of "a single senior resident" or chief who previously would have served as an information hub. This is an example of how the shortcomings of handoffs to night teams diminish their capability which, in turn, increases the workloads of attendings. What a service's resident team would have known in the past can no longer be assumed by attendings.

The reforms mean that attendings directly engage in more clinical work, such as dressing changes, pulling tubes, writing orders, and the like. Many attendings were quick to add that they have also become much more involved in the supervision of clinical work. Prior to the reforms, residents, especially chiefs, were expected to set attending-approved patient care plans in motion and ensure that they were accomplished in a timely and appropriate fashion. Chiefs, not attendings, were expected to do the necessary double-checking to ensure that requested care had been performed satisfactorily, that studies had been ordered, completed, and evaluated, that consults from other services were at least pending if not in hand, and so forth. Many attendings argue that the reforms have made resident awareness, engagement, and follow-through less predictable. During the field observations, one captured the concern well in saying that it is not clear that residents always "have their arms around the patients."

In response to the interview question about changes in their work activities and responsibilities, attendings used an expression also heard during the field observations: "I feel like a chief resident again!" The following comment is characteristic of this general expression and set of convictions:

> *Do you think that what you do and what you're responsible for has shifted because of the eighty-hour rules?* Yeah, I feel like a chief resident! *Can you expand on that?* Sure. I have to be more attentive. So again, I go back to my own training, which was considerably different, I would argue, it was considerably more rigorous in term of the expectations and demands on us. We'd never talk to our faculty, I mean the chief resident would talk to faculty, but the chief resident was it. They just ran the show. . . . I have to be more vigilant now. *Could you give me an example? On what sorts of things would you need to be more vigilant?* Oh, I follow up labs myself, I go look at x-rays with the radiologist myself because I can't rely on the interpretation that is being relayed to me. I examine patients. I'll frequently see patients multiple times if I'm concerned about the reliability of the information that I've gotten and that sort of thing. (A-M)

Several expressions used by this attending—such as more attentive and vigilant—capture well a heightened sense of responsibility for the day-to-day aspects of patient care. That increased responsibility tended to be wedded to subsequent actions, such as following up on labs, conferring directly with a radiologist, or re-examining patients. But it would be a mistake to conclude that it is significant only in leading to more direct clinical care on the part of attendings. Rather, the increased sense of responsibility in many situations becomes a nagging distraction, where things need to be kept on the mind and reviewed often. One attending in the fieldwork summed this up by saying that his post-reform clinical work required more "bandwidth."

A Diminished Allure for Academic Medicine?

The belief that workloads have increased because of the reforms might diminish the allure of academic medicine. Many surgeons described how academic surgeons face two main burdens: lower earnings than their non-academic peers and less efficient support systems. As one surgeon described his previous private-practice experience, everything was aligned in the direction of saving time and effort—streamlined records, support staff who were more directly accountable to the surgeon, OR policies and staff that facilitated and encouraged procedures rather than hindering them, and so forth. Less effort was required to yield the same or even greater output which, in turn, was rewarded more highly. In short, less produced more. During the field observations, attending surgeons often grumbled about both issues.

Residents can offset those burdens in two ways. First, they traditionally offered around-the-clock assistance that lightened the load of attending surgeons. At the least, residents could serve as what some attendings called their "eyes and ears"—additional staff to help monitor patient conditions. But ideally, as faculty described the past (and is evident in Bosk's analysis), residents *could*, and in many cases *did*, manage many aspects of patient care, thus freeing attending surgeons to pursue other activities. Second, residents offer attending surgeons a chance to teach a new generation the science and craft of surgery. There is no question that many attendings enjoy teaching residents, something that was observed repeatedly—and commented on by attendings and residents—during the fieldwork. As one attending put it during an interview, "although residents have traditionally provided service, they also provide joy and intellectual intrigue" (A-M).

Teaching runs the gamut from technical skills such as suturing and the placement of a central line to communication with patients and families. What to pay attention to, what counts as evidence for or against a line of thought and action, and what to do and how to do it represent the primary grist of surgical teaching and learning. That teaching, for the most part, occurs as residents and attendings interact—in the ongoing ebb and flow of actual patient-care work—rather than in lectures, group educational meetings, and surgical simulation laboratories. Those latter formats constitute an increasingly important, but still secondary, source of residency education. The act of doing surgical work together continues to be the primary way that critical knowledge and skills are passed to a new generation of surgeons.

There are several ways that the reforms bear on the experience and appeal of academic medicine. A first centers on time. Faculty often invoked a zero-sum logic, arguing that heavier clinical workloads meant less time for academic pursuits. Consider the following comment by a faculty member in a community-based program:

> *Do you think the eighty-hour rules have had any effect on patient care?* I'm going to
> say probably not, directly. I think the shifting has occurred to the attending side.
> I'm double-checking. I'm doing more of the non-productive patient care, the

computer work, the order entry, the rounding, the consults. And as such, I don't have as much time to do other things that used to be part of the big package deal, meaning committees, research presentations, national meeting participation, etc. So, in a way what we've done is taken the work away from the resident, put it on the attending which makes the attending work harder and be a little bit unable to do some academic things. I think, as a result, our interest in committee involvements in the hospital and research participation fall off, unfortunately. There's only so much time in my day, so something's getting cut out. (A-M)

The implication of this position is clear: more time devoted to clinical work means less time for academic pursuits. While not exclusively stated by those in community-based programs, this sentiment appeared more often in those interviews and might represent a distinctive perception. In community programs, faculty are for the most part private-practice surgeons who volunteer their time as surgical educators. Traditionally, the exchange was resident assistance for academic contributions, which included teaching as well as professional activity. That bargain has been jeopardized by the reforms.

The most common way faculty in all types of programs linked the reforms to a diminished luster of academic medicine involved a sense of detachment from residents. For many, the intensity of the working relationships they form with residents has waned. What used to be a collective enterprise, with residents always tagging along if not fully immersed in work with faculty, has become a less collective, more individual undertaking. Consider the following comment by an attending in a university-based program.

Do you think that your activities and responsibilities have changed because of the eighty-hour rules? Definitely. *Can you give me a few examples of how they've changed or what has changed?* Sure. We pretty much no longer rely on residents. In other words, I can write orders if I have to. If they show up, fine. If they don't, well that's fine too. Sometimes they don't because the intern who was on last night is gone today. They had to go home. So, you're never sure whether residents will be around or not. There are days we have no residents on our service that are available. The senior resident may be gone or might get pulled to another service. The junior resident was on the night before, so we have nobody. So, it's gotten to the point where I don't always go looking for them because you don't know if they're going to be there or not. So, the attitude is, and this has been a very devastating one among attendings, residents are undependable. Not because they don't want to be, just they can't be. So we just do it ourselves. That's what everybody's doing. There's a huge attitudinal shift. Having practiced in the eighties and nineties, you never did anything until the resident was there. And the resident was always there. Now they may be, may not be, they're not expected to be. So, somebody's got to take care of the patient, so it's going to be me. I'll do it. (A-M)

The transformation noted here is striking, from "the resident was always there" to "we just do it ourselves." What this and other attendings speak to is the sense that the "old team concept" has waned and that they now work more independently of residents. Faculty attribute this change to the reforms, and the need for residents to curb and suspend their involvements, rather than to indifference or disinterest on the part of residents. Consider the following comment on that issue, this time by a faculty member in a community program:

I really have completely changed—my relationship with the residents has completely changed. In the past, it was much more of an, "Okay, we're going to meet at a certain time. Present every patient to me. We'll go through it. We'll do some teaching, etc. And why weren't you in clinic? Why were you late to the OR?" That sort of thing. And very demanding. I don't do that anymore. . . . It's not the old team concept where my chief resident finds me and we run the list and he's responsible for everything and checks in with me. It's just not that way anymore. If they're around, great. If they're not around, I just do my own thing. (A-M)

As with the other comment, the main theme here is the idea that the attending's work is less integrated with residents, prompting the expression "I just do my own thing." Residents are welcomed but not really expected, and demands on resident involvement appear to have waned. What is lost in the transcribed text—and in many other interviews and fieldwork moments when this issue arose—is the unmistakable emotion conveyed in statements like this: "If they're around, great. If they're not around, I just do my own thing." What reads like casual resignation had the unmistakable sound of profound disappointment and loss.

Faculty emphasized a pattern of fragmented resident involvements as a final way in which their relationships with residents had changed. A centerpiece of traditional training was resident involvement in all stages of a patient's care, from preoperative clinic visits, where a surgical need is first determined, to postoperative care, even if that meant relatively short-term care for patients not admitted to the hospital. The reforms leave residents less likely to be present for all phases of any patient's care. With the greater fragmentation of residents' involvements, the concern among faculty is different from their new need to more frequently "do their own thing" and work independently. Rather, it suggests that training has been eroded. Consider the following comment about fragmented resident involvements:

> Where before, if they were going to scrub a case, we expected them to see the patient in the clinic so they knew what was going on. And then they would see the patient post op to see how they are doing. That just doesn't happen now—it's very rare. The resident literally becomes a technician who's disconnected from what comes before and after the OR. (A-F)

In this comment, the description is largely matter of fact. During the field-work, it was common to observe attendings become extremely upset with residents who were unfamiliar with patients because they had not been involved in earlier phases of their care. Knowing "what is going on" is viewed as critical in a way that is not fully conveyed by this surgeon's matter-of-fact style. Fragmentation was also linked by some to diminished interest in taking the time to draw out the educational aspects of particular patients that residents would probably not continue to follow:

> *Do you think that the rules have any effect, good or bad, on the skill and professional development of residents?* Yes. I think it's detrimental in that I think we're teaching people how to do operations and not teaching them how to operate. . . . We've lost the ability to teach them, at least in a way that I'm familiar with, the preoperative, intra-operative, postoperative, and then post-discharge continuity of care. . . . I think that makes residents feel somewhat inadequate as surgeons. That's one of the things that drives them to take on fellowships—they just don't feel like they know how to do anything. And I think it does impact my interest in teaching a resident how to take care of a case if they're not going to be around for the end of it. What's the point of going into any detail if they aren't going to be there? . . . I'm not teaching them with the same intensity as I did beforehand. (A-F)

Concerns about continuity of care thus surface again, as they have repeatedly in earlier chapters. Here, the concern is less with the quality of patient care than education, particularly the attending's interest in teaching if a resident's participation is partial.

It is important to emphasize that while attendings repeatedly spoke about a loss of teaching opportunities and intensity and increased clinical workloads and responsibility, not a single attending in the field setting or interviews even hinted at throwing in the towel and thus abandoning their residency program. For example, after discussing the need to come in more frequently while on call at night, an attending quickly added the following point:

> I don't mind coming in and teaching the junior residents. I don't think it's necessarily a negative to my job. I just think it's more involvement. Part of what I signed up for is to teach, and so I really don't view it as a negative. I just say it's more—I'm more involved because I can't just rely on my residents. (A-F)

Sentiments of this sort were common. Another example, which followed a discussion of changing workloads, is similar: "So there is an expansion of my day-to-day workload, but I can still get it done, and it's not something that's driving me out of my career. But it's certainly present" (A-M). The pattern is clear: note, grouse, and adapt. In our view, increased workloads are not a primary reason why attending surgeons struggle with the reforms.

Enter Advanced Practice Providers: A Survey-Based Overview

One obvious response to constraints on resident work hours and schedules would be to essentially back-fill lost hours with advanced practice providers (APPs). In that way, pressures on faculty to increase their workloads would be lessened. During the fieldwork and interviews, the possibility of "APPs as reform facilitators" surfaced frequently. We now turn to this possibility. We begin with Table 5.2, which explores how faculty view advanced practice providers and their fit with residents and surgical education. The fourteen questionnaire items were suggested by previous studies and grounded upon the field observations. The results are restricted to the 78 percent of faculty (N = 218) who have at least one advanced practice provider on their primary service. After each question, the overall percentage who "agree or strongly agree" is noted, followed by the contrast for program type (community versus academic). We do not present information broken out by gender or age because nothing varied substantially or significantly across those dimensions.

With respect to overall patterns, the strongest agreement occurred in response to items 1 and 2 (88 and 80 percent, respectively), which asked whether advanced practice providers reduce the workloads of faculty and residents and also help residents comply with reforms. Item 7 also shows strong agreement (71 percent) and indicates that faculty believe that advanced practice providers teach medical students and residents. In contrast, item 6

TABLE 5.2. Assessments of Advanced Practice Providers by Program Type among General Surgery Faculty

		% Agree or Strongly Agree		
			Program Type	
Item	Exact Question Wording (where APPs = nurse practitioners and physician assistants)	Total	Community	Academic
1	APPs decrease resident workloads and help facilitate compliance with duty hours.	88	77	95*
2	APPs decrease my workload.	80	72	85*
3	Most of what APPs perform is work that is viewed by residents as noneducational.	60	57	62
4	APPs reduce resident exposure to educationally valuable preoperative care.	53	51	54
5	APPs sometimes assist in the OR in a way that reduces opportunities for residents.	33	43	26*
6	The presence of APPs reduces the amount of teaching I do on the service.	18	16	19
7	APPs help to teach medical students and interns.	71	52	84*
8	APPs create some difficulties with respect to lines of communication on the service.	27	27	26
9	APPs reduce resident exposure to educationally valuable postoperative care.	48	49	48
10	APPs serve largely as "resident substitutes"—doing work residents would otherwise do.	63	63	63
11	APPs usually offer more knowledge and consistency than the rotating resident staff.	72	59	81*
12	APPs create some difficulties with respect to lines of authority on the service.	33	36	30
13	Attendings sometimes round and make decisions with APPs instead of the resident team.	70	59	77*
14	Some APPs redefine their role to become more independent and less helpful to residents.	47	44	49
	Sample Sizes	218	88	130

Notes. Notes: An asterisk (*) next to the second percentage for a pair of contrasts indicates a significant difference in the percentages at the .05 level; a plus sign (+) indicates significance at the .10 level (from Pearson's chi-square tests).

suggests that faculty largely reject (agreement of only 18 percent) the idea that advanced practice providers reduce the amount of teaching they do on their service. Together, these items point to a positive educational assessment: lowered workloads, the facilitation of duty-hour compliance, and contributions to teaching that augment what is offered by faculty.

Several items, however, suggest that faculty do not view advanced practice providers as a straightforward educational advantage for residents. For example, items 3, 4, 5, and 9 all suggest that advanced practice providers might reduce resident involvement in important activities. Item 3, for example, suggests that about 40 percent of faculty disagree that the work performed by advanced practice providers is viewed by residents as noneducational, whereas items 4 and 9 show that about half of faculty agree that advanced practice providers reduce resident exposure to educationally valuable pre- and postoperative care. Item 5, likewise, suggests that 33 percent of faculty believe that advanced practice providers sometimes assist in the OR in a way that reduces opportunities for residents. Lines of communication and authority on services (items 8 and 12) are also viewed by about a third of faculty as more difficult when advanced practice providers are present on their services. Faculty largely agree that advanced practice providers offer more knowledge and consistency than rotating residents (item 11 at 72 percent); they also at least occasionally round and make decisions with advanced practice providers instead of their resident team (item 13 at 70 percent). Taken together, these items suggest that advanced practice providers help lessen resident workloads, but that their help may come with a price for residents, namely less exposure to educationally valuable activities and a less central role in helping to care for patients and managing services.

The right side of Table 5.2 contains a contrast for program type. Overall, advanced practice providers are more common in programs with an academic affiliation (87 versus 68 percent). With respect to program type, six of the fourteen items differ significantly. Three of the items (1, 2, and 7) showed the strongest overall level of agreement, as noted earlier, and are now seen to be driven by very strong agreement among those in academic programs. For example, nearly all faculty in academic programs (95 percent, item 1) believe that advanced practice providers reduce resident workloads and facilitate duty-hour compliance. First assisting by advanced practice providers is more common in nonacademic programs (43 versus 26 percent, item 5), whereas the tendency to round and make decisions with advanced practice providers instead of residents is greater in academic programs (77 versus 59 percent, item 13).

Confidence *and* Concern:
Advanced Practice Providers and Resident Education

The three strongest patterns in the questionnaire data—that advanced practice providers decrease faculty and resident workloads, that they help residents with duty-hour compliance, and that they serve in a direct role as teachers—were also dominant in the interviews, surfacing in virtually all responses. Faculty were of one voice in saying that advanced practice providers reduced their workloads and those of residents. A typical example:

Mid-levels are essential—we just can't run the service without them. I was Chief of Surgery at one of the VA hospitals when the eighty-hour work week came in. Our residents were averaging more than eighty hours all the time. We hired a huge number of mid-levels. We couldn't do our jobs without the mid-levels. There would be no way—we'd all be working a gazillion hours a week! Things would be forgotten, neglected, and not done. God bless them all for taking care of everything! (A-M)

Many saw advanced practice providers as a necessary counterpart to the reforms. Comments often began with expressions like this: "Because of the duty-hour restrictions, we can't run the service without them [APPs]" (A-M). Without exception, attendings spoke of advanced practice providers as a welcome, even essential, presence on their services. The attending, quoted immediately above, continued by saying, as many others did, that "mid-levels are very much a positive and essential ingredient," even though he also voiced several concerns discussed below.

In our view, the positive aspects of advanced practice providers are readily grasped, whereas faculty concerns about their effects on resident education have received less attention and remain only partially illuminated by the questionnaire data. The concerns that faculty expressed about the fit of advanced practice providers with surgical education clustered analytically into three main areas, although any given comment often touched on more than one issue. Here, we overview concerns about patient care, responsibility and decision-making, and the dynamics of the surgical team. As one attending put it, "mid-levels are a great example of a solution that's also a problem—residents aren't getting the education they need!" (A-M) Due to substantial similarities in the responses of faculty in academic and community programs, distinctions by program type are not drawn out, although a few issues that seem especially salient for sub-specialty services are noted.

The character of residents' involvement in patient care is a common concern. Consider first the sort of "distance from care" noted by the following attending:

One of the problems with good mid-levels is that they sometimes create residents who are distant from the actual process of patient care. They just spend their time in the OR, but then don't understand pre-op or post-op management. It's all automated because there are good mid-levels. Those elements that are educational are maybe just learned in practice, not in training. They just don't leave programs with those skills. (A-F)

The ability of advanced practice providers to "get residents into the OR" became a concern if it meant that residents received insufficient exposure to pre- and postoperative patient care. The following comment on this was typical:

> My opinion is that the residents, if they are relying on mid-level providers, are going to lose an important part of becoming a surgeon—which is adequate patient workup and evaluation. You can teach a monkey to operate. Working up a patient and knowing when not to operate is an equally important skill set. With physician extenders, my worry is that residents are no longer going to have all the abilities to work up a patient from presentation to the operating room and then to carry them out. We're having all these mid-level providers do the H & Ps, doing initial evaluations. Residents will know the mechanics of that surgical procedure, but if they are no longer taking care of the patient postoperatively and are relying on a mid-level provider to do their orders and things, they lose out on all that, too. We're tempted to call it [the increasing number of advanced practice providers] a good thing, because they help with duty-hour restrictions, but that's not the only thing we need to keep in mind. I strongly believe that. (A-M)

The attending then went on to say that he believed resident performance on board exams had slipped in recent years because of the reforms and the increasing presence of advanced practice providers (this is the second epigraph that led off the chapter). Another attending was distinctive in providing rough percentage estimates of how much care on his trauma service was provided by advanced practice providers:

> We do a high volume of surgery. If there is an operative case, there is always a resident there. But for the hour-to-hour, day-to-day care—the admission, discharge, that type of work—the PAs do that. I think the PAs on our service manage on a day-to-day basis—which means rounding, writing the floor notes, taking care of the patients—probably 80 percent of the work and patients. Only about 20 percent of the patients truly are managed by the house staff. Unfortunately, the house staff's ability to do that, in my opinion, is limited, and I see that as an issue—they're not very efficient or knowledgeable. I hate that it's turned into that, but it became a safety issue for us. We just couldn't provide safe care with the house staff coverage on the service, especially with their experience level. We decided as a group of trauma surgeons to hire PAs and to pay them well enough to keep them around. (A-M)

Less exposure, in this view, means less acquired capability to manage the full range of patient care. More advanced practice providers were hired because of the reforms, but doing so then diminishes growth in the surgical skills of residents. Another attending pointed to the way advanced practice providers allow residents to dodge complex aspects of care, such as ordering total parenteral nutrition or TPN:

> Do APNs [advanced practice nurses] impair resident education? They're surely a way to avoid or dodge things. Maybe a resident isn't able to order TPN, but they can dodge that by having the APN do it. If the APN wasn't there, they'd have to figure everything out, so maybe they are at least a crutch for residents. I don't have any way to quantify that—it's just a sense, a feeling, and I can tell it happens. (A-M)

Unless advanced practice providers report resident help-seeking to attendings, they will not know how often or extensively residents use APPs as a "crutch."

Advanced practice providers lessen resident involvement in pre- and post-operative patient care. But they might also leave residents less responsible for patients and less centrally involved in decision making about their care. One attending described this in a general way by saying that while residents used to know all the patients on the service and would pretty much run the service, "now they're just passengers on the service—the go-to person will always be a mid-level" (A-M). An attending on a cardiothoracic service elaborated on the notion of responsibility and who has become the go-to resource for nurses:

> We have a mix of PAs and NPs. Over time, we've just shifted to where our service will run smoothly even if there are no residents around. The nursing staff in the hospital is used to working every day with our PAs and NPs. Often, if there are issues, the residents are no longer the first people who get called if somebody's got a pneumothorax, for example, and they need to talk to somebody. Whereas it used to be that they were involved from the beginning. The negative is that sometimes they get moved down the chain, depending on how aggressive the residents are, how much they want to be involved. They don't really have to make many decisions anymore or get involved in the front line of care. I think that's had a negative educational effect on residents. (A-M)

The attending went on to say that over time there had been a gradual shift of responsibility, with residents receding and advanced practice providers rising, a pattern that "isn't at all bad for patients or for me."

The decision-making skills of residents may also diminish as advanced practice providers assume the position of what some called "go-to staff." Attendings believe that residents defer to at least some advanced practice providers: "I've seen it here where they [advanced practice providers] reach such a level of expertise that the residents defer to the mid-levels who then, basically, usurp their decision-making role" (A-M). In that case, it is the perceived expertise of advanced practice providers that makes residents deferential. In other cases, faculty spoke about how advanced practice providers, in the face of pressing patient care issues, would formulate a plan and then present it to a resident, relieving the resident of the need to think independently.

> Residents need the experience of being on the front line instead of having things gift-wrapped and handed to them by a mid-level who says, "So and so has shortness of breath. I got an EKG and a chest x-ray. Here's the blood gas. The potassium is this, the magnesium is that. I think I'm going to give some Lasix." That eliminates the thinking for the resident. "Oh, that sounds right," instead of him going to see the patient who is short of breath the day after heart surgery to figure out what information they need to make a decision about therapeutic intervention before calling one of us. (A-M)

In this view, residents are in some cases relieved of the need to think through patient-care issues for themselves. Gift-wrapped information and decisions do not advance resident education.

Faculty identified two ways in which advanced practice providers disrupt the dynamics of surgical teams. A first involves the classic hierarchy, where information and responsibility flows up and down from attendings to interns. Advanced practice providers can and do become a first point of contact not only for nurses, but for attendings as well, and thus tread on the traditional turf of residents. A second centers on communication, and how it may be complicated or confused by the presence of advanced practice providers.

No attending spoke of a deliberate intent to change the information and responsibility dynamics of surgical teams. Rather, changes occurred for three main reasons: time pressures; perceptions of familiarity, knowledge, and availability; and the sense that residents were not particularly interested in a service (a pattern evident only for sub-specialties). Consider first the issue of time pressures, which combine in the following comment with the familiarity and knowledge of advanced practice providers to produce a communication preference:

> As an attending, when the day is falling apart around me, I'm going to communicate with the person I have the most confidence in, who is typically the most senior person. If my PA knows better than the residents how I work, how I get

things done, I call that person. If they go back to the team and everything is further communicated, wonderful. If there is a feeling from the resident pool that they're being left out, or vice versa, then there may be some issues. Communication is always an issue, especially with limited staff and when we're busy, running around like crazy people! (A-M)

This attending suggested that the chief resident could still be a first point of contact, in which case the dynamics would be flipped and advanced practice providers might feel left out. Another comment on the hierarchy also highlights time pressures, limitations in resident availability, and the consistent presence of advanced practice providers:

Our mid-levels have become our point of continuity. My residents get upset with me if I go make rounds with the mid-levels. But if they're post-call or at a mandatory teaching conference, what am I supposed to do? Sit down and do nothing? I'm responsible for my own time management. Frankly, residents rotate on and off—mid-levels are here all the time. They know the ebb and flow that we learned, painfully, during our own residencies. (A-M)

Time pressures were often but not always noted, as some focused on the predictable presence of advanced practice providers and their reliability. One, for example, simply said, "It's easier for us to call advanced practice providers because they're more likely to be on the floor than the residents are" (A-M). He noted that residents are often in the OR, with another attending, or across town at the other hospital they cover. More elaborate comments resembled the following:

Quite frankly, I usually call my mid-level on my way to work. I clarify things and get things ordered right away. The senior residents usually feel obligated to talk to me directly, which is fine. When they call or text, I can say, "Yes, I agree with that—I told her [the mid-level] to go ahead and get going on it." The reason all the staff communicate with the mid-level is because they're not in the operating room and they're available. You know they'll get the job done. You used to be able to call the intern because you knew they'd be on the floor. Not always, not anymore. (A-F)

Importantly, the attending initiates calls to her advanced practice provider, not her residents. A communication pattern of this sort surely marginalizes residents, as decisions have already been made and set in motion. Another attending connected those dots, saying that residents could easily become "bystanders to patient care," a point that merges with concerns about responsibility presented earlier.

> Mid-levels are more a constant presence on the team than residents. Attendings become very comfortable working with the mid-levels, so much so that some of the treatment algorithms and the conversations and the decisions start to bypass the residents. Residents aren't fully participating in that—and that takes away from their educational experience. So, in practice, mid-levels are typically engaged, things are happening, and the residents are sometimes becoming bystanders to patient care and not full participants. (A-M)

In addition to time pressures and the familiarity and presence of advanced practice providers, a third factor shaping team dynamics involved resident disinterest. Some faculty spoke about what they viewed as resident disinterest as a reason to involve advanced practice providers in a more fulsome way on their service.

> *I wonder if you've seen any evidence that attendings, maybe because of the press of daily work, start looking more to advanced practice providers and bypass residents to some extent?* We're not general surgeons [a vascular surgeon speaking about a vascular surgery service that was a required component of a general surgery program]. I think if we see the residents are coming to tick the box, that they're here because they have to do this rotation, that they're not invested and aren't taking ownership of patients, then absolutely I look to mid-levels and bypass residents. Absolutely. I want to do what is right for the patients and take care of them the right way. That's often through the advanced practice provider when residents aren't very interested or invested. (A-F)

No faculty on general surgery services spoke of resident disinterest in this way, which suggests that it may occur only on sub-specialty services.

A final issue involves communication. Choosing to contact advanced practice providers preferentially is one common pattern and concern, which we have already noted. But general uncertainty if not confusion as to who should be contacted, and who is taking care of what on a service, also surfaced. Consider the following comment, offered by an attending who claimed considerable experience in working with advanced practice providers:

There are a lot of communication issues. On our service [cardiothoracic], it's sometimes confusing for me to know who I should call to talk about an inpatient issue. A lot of times, a single patient is being seen by a resident and one of our mid-levels. Sometimes, both aren't sure who is taking care of what. We've had our mid-levels for a long time [one since 1990], and we've gotten pretty good at it, but communication issues like that come up every week, at least. (A-M)

Patterns of this sort are striking in light of the attending's long experience with advanced practice providers, and suggest that communication challenges may be endemic.

Reflection: I'll Present This One

Probably in every surgeon's experience, there is a single case, or perhaps several, that are indelibly imprinted in her or his psyche. Some such cases are ones where a key intervention perhaps saved someone's life, meaning death was deferred. More likely however, is the memory of the case that didn't go as hoped for or planned. Such was the case with Danny.

Danny was not dealt a very easy pass in life. He was born with congenital diseases including familial polyposis and hereditary hemorrhagic telangectasia. The former disease led to him having to have his entire colon and rectum removed at age nine, with a permanent ileostomy, or exteriorization of his small intestine to empty into a bag. It also predisposed him to polyps and cancers of his small intestine, one of which had already developed and required removal in his adult years. The latter made him prone to bleeding, and gave him enlarged internal blood vessels compared to a normal person. Whether for congenital or social reasons, or a combination of the two, Danny was not fully developed mentally. He could carry on a normal conversation, but had limited comprehension, lived by himself in a rural setting, and liked to tinker on car engines. A sister helped look after him, and he had no other friends or family.

I met Danny when he was in his forties. A local gastroenterologist asked us to see him when he found such a heavy load of new precancerous polyps in his duodenum that he couldn't remove them with an endoscope, therefore dictating surgical removal. This had developed after Danny had fallen off the surveillance bandwagon for a few years and built up a large number of polyps, essentially replacing the entire lining of his upper intestine. Because that part of the small intestine is where the pancreas and bile duct connect to the intestine, and because biopsies showed advanced precancerous changes (called high grade dysplasia), the operation needed was a complex one known as a Whipple procedure, involving removal of the duodenum, part of the pancreas, part of the bile duct, and the gallbladder, and then performing a series of reconstructive new connections to replace those removed.

Danny and I met several times to discuss this, weighing the magnitude of the surgery and his understanding of what could be involved, vis-à-vis accepting the virtually certain progression to cancer, if not already present, that not operating would entail. He eventually was able to say he wanted to do the surgery. He did well initially after the operation, but had an episode of vomiting a small amount of blood on the day of planned discharge while waiting for his ride home. Without belaboring the details, Danny ended up having a long and complicated course that began with bleeding from an aneurysm that formed from one of the enlarged arteries in his abdomen, and included eventual breakdown of his intestine into his abdominal wound requiring months of intravenous feeding, repeat operations, consultation with colleagues locally and nationally, and other advanced care. Given his social situation and the complexity of his wound care, nearly all of this, for a period of five hundred days, involved continued hospitalization.

One of the hardest things for a surgeon to do is face his or her complications. The suffering a patient goes through, and the "could've or should've or would've" questions the surgeon has to process are not easily managed. In Danny's case, trying to help him process the nuances of why he couldn't eat, why we couldn't just re-operate right away and fix his exposed and leaking intestine, and when this would all be better seemed a form of torture for him, and for me.

At the darker times in his prolonged course, I would sometimes after an overly full day get by his room late in the evening. He had been seen by the resident team already that day with whom I had already communicated, but I needed and wanted to pay my visit as well. A number of times in those evening hours, when he and I were both spent from our days, I would find his "wound manager," a complex conglomerate of plastic, protective materials, and suction devices, failing and in need of being replaced. This was a twenty-minute exercise with multiple steps, now being done with the resident team and the nurse who was available to perform such care being long gone for the day, and the night team on duty well deployed and preoccupied with other, more acute duties. In such moments, Danny and I would spend an extra period of time together, often without many words, as I replaced his manager so his abdominal wall would be protected overnight from his own digestive juices. It was the last thing I wanted to do at that point, but with the resident team gone and the night team often very busy, the need at hand, and my own responsibility for his care, it was quite simply the thing that needed to be done.

Danny eventually became sicker, had a neurologic event, and ended up on a ventilator, and after discussions with his family, passed away after those five hundred days. Truth be told, my emotions included a profound sadness, and a sad sense of relief that his physical suffering, and my day-to-day challenge of living out our therapeutic failure, were over. After all that had transpired and the fact that nearly every resident in our program had at one point or another rotated on our service and assisted with Danny's care, I said to the residents as we prepared to discuss his case at our weekly "morbidity and mortality" conference where all deaths and complications were reviewed, "I'll present this one." I presented the case, commiserated with colleagues, shared some precious times of reflection with his sister, and moved on. Shortly after that presentation, my chairman called me aside. He asked if I knew what the most important part of the case had been. Acknowledging I wasn't myself sure of that, he said it was the residents seeing my continued commitment to my patient, doing my best to care for him, even when it meant facing my failure, day after day.

What is the point of such a story? Someone is ultimately responsible, and responsibility is being there when there is need. As the research presented has pointed out, the duty-hour restrictions haven't taken away need, but they have redefined the parameters around which that need is adjudicated amongst the providers. Given the realities of patient care in complex settings, the appropriate ultimate responsibility of the attending surgeon often dictates increased workload on that person's part to compensate for the required schedules of the rest of the team. One of my former colleagues presented a study on practicing surgeons, and found that most of them worked more than eighty hours per week, in some cases because that was the price of ultimate responsibility.

I am certainly not a fan of going back to the pre-duty-hour-restricted era of graduate medical education. As some of these reflections have outlined, that world had some real liabilities, and it is far too easy to forget the truism that "the past remembers a lot better than it ever lived." What I would say is that someone does have to be ultimately responsible for a patient's needs, and responsibility doesn't operate on a time clock. Increased faculty workload will continue to be part of the solution to duty-hour limits for trainees, and that is the real price of caring, and of care.

CHAPTER 6

Revisions Imposed and Rescinded
The Sixteen-Hour Shift Limit for Interns

I was a chief resident the first year of the intern cap. I think the supposition that under-lies the rule is that people who are younger and inexperienced are the primary mistake makers. But are interns really a big source of medical error? No. I don't think the source of medical error is interns entering orders for potassium and writing notes and closing skin in the OR. If the goal is to address medical error from fatigue, I don't think that limiting the shifts of interns addresses that question one bit. (A-F)

In 2011, the ACGME rolled out the first substantial revision of the reforms implemented nationwide in July of 2003. The most notable and provocative change was a reduction in the maximum shift length permitted for interns. Residents in their second and subsequent years would continue to be allowed to work for twenty-four hours, with up to four additional hours (down from six) for the purpose of maintaining continuity of care with particular patients (henceforth "24+4"). But intern shifts were capped at sixteen hours (hence-forth the "sixteen-hour cap" or the "cap"), with no additional hours allowed for continuity of care. The cap was a compromise on the part of the ACGME, which initially considered implementing a recommendation from the In-stitute of Medicine report that duty periods be capped at sixteen hours for *all residents*, not just interns (Ulmer, Wolman, and Johns 2008). The IOM's recommendation was based on research that suggested clinical performance wanes, and errors increase, after sixteen hours of wakefulness. The cap and the logic that drove its formulation and imposition were not just a change, but a notable tightening of the work-hour rules.

The rationale for the cap involved more than the notion that performance wanes as hours of wakefulness accumulate. An ACGME document (Riebschleger and Nasca 2011, 31) titled "New Duty Hour Limits: Discussion and Justification," draws the rationale out more fully:

> Duty periods of PGY-1 residents must not exceed 16 hours. . . . It takes into account the differences between PGY-1 residents and their more senior colleagues, and the consensus that very junior learners would benefit from a more supported and regulated learning environment. PGY-1 residents may not have sufficient experience and skills to provide high-quality, safe patient care, while research indicates that under the current standards, this group works the longest hours of any cohort of residents. . . . In addition, PGY-1 residents make more errors when working longer consecutive hours. Entrusting care to residents with inadequate experience is neither good education nor quality, safe patient care. . . . The ideal is a first year of education with more protected hours.

Interns are viewed as a distinctive group who may not have the requisite skill, experience, and judgment to provide good and safe patient care. They have also traditionally worked the longest hours among residents. In addition, the ACGME was strongly influenced by research we reviewed in the opening chapter that found interns made more medical errors in intensive care units on long shifts (Landrigan et al. 2004; Lockley et al. 2004). Together, these concerns led the ACGME to view the intern year as transitional and interns as needing special protection.

Two streams of research have explored the sixteen-hour cap. A first examined potential links between the cap and a broad range of health outcomes for patients. Since the primary rationale for the cap was rooted in concerns about intern errors and patient welfare, studies of this sort are clearly important if not essential. Early studies invoked a before-and-after design, comparing patient outcomes from one or more residency programs before and after the imposition of the cap. The results generally support the conclusion that the sixteen-hour cap did not improve patient outcomes (Patel et al. 2014; Rajaram et al. 2015; Scally et al. 2015). The most compelling and recent pair of studies invoked a randomized design, where a large pool of residency programs was split into a group that abided by the sixteen-hour cap for interns and the 24+4 limit for residents and an intervention group that was permitted flexibility over shift lengths and rest periods between shifts. Results show that outcomes in programs that purportedly abide by the sixteen-hour cap and the 24+4 rule are indistinguishable from those with shift-length flexibility (Bilimoria et al. 2016 for surgery; Silber et al. 2019 for internal medicine). Importantly, none of this research permitted programs to officially relax the eighty-hour weekly work limit. Shift lengths, not overall weekly hours, were allowed to be more flexible, as were rest periods between shifts.

A second stream of research has explored the views and experiences of residents and faculty, asking in essence whether the cap has been a good, bad, or mixed policy for residents, residency programs, and patients. Research of this sort is also essential, as it sheds light on how the sixteen-hour cap altered important aspects of the residency experience—such as technical education or professional development—that might not bear on short-term patient outcomes. Published studies have been critical of the cap, pointing out a range of concerns on the part of both faculty and residents across many specialties (e.g., Ahmed et al. 2014; Bolster and Rourke 2015; Desai et al. 2018).

This chapter contributes to this second stream in two ways. First, most studies of the sixteen-hour cap were either done before the change took place— asking what faculty and residents *anticipated* the cap might be like—or shortly after the cap's introduction—thus asking about *first impressions*. While those approaches have merit, there are obvious advantages to a research design that allows faculty and residents to experience and adjust to the sixteen-hour cap over several residency years before exploring their assessments. Our research design, which collected data after the cap had been in force for three and a half years, thus permits a more substantial experiential foundation for the views of faculty and residents on the sixteen-hour cap. Second, our design permits insights into the ways resident status and faculty tenure might influence experiences with, and assessments of, the cap. With respect to resident status, all interns and junior residents (PGY2–3) in our study experienced directly the sixteen-hour cap, and a portion of PGY4s did as well. Junior residents and the PGY4s who also experienced the sixteen-hour cap as interns are perfectly positioned to address their experiences with both sixteen-hour and 24+4 shifts. We explore the possibility that interns, junior residents, and senior residents view the sixteen-hour cap differently. In addition, faculty fall into three groups based on tenure: those who trained entirely during the era of the ACGME duty-hour restrictions; those who trained at least partly during those restrictions; and those who finished training before the restrictions emerged nationally in 2003. No published research has explored the possibility that faculty tenure might shape experiences with, and assessments of, the sixteen-hour intern cap. Are those who "came of age professionally" during the reform era more supportive of the cap than their older peers?

The evidence drawn upon here was collected from both residents and faculty during the third wave of the study. Questionnaire items about the merits and demerits of the sixteen-hour cap were adapted from previous studies or generated on the basis of discussions with residents and faculty. The eighty-two interviews allowed us to probe in detail both how and why residents and faculty view the sixteen-hour cap on intern shifts as a good, bad, or mixed policy for surgical residents and residency programs. Those interviews, we add, amount to more than six times as many interviews as a small exploratory study of similar issues (Kreutzer et al. 2017). In both prongs of the analysis, we draw fully on evidence from both residents and faculty. As we describe at the end of the chapter, the ACGME rescinded the sixteen-hour cap on July 1, 2017. Our data, which was collected in advance of the ACGME's decision to lift the cap, thus explores and documents experienced-based assessments of the cap on the eve of its revocation.

A Survey-Based Overview

Table 6.1 presents fifteen questionnaire items along with results for faculty and residents. Looking at the table as a whole, the views of residents and faculty often differ, with twelve of fifteen percentage differences indicating significant gaps. Items 1 through 3 ask if the sixteen-hour cap is supported by credible evidence, represents a positive change, and should be extended to include all residents. The results indicate weak support, as no more than 26 percent of either group is in agreement. The lowest percentages in agreement—14 for residents and a mere 4 for faculty—are for item 3, which asks if the sixteen-hour cap should be extended to cover all residents. Results for items 4 through 7 show that a minority of both residents and faculty (42 and 39 percent) believe that intern fatigue has been reduced (item 4), and even fewer (27 and 9 percent) see any improvement in patient safety due to reduced intern fatigue (item 5). Conversely, a majority of residents and faculty (55 and 77 percent) express concern that the cap has worsened patient safety due to handoff-related problems (item 6). Interestingly, only about half (48 percent) of faculty and residents believe that the quality of life and well-being of interns improved with the cap (item 7).

Items 8 through 15 probe various aspects of the professional development of interns and team dynamics. Few residents and faculty (17 and 19 percent) believe that the sixteen-hour cap has promoted education over service obligations (item 8). Results for items 9 through 12 suggest concerns about the professional development of interns and significant gaps between resident and faculty views. Both groups express concern about how the cap might foster a

TABLE 6.1. Assessments of the Sixteen-Hour Intern Shift Limit by General Surgery Faculty and Residents

	Exact Question Wording:	% Agree or Strongly Agree	
Item	"The sixteen-hour duty period limit on interns . . ."	Residents	Faculty
	PANEL A: GENERAL ASSESSMENTS		
1	is supported by credible evidence that performance diminishes after sixteen duty hours.	26	18*
2	represents a positive change for surgical residency programs.	26	12*
3	should be extended to include all residents, not just interns.	14	4*
	PANEL B: FATIGUE, PATIENT SAFETY, AND QUALITY OF LIFE		
4	reduces intern fatigue at the hospital.	42	39
5	improves patient safety by reducing fatigue among interns.	27	9*
6	worsens patient safety due to problems with information transfer and communication.	55	77*
7	improves the quality of life and well-being of interns.	48	48
	PANEL C: PROFESSIONAL DEVELOPMENT		
8	promotes education over service obligations.	17	19
9	encourages an unprofessional "shift mentality" among interns.	57	81*
10	makes it difficult for interns to learn to place patient needs above self-interest.	38	69*
11	diminishes interns' clinical competence and fund of knowledge.	44	72*
12	diminishes the preparation of interns for more senior roles.	60	87*
	PANEL D: CARE TEAMS		
13	makes it more difficult for interns to function as members of a care team.	39	74*
14	worsens relationships between interns and more senior residents.	32	39+
15	shifts some work from interns to other residents or attendings.	69	90*
	Sample Sizes	*291*	*279*

Notes. An asterisk (*) next to the second percentage for a pair of contrasts indicates a significant difference in the percentages at the .05 level; a plus sign (+) indicates significance at the .10 level (from Pearson's chi-square tests).

"shift mentality" (57 and 81 percent on item 9) and diminish intern preparation for more senior roles (60 and 87 percent on item 12). Majority agreement is found among both residents and faculty that the cap shifts some work from interns to residents or attendings (69 and 90 percent on item 15). A minority of both residents and faculty (32 and 39 percent), however, believe that the restriction on intern shifts worsened relationships among interns and more senior residents (item 14).

The results in the table mask a strong pattern because they present over-all figures for residents and faculty. Additional analyses split attendings into

TABLE 6.2. Assessments of the Sixteen-Hour Intern Shift Limit by Surgeons by Experience and Status

Item	Exact Question Wording: "The sixteen-hour duty period limit on interns . . ."	Residents by PGY			Faculty
		1	2–3	4–5	All
	PANEL A: GENERAL ASSESSMENTS				
1	is supported by credible evidence that performance diminishes after sixteen duty hours.	48	28	10*	18
2	represents a positive change for surgical residency programs.	51	28	8*	12
3	should be extended to include all residents, not just interns.	32	14	3*	4
	PANEL B: FATIGUE, PATIENT SAFETY, AND QUALITY OF LIFE				
4	reduces intern fatigue at the hospital.	61	50	21*	39
5	improves patient safety by reducing fatigue among interns.	55	29	9*	9
6	worsens patient safety due to problems with information transfer and communication.	36	55	65*	77
7	improves the quality of life and well-being of interns.	61	52	37*	48
	PANEL C: PROFESSIONAL DEVELOPMENT				
8	promotes education over service obligations.	27	20	8*	19
9	encourages an unprofessional "shift mentality" among interns.	29	57	76*	81
10	makes it difficult for interns to learn to place patient needs above self-interest.	23	32	56*	69
11	diminishes interns' clinical competence and fund of knowledge.	30	38	57*	72
12	diminishes the preparation of interns for more senior roles.	36	55	79*	87
	PANEL D: CARE TEAMS				
13	makes it more difficult for interns to function as members of a care team.	15	34	58*	74
14	worsens relationships between interns and more senior residents.	15	33	41*	39
15	shifts some work from interns to other residents or attendings.	47	69	82*	90
	Number of cases (cases with missing values were deleted):	*66*	*113*	*108*	*274*

Notes. An asterisk (*) next to the third percentage for a set of contrasts indicates a significant difference in the percentages at the .05 level; a plus sign (+) indicates significance at the .10 level (from Pearson's chi-square tests).

three groups based on how long they had held that status in a residency program (one to five years, six to twelve years, and thirteen or more years). Those groups contrast attendings who trained entirely under the ACGME reforms (the one-to-five group), those who trained at least partly under those conditions (the six-to-twelve group), and those who trained prior to the restrictions (those with thirteen or more years of tenure). The results showed no significant or substantial variation in the views of faculty for any of the fifteen items. We also split residents into three groups, namely interns, junior residents (PGY 2–3), and senior residents (PGY 4–5). In striking contrast to the pattern for faculty, the results in Table 6.2 for all fifteen questions show that resident views of the cap vary significantly and often dramatically across PGY levels (the average intern versus senior-resident gap is 35 percentage points). While faculty views are homogenous, resident views are not.

The results across PGY levels for residents suggest two more specific patterns. A first is that there tends to be a shift across resident levels, not just a gap between the least and most experienced. For example, when asked if the cap has been a positive change for surgical residency programs (item 2), 51 percent of interns agree, but that percentage drops to 28 percent for junior residents and 8 percent for senior residents. Likewise, the results for item 12, which asks whether the cap diminishes the preparation of interns for more senior roles, indicate agreement among 36, 55, and 79 percent of interns, juniors, and then senior residents. A second pattern is that the views of senior residents are more closely aligned with faculty views than is the case for their less-experienced peers. In some cases, such as items 1, 2, and 3, senior residents are slightly less supportive than faculty of the sixteen-hour cap. For other items (e.g., 9–13) senior residents continue to differ modestly from faculty in seeing fewer problems with the cap.

Table 6.3 provides a final consideration of the role of gender. Much like previous chapters, the results indicate only occasional and relatively small differences between men and women. For example, female attendings are less likely than their male peers to see the cap as a positive change (item 2), more likely to believe it worsens patient safety (item 6), and more likely to link the cap to a shifting of work to other residents and attendings (item 15). While each difference is modest (the largest is 12 points), women, not men, express more discontent with the cap on intern shifts. A similar pattern is found for residents. Women differ significantly from their male peers on four items (4, 8, 11, and 12), but the differences again tend to be modest and point to women being more discontented with the cap. As in previous chapters, gender does not strongly shape the views and experiences of surgeons in training or in practice. The modest differences that emerge suggest that women harbor more concerns than men.

TABLE 6.3. Assessments of the Sixteen-Hour Intern Shift Limit by Surgeons by Gender and Status

		% Agree or Strongly Agree			
		Attendings		Residents	
Item	Exact Question Wording: "The sixteen-hour duty period limit on interns . . ."	Men	Women	Men	Women
	PANEL A: GENERAL ASSESSMENTS				
1	is supported by credible evidence that performance diminishes after sixteen duty hours.	19	14	28	22
2	represents a positive change for surgical residency programs.	14	6*	27	23
3	should be extended to include all residents, not just interns.	5	1	13	15
	PANEL B: FATIGUE, PATIENT SAFETY, AND QUALITY OF LIFE				
4	reduces intern fatigue at the hospital.	38	38	46	34*
5	improves patient safety by reducing fatigue among interns.	10	8	28	26
6	worsens patient safety due to problems with information transfer and communication.	74	86*	53	57
7	improves the quality of life and well-being of interns.	48	44	49	46
	PANEL C: PROFESSIONAL DEVELOPMENT				
8	promotes education over service obligations.	20	16	20	12+
9	encourages an unprofessional "shift mentality" among interns.	80	84	57	58
10	makes it difficult for interns to learn to place patient needs above self-interest.	70	67	35	44
11	diminishes interns' clinical competence and fund of knowledge.	70	77	37	54*
12	diminishes the preparation of interns for more senior roles.	85	92	56	66+
	PANEL D: CARE TEAMS				
13	makes it more difficult for interns to function as members of a care team.	73	77	38	40
14	worsens relationships between interns and more senior residents.	41	36	29	36
15	shifts some work from interns to other residents or attendings.	87	96*	69	69
	Sample Sizes	203	73	177	108

Notes. An asterisk (*) next to the second percentage for a pair of contrasts indicates a significant difference in the percentages at the .05 level; a plus sign (+) indicates significance at the .10 level (from Pearson's chi-square tests).

The interviews allowed us to explore more fully how and why residents and faculty view the cap as a good, bad, or mixed policy for surgical residents and residency programs. We focus here on four main issues that serve best to elaborate and extend the patterns found in the questionnaire evidence: concerns about educational losses from shorter shifts; difficulties when interns assume second-year responsibilities; how intern shifts may be more fatiguing than expected; and how the relatively rare positive evaluations of the cap tended to be framed. We omit from consideration a key pattern, namely a perceived clash between shorter shifts and professional values, because it largely overlaps with evidence drawn out in previous chapters.

Shorter Shifts and Educational Losses

A pervasive comment, found in virtually every interview with faculty and nearly all residents, was that interns "missed out" on valuable learning opportunities because of the cap. For interns, complaints centered exclusively on foregone chances to get into the operating room, as in the following comment:

> The biggest negative for me is when it limits educational experiences. I've been working a week of night float. There were several cases that came in overnight. I was the first person to see it in the emergency department. I was the person who worked the patient up to get them to the OR. Then I hear, "Oh, hey, by the way, it's the end of your shift—you can't stay to do part of this case because you're approaching your limit." That, to me, is a really big limitation—having a very hard and set time limit. It can interfere with a good educational experience. (PGY1-M)

They also noted that "it's not like interns are doing these cases—you are mostly watching and always have someone behind you" and that the "sixteen-hour rule limits how much we're able to see" (PGY1-M).

Junior residents made similar but retrospective comments, such as the following: "Just based on the range of things I have seen and learned in my six months as a second year that I did not have an opportunity to see when I was an intern, I mean, that has experientially illustrated to me the huge loss in clinical exposure for interns" (PGY2-F). Senior residents tended to emphasize how interns need clinical exposure and how they have substantial back-up support:

> *Interns are the least skilled clinically and many didn't experience long hours in their medical schools. Do you see merit to the sixteen-hour shift as a bridge experience*

from the lower hours of medical school to the longer hours of residency? It's absolutely dumb. It's like the ACGME guys never did a residency, or are now so old they forgot what it meant. What interns need is exposure and experience. They don't need to be coddled. They need to see things as they are. They also need to understand there are chiefs to call and there's an attending to call. There is always help available one way or another—no intern is ever on their own. The thought shouldn't be to give newcomers less exposure to patient care. The thought process should be that we make sure they have as much exposure as possible with as much support as they need. (PGY5-M)

Faculty spoke about how the shorter and more rigid shifts of interns interfered with the development of pattern recognition and judgment. A common argument was that there was much to be gained educationally by following particular patients over longer periods of time to more fully observe their course. Efforts to "piece" or "stitch" together partial experiences with several patients were not viewed as comparable. The following observations were typical:

Even though an intern isn't there for a patient's entire course, can they still stitch things together across various cases? Is observing portions of cases A, B, C, and D about the same as observing the full course of patient A? No. I totally disagree with that. You can't stitch experiences together like that. *Why?* Continuity is really important in patient care, especially in surgical patient care. So if you're not following the patient from beginning to end, you can't really stitch together different patients' experience because they're all different. A lot of this is pattern recognition. So when you're learning from a disjointed view then it's hard to recognize those patterns. I very strongly believe in allowing residents to follow a patient all the way through as much as possible. (A-M)

Several faculty noted that the value of "following a patient all the way through" was especially important for interns, as they were just beginning to recognize patterns. Consider the following observation about the value of continuity for interns:

Say an intern admits an appendix from the ER, but they have to go home before the case goes. They don't get to see the result of what that patient's exam looked like versus what the appendix looks like, what things look like on the inside. They come back the next day. They may discharge them, but they don't know all the nuances of the case that might impact what their follow-up or discharge instructions should be. *I wonder—can you segment a case into parts? Maybe appendicitis*

has five parts to it. If an intern sees the first two with one patient, the third with an-
other, and the last two with yet another patient, can they mentally stitch the experi-
ences together in a way that makes it like seeing it all with one patient? I agree with
that with more advanced learners, but not for the interns. The intern needs to
see specific cases, all steps of the case, throughout, to develop a good sense of the
whole sequence. More advanced learners can integrate in the way you describe,
but that's only when they already have a good sense of the whole sequence. (A-F)

A final way faculty conceptualized the educational value of continuity involved
the development of judgment. Judgment is seen as being founded upon knowing the implications of the many patient-care decisions that are made, as in
the following comment:

Educationally, we are not producing the same residency product. Technically, residents are fine. The problem comes with judgment—it's very hard to learn judgment,
which comes from experience and unfortunately some bad judgment. If you make
decisions and you don't get to see how they play out because you go away, you don't
learn the natural history of diseases, and you don't learn judgment. So with this
coming and going, and now the shorter intern shifts, they don't see the whole arc
of all the little things that came up with these patients. You make a series of micro-
decisions and they have these implications—that's the basis of judgment. That's the
deficit that people talk about when they hire young surgeons out of residency. It's
not about technique. It's about judgment—about knowing what to do. (A-F)

Most comments of this sort were paired with observations about how the
cap had amplified concerns already present with the reforms. For example, "I
think they're missing out on a lot of the initial pre-op and then the post-op
care experiences as well. The eighty-hour rules curb some of that, but the sixteen really does" (A-F).

A More Difficult Intern-to-PGY2 Transition

A prevailing observation among surgeons centered on traditional expectations for those entering the second year. Put simply, clinical and operative
responsibilities and the need to teach and oversee medical students and interns all increase substantially with the transition to the second year. At the
same time, support from more experienced residents diminishes. Because of
those new demands, the second year is viewed as a poor time to first encounter long shifts. A second-year resident comments on these issues:

Could you speak to what you see as the good or bad aspects of the sixteen-hour rule? I feel it's mostly a negative. I would prefer on balance not to have the sixteen-hour work limit. The intern year is the most supervised year. You have all the other levels above you. No one expects you to be as great at your job as everyone else. So, I think that learning how to handle the fatigue and working while tired is more important when you are more supervised. It seems odd to put limits on interns and then expect you to learn how to work long days as an upper level. (PGY2-F)

As we described earlier, fatigue and working while tired are viewed as a reality of life among surgeons and a necessary developmental encounter for residents. Surgeons believe that they can learn to recognize, mitigate, and overcome fatigue, all of which should take place when responsibilities are limited and support is not. A chief elaborates:

You learn coping mechanisms for being on long-call shifts—ways to deal with being tired safely, ways to work through things in a more deliberate pace, or lean on other support systems or other people you have in the hospital. I feel like intern year, as painful as it is because there are so many adjustments, is the right time to learn to deal with long shifts because you are always on call with an upper-level resident. You develop coping mechanisms in a protected way. Now, the transition to being a 2 [a second-year resident] is much harder for interns. They have to figure out those coping mechanisms for the first time, but often at a time when they're the only people in the hospital. There is no upper-level resident that they're on call with to lean on, get feedback from, or get advice from. They have to adjust to that and do it in a more isolated way than if they had learned those things when they were interns. (PGY5-M)

Although yearly didactic presentations about fatigue and fatigue-mitigation strategies are now required features of all residency programs, the chief resident quoted immediately above summed up the experiential basis of learning to work while tired in this way: "you can't learn what it's like to work or stay efficient when you're tired unless you do it."

Faculty comments mirrored those of residents in pointing out how the need to learn to manage long call should not occur at the same time as responsibilities increase and support decreases. They also tended to suggest that patient safety and care is not enhanced by delaying the experience of long call until the second year.

I'd like to ask about the sixteen-hour rules for interns. Do you see that as a positive development, a negative one, or a mix of the two? That has been a negative. *Why is that?* Well, they are not exposed to long call. And then, when they get into the second year, they haven't learned to work with the physical limitations of fatigue or even knowing when they're fatigued or what to do when they're fatigued. Interns miss that. It's a big change for them, especially with the change of responsibilities from an intern to a junior. A junior usually has a lot of responsibility in most programs. So, you have the responsibility plus the extra hours that they have to work. They crack easier. (A-M)

The ominous expression "crack" was echoed in the statement of another faculty member, who summed up this new second-year challenge as "in nobody's best interest" (A-M).

The Fatiguing Character of Shorter Shifts

Faculty commonly addressed the previous two themes, but none noted what was a common and striking observation among junior residents: that shorter shifts can *exacerbate* or *induce*, not lessen, fatigue. Workplace fatigue, of course, can be acute—induced by a single long period of work—or chronic—induced by a string of demanding days and insufficient rest. Several junior residents referred to the intern year as a "grind," an idea described by the following resident:

> *Was it your sense that you were able to be more rested and less fatigued during your first year than when you became a PGY2?* I think I was more rested, but also more fatigued. *Can you explain that?* I consistently got sleep at night, but you're working long days, from 5 a.m. to 7 p.m. every weekday. You never have a post-call day. You never have a day to catch up. You never have a weekday to get a haircut or go to a bank or get your car fixed. It really wears on you and becomes a grind. I think by month seven, eight, and nine, you are constantly fatigued by that schedule. (PGY3-M)

These observations have three key components. The first is the sense that a string of back-to-back shorter shifts is perceived as more fatiguing than a schedule occasionally punctuated by long call. A second-year resident comments on this:

> Compared to this year, it felt like I was working more last year. You would work fourteen or sixteen hours in a row and have to be there right away again the next

day. If you were there all day every day for five or six days, up to eighty hours, you just felt busier and more tired than you would if you were there overnight one or two times and then you have the next day off. I feel like I have more time this year than I did during my intern year. (PGY2-M)

A second factor driving this perception is the sense that a post-call day, where residents leave in the late morning, provides more than just a chance to do what they commonly call "normal-person things" like get a haircut or have a car repaired. Rather, it offers a chance to catch up on sleep and relax. And third, the shorter shifts of interns tend to be packed and busy. Long-call shifts can be like that too, but they are more likely to have lulls and thus opportunities for sleep. A second-year describes these latter two factors:

I felt more fatigued last year. I believe that you can catch up on sleep if you have more hours off in a row. I think that I am less tired because of post-call days where I'm going home at 10 a.m. or 11 a.m. and I don't have to be back until six o'clock the next day. That, to me, is more of a break than having eight hours between every day as an intern. So, that's one aspect of it. Another is that on a sixteen-hour shift, you're almost never going to take a nap. On twenty-four- or twenty-eight-hour shift, there are nights when you'll get an hour, two hours, three hours of sleep. You can't count on that, but with that power nap, I don't feel tired at all, and then I get the next day off. (PGY2-F)

For interns, back-to-back shorter shifts, few chances to do normal-person things during the week, little opportunity for long periods to relax and catch up on sleep, and the steady pace of work during their shifts combine to produce at least the perception if not the reality that their work schedules may be more fatiguing than the schedules of residents.

Why Some See Merit in the Cap

As is evident in some of the quotes drawn upon above, we approached the issue of the cap by asking whether surgeons saw it as a change that was good, bad, or a mix of the two. In many cases, they expressed a variation on this response: "What could be good about the cap?" They then launched into comments about one or more of the issues discussed above, offering nothing in the way of perceived merits. But in a few interviews with attendings, and especially those with interns and to a lesser extent second-year residents, comments touched on the merits of the cap. Comments of this sort stand in stark contrast with the concerns and critiques that were the most prevalent perspective on the cap. In this section, we describe the common themes in these supportive comments about the cap. It is important to note, however, that in every case observations about perceived merits were accompanied by expressions of concern, meaning that the cap was seen as a mixed policy. But given the strongly negative assessments described thus far, what were the grounds for at least a measure of support?

Faculty and residents differed in the merits they identified. For a few faculty, resident safety, education, and separating the twin challenges of learning to manage long call and gaining clinical knowledge were noted as strong positives to the cap on intern shifts. Consider the following comment by an attending about safety and learning:

> *Do you believe that the sixteen-hour cap on intern shifts has been a good thing for surgical residents and surgical training, a bad thing, or is it a mix of the two?* It's a good thing. It has drawbacks, but on balance, it's a good thing. *Can you articulate a bit what you see as good?* When I was in med school, one of my sisters went into pediatrics. Not a blood relative—we had mentors who were called our big brothers and sisters. She was an upperclassman. During her internship, she was driving home after a thirty-six-hour shift and she drove under a truck and died. That was directly attributable, in my mind, to the lack of work-hour restrictions. I've experienced near misses myself where I've fallen asleep at the wheel. I stopped when I ran into somebody else. *Okay. So, one positive would be safety on the part of the resident himself or herself.* Yes. Sure. *Other positives?* I've seen a lot of studies that acquisition of new information, whether it was a rote memorization of facts or duplication of a mechanical task or a perception task, such as discerning wavy lines, how close they are. Those abilities decay—the acquisition of new information and performance isn't good when we're fatigued. (A-M)

Given what is known about the risks of driving when fatigued, it is surprising that this comment about those very real risks—and the death of a friend—is the only one made by an attending during any round of interviews. Almost uniformly, surgeons turn attention away from personal safety to how shift limits interfere with what they see as good care and training. Here too is the rare observation, which is also well grounded in research on learning, that fatigue diminishes not only cognitive performance but also the ability to grasp and retain information (Doyle and Zakrajsek 2013). For this attending, long shifts put residents at risk and diminish the educational value of their clinical experiences.

The other way faculty expressed support for the cap was to suggest that the traditional twin challenges of the internship year—managing fatigue and gaining clinical knowledge—should be decoupled. The jump from the final year of medical school to the internship year is considerable. Work hours in medical school tend to be shorter, with few really long and demanding days on rotations, and of course there is much less direct responsibility for clinical matters or expectations about medical knowledge. One rationale for the sixteen-hour cap was to split these two so that the internship would become a bridge between medical school and residencies. The following attending essentially embraces and articulates this perspective:

> *Do you see the sixteen-hour limits on interns as a positive development, a negative one, or something that's a mix of the two for surgical residents?* I think that it's mixed. I think that in the past the interns have been easy prey to mistakes due to inexperience and due to prolonged hours of work and getting tired or overwhelmed. I truly think that limiting that risk factor by having them come in fresh every day, work sixteen hours, and then having somebody cover the night is better. The disadvantage of that is that the process of them getting experience and getting better at what they should be doing is going to be longer. So, I would think that if we could get the medical students to graduate with better clinical experience this system is actually very good, but because the medical students actually don't have much experience when they become interns, it just prolongs the process significantly for them to get experience. But I think it's safer. *So you see the cap on intern shifts as something of a bridge experience between being a medical student and the full on 24+4 shifts of residents?* Yes. I'd rather train somebody to have ways of dealing with clinical problems—and then train them to have the stamina to work long hours. Traditionally, we've tried to do both at the same time. That just risks problems. (A-M)

Safety surfaces again, but here the focus is on fatigue-related mistakes that interns are prone to make given their insufficient fund of medical knowledge and experience of working while fatigued. If the cap did in fact remove fatigue from the intern experience, which is doubtful given the observations offered earlier in the chapter, splitting the two would allow interns to become more skilled clinically before taking on the challenge of working while fatigued.

Interns and second year residents were among those most likely to describe the cap as a positive development. They framed this in three ways: the cap as a bridge experience; how the cap made a more normal schedule possible; and how their unfamiliarity with hospital systems, not so much a deficit of clinical knowledge, made the intern year a formidable challenge. The notion of capped intern shifts as a bridge experience was a common sentiment among those in their intern year. Consider the following comment:

> *My understanding is that you're an intern now. Is that correct?* That's correct. *Do you see the sixteen-hour limit on interns as a positive development, a negative one, or something that's a mix of the two?* Well, I think that one of the benefits of the sixteen-hour rules is that it does give more study time, especially on the weekends, on weekend call. Having to take just a day or a night call usually helps with having some free time on the weekends. Also, it does help, especially early on in the intern year, I felt like it helped with avoiding getting overwhelmed. Going straight from medical school into residency, you're just not used to doing anything past eight to twelve hours. I feel like going straight into a twenty-four-hour call would've been a lot more difficult. *Did you work any long shifts in medical school?* It depended on the rotation. Typically, I wouldn't do anything more than twelve hours, and that wasn't often. A few times on surgery I stayed that late. *Okay. So, you had a little insight into that, but not much.* Yes, and I think I'm like others—I don't think anybody's medical school experience was anything like the intensity of residency. (PGY1-F)

The statement that the cap helped the intern avoid "getting overwhelmed" was echoed by a few other interns. Medical school, they say, is not like residency, and capped shifts ease the transition as the policy had intended. The caps on intern shifts also permitted a more normal schedule than what was typically possible for residents in their second and subsequent years.

> *Could you describe a bit what you see as positive about the sixteen-hour rule for interns, what's negative, and how you see it on balance?* I'll start with the positives, but there are negatives too. Being there only sixteen hours, or at least having the potential of only being there sixteen hours, is a little bit more reasonable in that you have a similar schedule, for the most part, most weeks. You have a slightly more predictable schedule. That can kind of translate into the opportunity to have a more structured outside-of-the-hospital life. You can interact with other people in a little bit more structured way because you can say, "I'll be done by such-and-such time." With regulations in place, you'll be off by that time. You will be able to do whatever you want. I can't rely on that this year just because of the unpredictable call schedule and shifts that we have and a lot of programs have. (PGY2-F)

For this resident, predictable schedules were described in a wistful way, and their loss was a notable and lamentable feature of the move up to the second year.

Like attendings, residents also described the importance of newness and unfamiliarity with clinical matters during their first year. But their comments tended to put much less emphasis on what attendings call a fund of medical knowledge. Instead, residents emphasized the many more nearly organizational routines and procedures that needed to be mastered in order to get anything accomplished. In short, matters as simple as where supplies are kept, how to get them restocked when needed, how to get a CT scan ordered and completed in a timely manner, and how to gain the trust and support of particular nurses were challenges that residents had to encounter and surmount. In short, *getting things done* involved far more than simply knowing how to assess a clinical situation and make a medical decision. For newcomers, practical matters compounded the challenge of gaining clinical skills.

> I think sixteen hours is probably a pretty good cap, especially starting out. It really is different from this year to last in the sense of my comfort level. I now know how every system works in the hospital. I know how to identify a truly sick patient. There's not much that I haven't seen yet or wouldn't know who to take it to. So I think there is some judicious value in keeping that for the interns. *So you agree with the idea that it makes sense to have people who don't know what they're doing, haven't worked a lot yet, to have shorter shifts?* I do. When you start, you really are inefficient. It's not because you're dumb. There is a pretty steep learning curve for how each service works, learning how to interact with the ED, learning how to interact with the operating room, learning how to interact with different types of consults, even getting things ordered. There's such a steep learning curve even outside the whole medical aspects of it. I think the more things that are new to you, you are more easily exhaustible. Right now, working twenty-eight hours, it's not fun, but it's not that big of a deal. There's not a whole lot that's entirely new. I can navigate it. I'm not as exhausted by trying to figure out how everything works and having all these new things that I'm encountering for the first time that I don't know how to navigate. As an intern, even if you know what to do—like the medical aspect of something—getting anything done depends on knowing a ton of things that are different on each service! When you have that kind of newness everywhere, your brain is working more and you get overwhelmed and really tired. Now, I can navigate everything. It's not an issue. (PGY2-M)

As interns and junior residents described the value of a cap, they also made two other points. The first emphasized that the cap was most valuable and justifiable during the first few months of the internship. For example, one of the interns, quoted above, noted explicitly that "it does help, especially early on in the intern year" (PGY1-F). As the year progresses, and interns become familiar with the many things they need to know to accomplish clinical work, the need for the cap wanes. A second emphasized that the cap had merit but was not essential. The second-year resident, quoted directly above, concluded with this observation:

> Although, if it were to go away, our program is set up such that I don't think it would put anyone at risk. I feel like we are pretty good about mid-levels and the upper levels being aware of what's going on. The intern is not left with enough responsibility that they could really screw something up. I think I liked it how it was. If it were my decision to make, I think I would keep it that way. But if that were to change and it were to go away, and interns were stuck with longer shifts, I think that would be okay too. (PGY2-M)

All told, the comments in this section and the results of the questionnaire data presented early in the chapter suggest that some saw merit in the cap. That support, however, was not common or strong, and it was largely overshadowed by passionate and sustained criticisms.

Revisions Reconsidered and Rescinded

The ACGME issued new program rules for residencies effective July 1, 2017 (ACGME 2017; Burchiel et al. 2017). Although the new rules include a number of changes that purport to foster teamwork and physician welfare, the changes that were most consequential for those in general surgery centered on work hours. The cap on intern shifts was lifted, the mandatory rest periods between shifts were allowed to be more flexible (for both regular shifts and long call), and shifts reverted to 24+6, where the extra six hours was earmarked (as with the +4) for continuity of care. The eighty-hour work week, however, remained. The 2011 effort to more strictly limit shift lengths and prescribe rest periods was thus reconsidered and rescinded.

As part of its reconsideration of the work-hour rules, the ACGME sought and received feedback on the rules from faculty, residents, and a host of advocacy and medical-professional organizations. As described by the task force formed by the ACGME to reconsider program requirements, comments were easy to summarize: "The Task Force was presented with a consensus recommendation from senior residents, specialty societies, and the GME [graduate medical education] community to eliminate the 16-hour requirement for first-year residents due to its unintended negative effects" (Burchiel et al. 2017, 694). The three main professional organizations for general surgery—the Association of Program Directors in Surgery (APDS), the American Board of Surgery (ABS), and the American College of Surgeons (ACS)—prepared and presented position papers to the ACGME in January of 2016. All three recommended that the cap be retracted. The APDS (2016) described the cap as "the most detrimental of the 2011 implements" while the ABS (2016) argued that "specific requirements regarding shift lengths and time off are overly rigid" and "inappropriate in the context of the professional clinical responsibilities." The ACS (2016), which claims to be "the premier professional organization of surgeons in the US," went the farthest of the three organizations in advocating for the repeal of all but one work-hour rule:

> There is widespread concern regarding the training of surgery residents and their preparation for practice. Deficiencies in residents' surgical skill, judgment, and a variety of other competencies have been reported in the literature. . . . Based on the reported studies, the concerns being expressed nationally, and feedback from key stakeholders, ACS believes that the current duty hour restrictions have not improved surgical care and have negatively impacted the training of the next generation of surgeons. . . . ACS would recommend that the only restriction on resident duty hours be a total of 80 hours per week averaged over a 4 week period, with no other restrictions. This will provide sufficient flexibility to deliver the best care to patients and offer residents optimal training opportunities under guided supervision from surgery faculty.

Although specific points of emphasis vary, there was substantial consensus among the three organizations that strict shift limits undermine professionalism, hamper the development of skill and judgment, and lower the quality of patient care. Rescinding the cap was wholly consistent with those views, and the move was "endorsed" and "applauded" by the surgical organizations.

Reflection: Don't Share that Information with Patients

It is very easy to pontificate about the perceived merits of a duty-hour unlimited training environment when that is the world one grew up in. As has been outlined in this chapter, faculty of my own era see the duty-hour restrictions as undermining the development of key elements in surgical maturation, including pattern recognition, judgment, time management, continuity of care, and professionalism. That being recognized, and as we've stated before, the past remembers often better than it lived.

During my internship year, one of the second-year residents in our program had an unusually busy duty period in which he was up without sleep for close to forty-eight hours. At the end of the shift, he walked into a patient's room to check on the patient, and one of the family members present looked at my colleague and commented that they thought he looked worse than their relative in the bed. The resident responded that he was sorry for his appearance, and acknowledged he hadn't slept in two days. The patient wrote on their hospital experience feedback form that it didn't improve their confidence in the care they received to learn that the physician caring for them had worked forty-eight hours without sleep. This feedback percolated up to the surgery department chair, who was an internationally prominent surgical leader, and a person many of us appropriately looked up to as a key role model. The chairman sent all of the residents a letter in which he outlined that while the program "supported the principle of meaningful family and personal time," we should not "disclose information such as how long we had worked to our patients," as it might undermine their confidence in our care. No lie.

Fast forward now to a recent conversation I was having at a national level board meeting with a prominent colleague who had been part of my intern class and now has a well-deserved and strong national reputation. We were catching up on residents we had known and worked with together. Prominent on the list of acquaintances we were catching each other up on were colleagues who had left clinical medicine early, struggled through marital and other challenges common in our profession, and suffered other hardships, alongside some who had enjoyed long and fulfilling careers and personal lives.

One particular resident in my memory was one of my chief residents who for the purposes of this discussion we will call Gene. Gene had the unusual ability to speak in cogent but contextually inaccurate sentences on the phone while still asleep, requiring us to force him to get out of bed at night when calling him for advice, before allowing him to guide us on what to do. I had once bumped into him on an elevator late in his chief residency year, and asked him what he was planning to do the next year following his graduation from residency—a fellowship, or a great job opportunity somewhere he hoped to live? His answer was that of a worn-out warrior: "Hopefully nothing." The pace of that year of ultimate responsibility, in an era where attendings may not even have come in to the hospital to help with a case at night while he as chief resident had not gone home at all for days at a time, had clearly drained any joy in the journey out of him. Someone who no doubt a few years earlier had been brimming with enthusiasm and joy to pursue his chosen career path at a prominent institution was at that point simply enduring, with no future goals other than recovery from the training experience. When I asked my former internship colleague if he knew what had become of Gene, he relayed that Gene had committed suicide.

So how does one process the debate around duty hours and shortened shifts and their impact on professionalism, patients, providers, and what we all are—persons? It is no longer an academic exercise for me and for many who have lived on both sides of the divide between the "good old days" of autonomy and independence and the current era where we discuss the nuances of fatigue and function as a product of sleep and wake cycles. I obviously don't have simple answers to the complex questions herein explored around how to train the next generation of surgeons with a view to both the requirements of their duties and their human capacities and frailties. What I would say is it is not so much about the clock as it is the culture of how we train, and the character of both those who train and are themselves undergoing training. It is about an ethic centered on the patient and their service, both in the here and now, as well as decades hence when our trainees will be the leaders of the field with their own stories of development, growth, success, and failure. I would like to offer a simple answer and regret to admit I have none. Perhaps the best I can say is that as we move forward in determining how best to train the next generation of physicians and surgeons and do the more complex but critical work of balancing the Herculean demands of good health care with the realities of our human failings, we may do best to focus on the following truth, which years in medicine have taught many of us privileged to practice it. Do to and for others, and especially your patients, as you would have them do to you, or your family. For you see, while sleep and work, teamwork and ownership, life balance and duty are all important, caring for another life is a matter of conscience. God grant us sufficient courage and commitment to continue to keep it such.

Policy to Practice
Muddling through Work-Hour Reforms

I remember working forty-eight, sixty hours in a row as a resident, and in thinking about it now I'm sure I was impaired. The way I was trained was not safe!
The past was no golden era we should try to reclaim. The question is whether
we have swung the pendulum too much the other way. . . . We haven't found the
right middle ground yet. (A-M)

Most of us don't keep track of hours because it's pointless. They're still important—
and something we like—in a way I can't, I guess, explain. It's sort of like just by
making a big deal out of them, we're better off—even if we mostly blow them off.
Seems like it needs a hashtag—maybe #BlownOffRulesMatter? (PGY3-M)

"Medical practice is a moral activity, you know," uttered the attending on our
walk back to his office after a long clinic session that I observed early in the
fieldwork. He had a disarming, jocular way of interacting with patients, and
it was clear from the facial expressions, tone of voice, and easy conversation
that his patients were comfortable with him and appreciated his care. "I try
hard to be easy to relate to, but being a good doctor mostly means putting
the welfare of patients first, practicing with careful attention and thorough-
ness, doing whatever I can to keep them safe, and of course doing my best to

model all of those things as much as I can for our residents and medical students." After talking about those issues for a few minutes, I asked if he saw tensions between medical practice as a moral activity and what seemed to be a crushing workload, pressure to get clinic and hospitalized patients seen and discharged quickly, and scrutiny of work hours. "Absolutely," he said with a broad smile before quickly adding, "but we muddle through it—just watch and learn." In muddling, and even when residents "mostly blow them off" per the second epigraph, the reforms have taken shape, though perhaps not as intended.

Our book has explored that muddling, particularly as it relates to the way the work-hour reforms intersect with the work and training of surgeons. Our aim in this final chapter is to weave together the results of that muddling to provide a broader perspective in terms of scholarly contributions and those that are more practical. Readers will have noticed that we skirted end-of-chapter conclusions as we progressed through the six core substantive chapters. We did that because it made more sense to wait until this chapter to avoid redundancies and to have the empirical foundation fully in place. We begin by addressing some arguments about potential sources of resistance to the reforms that we believe fall short. One of these was discussed in the introduction, but others seem sufficiently credible, may be on the minds of readers, and merit discussion. We then develop our main explanation for why surgeons struggle with the reforms—namely, that the reforms fit poorly with key aspects of the social organization and culture of surgical work and training. We develop each concept in turn, but emphasize that many aspects of surgical culture and social organization interlock. We discuss a few ways to address the concerns surgeons have with the reforms, but we note here that we have no magic bullets to easily overcome these cultural and organizational impediments.

Explanations That Fall Short

We begin by reviewing several lines of thought that are plausible but largely unhelpful in explaining why surgeons struggle with the work-hour reforms. In the introduction, we briefly reviewed Kellogg's (2011) *Challenging Operations: Medical Reform and Resistance*, in which she argued that "virtually all" attendings opposed the reforms while residents split into two camps, a minority who opposed the reforms ("defenders") and a majority who supported them ("reformers"). In her analysis, women, primarily, but also men who could not fully embrace the Iron Man ideal, were drawn to support the reforms. In our analysis, we found it difficult to clearly and consistently categorize residents, in particular, but also faculty as either supporting or resisting the reforms in theory or practice. For example, the attending quoted in the first epigraph of this chapter dislikes many aspects of the reforms, but sees value in the effort to regulate work hours. Likewise, the resident quoted in the second epigraph suggests a deeply complex view, admitting to both a lack of adherence to the reforms but also a conviction that they matter and are a good development.

Those views dovetail with the results presented by Brooks and Bosk (2012), who found that residents often held complex views of the reforms and how they influenced their work and education. Importantly, their data included internal medicine residents, which suggests that the complexity is not limited to surgeons. We extend the insights of Brooks and Bosk (2012) by also exploring faculty, finding that they hold similarly varied and complex views. Instead of following Kellogg's strategy of categorizing residents and faculty as supporters or opponents, and then trying to explain why they fall into one or the other group, we instead tried to grasp how the reforms were understood and experienced by those learning and teaching surgery. What do residents and attendings struggle with? How do they muddle through—in the words of the attending quoted in the opening paragraph—the reforms?

A clear and pervasive finding across the chapters is that we did not find gender to be a primary, or often even substantial, factor in shaping interpretations and behaviors regarding the reforms. Although there is no question that aspects of the occupational culture of surgeons are infused with elements of what is conventionally considered "machismo," women and men alike struggle with the reforms. In most of the survey-based analyses presented in the chapters, gender played a minor role, and when differences did emerge they were not the simple "men oppose and women support" pattern suggested by Kellogg (2011). The fieldwork data and interviews similarly showed that women voiced strong concerns about the reforms, thus suggesting that surgeons struggle with the reforms in a collective way, not split along gender lines.

In our view, it is possible that gender was an important dividing line at the time Kellogg collected her data before and then shortly after the reforms were implemented, as that was mostly a time of anticipating the reforms and then experiencing them during the first year. Our earliest evidence was also most likely to show some evidence of gender differences. As we argued about previous studies of the sixteen-hour cap, first impressions are often different than those based on years of experience with how the reforms play out in the world of surgical training and practice. It is also possible that the three programs she studied were simply unusual, perhaps because they were elite, urban, or in the Northeastern United States. Ours span from coast to coast and include prestigious academic programs along with those with a community orientation and more local or regional standing. Overall, we find that the struggles are remarkably similar across programs of all sorts, which makes the "local culture" explanation for her distinctive findings less compelling. We examined all of our evidence—field observations, interviews, and surveys—systematically and exhaustively, but find no evidence that gender drives beliefs and behaviors in the way suggested by Kellogg.

Make no mistake, however, that gender matters greatly in surgery, even though it does not bear strongly or systematically on beliefs and behaviors relevant to the reforms among residents and attendings. Surgery remains a male-dominated field (Epstein 2017; West et al. 2018), and there are many ways gender comes into play more generally. For example, many medical students who rotated onto the services that Coverdill observed were utterly daunted by the work hours and schedules they observed among both residents and attendings. They were also struck by the longer period of residency training that is required of surgeons relative to most other fields. No doubt, observations of this sort induced a selection effect which surely deters more women than men from choosing surgery. As one female attending put it, "it's the wrong field if you want to make cookies after school with your kids." Gender, in short, matters for understanding who enters residency (de Costa et al. 2018).

Women residents in the fieldwork program were also more likely to talk about, and then pursue, more time-constrained fellowships and forms of practice after completing their residency. Breast surgeons, per the conventional view, have little nighttime call and more controlled schedules. Gender thus matters in terms of fellowships, sub-specialty choices, and practice patterns. Gender is also evident in the work lives of women, who would often pair their comments about "what the job requires" with matter-of-fact comments that suggested gendered forms of suffering. A constant for surgeons, both men and women, is that everyone misses family events and has less time at home than they might like. But a few female attendings described it in strikingly gendered ways, as in this comment: "My son says to his friends that it's like mom and dad got divorced and dad got custody." Given prevailing cultural notions of motherhood and fatherhood, that sentiment surely invokes more discomfort—if not pain—than one that ends with "mom got custody."

There is thus no question that gender matters in a general way. But the fact of the matter is that gender simply does not play much of a role in shaping how residents and faculty view or respond to the reforms, the primary thrust of the book. We make this clear with the survey analyses, which often show few differences in the responses of women and men, whether they are residents or practicing surgeons. The qualitative evidence showed the same pattern, which we tried to make accessible and obvious to readers by noting the gender of residents and faculty in our excerpts from the interviews and field notes. Many of the most critical comments about the reforms come from women. In our view, our findings attest to the incredible power of the culture and social organization of surgical training and work, which combine to overshadow the role that gender might otherwise play in shaping beliefs and behaviors regarding the reforms.

A second line of argument that we find unhelpful suggests that surgeons might simply be poised to resist reforms. For example, Hughes (1984, 293), a giant in the sociological study of work and organizations, argued years ago that one should "expect occupations of long standing to resist attempts, especially by outsiders, to determine the content of their work or the rules governing it." Likewise, Freidson (1988), also a giant in the sociological study of medicine and the professions, noted that physicians "have the special privilege of freedom from the control of outsiders" (xii) and the "freedom to manage their knowledge and work in their own way" (137). Although the "freedom from control" noted by Freidson has been under siege and receding for some time now, it remains plausible to suspect that surgeons' struggles with the reforms might be more nearly a reflex than a response based on experience and reflection.

Similarly, evidence suggests that physicians and other staff in health care settings have not consistently embraced other risk-reduction innovations. For example, healthcare-associated infections, acquired during a hospitalization, increase a patient's risk of morbidity, mortality, and a prolonged stay, and the hand hygiene behavior of physicians and other staff can substantially curb such infections (Van Dijk et al. 2019). Yet, worldwide, adherence to hand hygiene protocols rarely exceeds 50 percent (Oliveira, Gama, and Paula 2017, 63). More broadly, research by Sekimoto and her colleagues (2006, 1) explored how physicians responded to evidence-based care guidelines and concluded that "scientific evidence alone cannot easily change physicians' clinical practices." Timmermans and Berg (2003, 97) offered a similar conclusion: "All in all, evidence-based guidelines seem to be one of the many impulses pushing professionals in a specific direction—and not a particularly successful one at that." One response to our findings is that of course surgeons struggle with the reforms—that is what physicians of all sorts do in the face of efforts to implement change!

There is undoubtedly some truth to that notion both generally and in the case of work-hour reforms. The reforms disrupted many routines of training and practice that had been in place for decades. But in our view, even if surgeons were poised to dislike the reforms, their encounters with them over nearly two decades have provided a wealth of experience with how the reforms pan out in actual practice. We do not dismiss their views as "legitimating accounts" or mere rationales intended to justify resistance to the reforms (Kellogg 2011). Many, as in the epigraph that led off this chapter and the chapter reflections by Mellinger, do not see the pre-reform era as some sort of golden age. Their "lived experience," as sociologists are often quick to note, should be acknowledged and explored, as we have tried to do here. In our view, there are specific and substantial reasons for their struggles, which we now highlight.

The Social Organization of Surgical Work and Training

The conditions under which surgeons work and train are critically important in shaping their responses to the reforms. Many of these pre-date the reforms, while others emerged largely with the reforms. It has long been recognized that residents are routinely overworked, a point emphasized in the first systematic study of residencies published in 1940 (cited in Ludmerer 2015, 274). For both residents and attendings, there has not been a tradition of having anything like "floaters" or a "bench," whereby capable colleagues can be called upon when a staffing shortfall arises. This lack of a bench was often noted as a substantial constraint that prompted both residents and attendings to work while fatigued. Even when a partner could be called upon by an attending, for example, they admitted that to do so with any regularity would not be acceptable if it was even possible. With residents, the loss of a colleague for whatever reason—a conference, illness, vacation, or being over hours—means that person's work is shouldered by those who remain. In addition, the conditions of work differ during the night and day. Surgeries are traditionally scheduled for daytime hours, and the full range of ancillary hospital staff and services is available during the day, but rarely at night. Nights have long offered less staffing support, typically creating a need for residents to call attendings at home when needs arise. None of these situations is new in the reform era.

The most significant aspect of the social organization of residencies that changed with the reforms was the widespread adoption of night float and cross coverage of patients at night. As we described it in an earlier chapter, many programs adopted night float, which involves a team of residents who start work in the evening (often at 5 or 6 p.m.) and leave in the morning (often at

6 or 7 a.m.). Commonly, residents are assigned to night float for a month or more and cover patients on all of the surgical services, thereby engaging in what is called cross coverage. Another format for night coverage of patients used mostly in smaller programs is long-call cross coverage, where a small number of residents who worked a regular day shift on particular services stay for the night and cover all patients, not just those on their day service. The use of night float and cross coverage mean that night residents now care for a wider range of patients, many of whom are unfamiliar, and the split between day and night staff has been sharpened. Day residents know their patients and participate more fully in their care; night residents are less familiar with their patients, see themselves as secondary care takers, and mostly aim to maintain the status quo until day teams return in the morning.

The social organization of care has profoundly diminished the viability of the reforms. The reforms, which sparked passionate editorials that foretold the "death of professionalism" in surgery and other disciplines (Barone and Ivy 2004; Rosenbaum 2004), were buttressed to some extent by those who argued for the emergence of a "new professionalism." Exemplified by the eloquent statement of Van Eaton, Horvath, and Pellegrini (2005), proponents of a new professionalism suggested that traditional conceptions and enactments of patient ownership by residents could and should be replaced by new understandings and practices based on the principles of teamwork. Individual patient ownership, founded on residents knowing everything about their patients and doing everything for them, would give way to team ownership. The new professionalism would be nurtured though clear guidelines as to what residents would be expected to know and do for their patients and those they cross-cover, along with instruction in how to conduct handoffs and hence safely transfer care across shifts.

Our results bear on the state of a new professionalism and the role of social organization in shaping professionalism and the prospects of reform. Two keys to the new professionalism are the *ability* and *desire* to pass work across shifts by residents who embrace the team ownership of patients. Our results point to the continued salience of a traditional professionalism in a reluctance to pass work from day to night teams, unclear guidance regarding stayorgo decisions during shift transitions, little (but growing) educational emphasis on handoffs, and the practice of long hours in the name of professionalism. The interviews and field observations, in particular, highlight the role of discretion, concerns about night staffing, and perceived professional obligations. The emergent, resident-generated notions of team and what it means to be a team player inhibit the passing of work across shifts. "Team players" respect their peers by not dumping and by passing very little, if any, work across shifts. Nearly two decades after the introduction of the reforms, a new professionalism represents a stalled revolution among general surgery residents in programs large and small, prestigious and relatively unknown.

The results imply a need to consider carefully and realistically how social organization impedes cultural shifts like those entailed in the new professionalism. As described by Leape (1997), systems issues—what we are calling social organization—are failures in the design of work tasks, training, and the conditions of work. Even if residents were completely sold on the virtues of a new professionalism, it is hard to see how those ideals could routinely translate into action given the prevailing workloads and staffing of residencies. Staffing at night is simply not the same as in the day, a pattern that aligns with Melbin's (1987) observations and evidence. As one resident memorably described it, night teams "put a finger in the dike until the morning," hardly a characterization of equal status with day teams. The dramatic disjunction between day and night staffing leads residents to conclude that passing off work to night teams can be, in at least some situations, tantamount to shirking professional obligations to patients and families, risking inferior or delayed care, and dumping on fellow residents.

It is unrealistic to expect that improved handoff practices and protocols can do much to improve shift transitions without additional attention to staffing issues and workloads. Although it is becoming more common, few surgical programs in our study taught residents how to conduct handoffs, a pattern that may indicate resistance on the part of faculty or a hidden curriculum opposed to a new professionalism. However, what dominated the analysis was a *reluctance* to pass off work, not a perceived *inability*. It is widely viewed as "easier and more efficient" to simply finish work than to explain what needs to be done to another resident. Work passed to the night team can easily become burdensome or overwhelming. Such concerns will simply not diminish as handoff protocols and training improve. Likewise, the Institute of Medicine's (Ulmer, Wolman, and Johns 2008) proposition that handovers can be an opportunity to reassess patient care and catch errors may be good in theory, but it assumes relatively equal teams across the day-night transition, not the finger-in-the-dike reality described by residents.

Abstract notions of professionalism guide action within particular social contexts, and those contexts help or hinder their realization. Schein (2004, 8), a leader in the study of organizations and culture, argues that whether or not a culture is functionally effective "depends not on the culture alone, but on the relationship of the culture to the environment in which it exists." Hafferty and Castellani (2010, 294) similarly emphasize that professionalism "does not take place in a vacuum." To be fully realized, the cultural transformation represented by the team-based new professionalism must be supported by the social organization of training and practice. Residents commonly speak as though they make the call to pass work off to night staff or delay their departures to finish it themselves, but our analysis suggests that a main determinant of delayed departures is sparse night staffing. How nights are staffed is an *organizational issue* for which programs—not residents—are responsible. It is unrealistic to expect change in the pattern of delayed departures until programs take seriously the imbalance between night and day staffing and devise ways to bridge that gap. Culture is but one part of an interdependent system.

Residents also face headwinds when it comes to balancing extra hours one day by cutting hours on a subsequent day. Many do not regularly seek to trim hours, a pattern that squares with the claim by Bosk and his colleagues that residents do not give "much thought to the clock or the number of hours worked" (Szymczak et al. 2010, 359). An effort to trim might be viewed as evidence that the resident is lazy, weak, or inefficient; attributions of that sort can lead to serious and feared consequences like remediation or retaliation (Yaghoubian et al. 2012; Hafferty and Tilburt 2015). These concerns may be even stronger than those that inhibit requests for clinical support, where asking too frequently or for too much support threatens professional credibility, but asking for "appropriate" support does not because it suggests an awareness of one's limits (Kennedy et al. 2009, 4). Adding hours to accommodate patients, staffing shortfalls, or education aligns with professional values (Carpenter et al. 2006; Bryne, Loo, and Giang 2015), but there appears to be no "appropriate" level of trimming. As currently understood, professionalism encourages and applauds addition, but not subtraction, and in that way undermines the reforms.

The social organization of surgical work bears on the possibility of trimming hours in three particularly striking ways. First, trimming is best accomplished on services in which residents are least likely to exceed their hours. Given that most rotations are longer than the four-week average used by the ACGME to measure work hours, rotations that require fewer hours cannot readily balance out busy ones. Second, the predictability and quantity of time that can be subtracted are insufficient to counter the frequency of delayed departures and the number of extra hours residents work. To balance extra hours, opportunities for trimming must be frequent and yield meaningful reductions. And third, the recurring daily rhythms of surgical work suggest a trenchant instance of what organizational theorists call temporal structure

(Zerubavel 1979; Barley 1988; Orlikowski and Yates 2002). Every day is just a "new thing with its own demands," where the patterning of activities in time is experienced as a strong external constraint. Institutionalized norms regarding time and behavior early on weekday mornings—prior to and then when scheduled cases in the operating room begin to progress—render delayed arrivals particularly problematic. Time is seen as largely inflexible.

Bolstering staff might seem like an obvious and relatively straightforward solution to some of the most pressing problems facing the reforms. Adding more residents, which was *never* raised as a solution among surgeons, would be difficult given resource limitations. It would also reduce operative experience and thereby the education residents receive. Advanced practice providers are a more promising source of support. Our results show that they are thought to lessen workloads for surgeons, help residents comply with the reforms, and provide some teaching, patterns that align well with previous research. Also pervasive is the conviction that they provide much-valued continuity and familiar faces for patients (both new and returning), thereby improving care and (most likely) patient satisfaction with that care. But concerns about the educational impact of advanced practice providers are also evident, all of which hinge on a vexing assessment: how deeply and frequently do residents need to be involved in some aspect of patient care to achieve expected educational outcomes?

What amounts to "service work" or "scut" and what holds educational value is contested (Reines et al. 2007; Sanfey et al. 2011), but sorely needs more attention and clarification. Faculty who fear that residents do not see enough postop checks, for example, need to spell out in a more comprehensive way what residents need to encounter and learn to manage. Otherwise, the *possibility* of something rare, and educationally valuable, implies that anything short of being involved in every possible postop check will fall short. Likewise, does resident involvement need to be complete, with residents fully responsible and making all decisions in consultation with their attendings, or can it be scaled back to allow advanced practice providers to shoulder at least a portion of that work? Can faculty at least occasionally use advanced practice providers as a first or main point of contact and round with them exclusively without compromising in some fundamental way the professional development of residents? If so, how often or fully?

The interviews suggest that there are lines that faculty have vaguely drawn in their minds, but these need to be developed and articulated, and policies need to be crafted to protect resident education and development. Otherwise, a substantial number of faculty will continue to view residents as "passengers" or "bystanders" on their services, say that they are "distant from the actual process of patient care," and that information and decisions are "gift wrapped" for residents by advanced practice providers. Expressions of that sort point to educational failures, not triumphs, and surely suggest that adding staff is no simple solution to the challenges posed by the reforms.

Occupational Culture in Surgery

Culture combines with social organization to matter greatly in shaping the way surgeons have responded to the reforms. While social organization involves the conditions of work, where workloads, staffing arrangements, and timing norms loom large, culture centers on how we understand the meaning and significance of our words and deeds. Here, we are focused on the occupational culture of surgery, and highlight three primary threads: cultures of professionalism, fatigue, and efficiency. All are long standing, pre-dating the appearance of the reforms, and the first two are modern renditions of cultures that have existed for a hundred years. The culture of efficiency, first drawn out by Szymczak and Bosk (2012), has changed in more recent years, but also pre-dates the reforms. All of these aspects of the occupational culture of surgery represent stiff headwinds for the reforms.

CORE ASPECTS OF PROFESSIONALISM

Two aspects of professionalism drive the reactions of surgeons to the reforms. A first is the traditional notion of putting patients first, of surgeons accepting the inconveniences brought by the unpredictability of illness and injury. This notion, described as present in the early 1900s in the historical analysis of Ludmerer (2015), is clearly evident in our data and is seen by many as clashing with the reforms. Surgeons, according to this culture, are "on" when patients need them, not according to the hands of the clock. This, of course, is what sparked a sustained uproar among surgeons about "clock watchers" and "shift workers." The reform's strong emphasis on time and the clock make this clash inevitable, even when residents do not always—or even routinely— abide by the clock. A second key component of professionalism involves Bosk's (1979) concept of normative error, which is based on the idea that surgeons should know everything about their patients and do everything they can for them. The reforms foster normative error, as we argued in our earlier chapter. For attending surgeons, a reform that challenges the notion that patients come first, unleashes a torrent of normative errors in residents, or both, is bound to induce consternation if not distress.

Our analysis of continuity of care, medical records, and transfers of information about patients across caregivers goes to the heart of this matter. Abstractly, the results bear on the issue of professionals and functional interchangeability, the ability of one person to substitute in a relatively seamless way for another. Zerubavel (1979) argued that temporal flexibility and patient charts were key to the realization of functional interchangeability among physicians and residents. In his view, the hospital "worked" as an organization because its most skilled workers put in unlimited hours, could return to the hospital or provide advice as needed, and had an effective device for transmitting information, namely the patient chart.

Our results suggest that functional interchangeability is an uncertain accomplishment, especially when patients are complex, unstable, or both. Various forms of tacit knowledge, intuitions, time pressures, and the practical shortcomings of patient records, the operative note, and oral handoffs compromise if not undermine functional interchangeability. The evidence is consistent with Hunter's (1991, 85, 91) claim that medical charts are best understood as "minimalist accounts" and that entries are made and read selectively. At least for surgeons, it is a dramatic overstatement to say, as Zerubavel did (1979, 45–46), that patient charts or operative notes represent an "effective mechanism" for attaining functional interchangeability. That problem is exacerbated by the increasing lack of official temporal flexibility, especially the ability of residents to delay departures or return to the hospital when needs arise.

The results dovetail with previous research that has highlighted the importance of tacit knowledge and intuitions that may be difficult if not impossible to articulate, let alone transfer smoothly and fully from one person to another (Harper 1987; MacKenzie and Spinardi 1995). Wilensky's (1964, 149) comment that professional knowledge is "to some extent tacit" and that professional work could produce understandings or insights "which we cannot fully report" remains strikingly prescient, as does Polanyi's (1962, 601) claim that "there are things that we know but cannot tell." Our results suggest that functional interchangeability is more fiction than fact, with much that matters becoming inaccessible when the primary caregiver leaves the hospital. Difficulties with interchangeability support and encourage long duty periods and call arrangements that traditionally served to minimize discontinuities in patient care. In this view, the organizational problems associated with handoffs and medical records may have spawned a particularly greedy notion of professional commitment (e.g., Coser 1974).

A CULTURE OF FATIGUE

Our research explored the surgical culture of fatigue, a set of beliefs about the meaning and experience of fatigue, and norms about working while tired. Prior research has largely overlooked this aspect of surgical culture. According to the culture of fatigue, residents *can* and *must* encounter fatigue and learn to assess their level of fatigue, how to function effectively when fatigued, and when they have reached their limits. Encounters of that sort are thought to be best initiated during training, not practice, when back-up wanes and responsibilities mount. Given that most believe that the practice of surgery *requires* the ability to work while fatigued, encounters with fatigue during residency are seen as essential to a proper education. To our knowledge, our study is the first to explore empirically an important conceptual framework in the study of work-hour reform, described as "successful sleep-deprived practice is a skill" (Schwartz et al. 2009, 22).

Fatigue culture among surgeons clashes with both sleep science and ACGME policy, where fatigue is seen as jeopardizing patient care and worker safety and is something to minimize if not avoid entirely (ACGME 2010). Fatigue-focused educational programs based on those convictions will almost certainly be ineffective in surgery because most faculty do not embrace or model those views. During the fieldwork, there were many long, obligation-driven workdays (and nights) among attending surgeons, which were noted by residents. A survey of practicing general surgeons corroborates those patterns, with an average of 2.6 nights on call per week and 20 percent routinely working more than eighty hours a week (Gadacz and Bason 2005). As noted by Krueger and Halperin (2010, 1843), "we are teaching doctors to minimize medical mistakes and personal stress by working fewer and less sporadic hours without providing them the necessary resources or coordination of services to meet these goals once they have completed their training." Fatigue culture aligns with practice, but it seems anachronistic relative to modern sleep science and ACGME policy.

A transition to a "safety culture" (Vogus, Sutcliffe, and Weick 2010) that recognizes and minimizes fatigue will likely require three sizable steps. A first step involves the need to address inconsistencies and gaps in the scientific literature on fatigue and performance. The existence of studies that appear to show little-to-no adverse effects of fatigue on at least some forms of simulated and real clinical work bolsters the culture of fatigue. As we see it, the preponderance of evidence points to fatigue as a risk factor, but it is not as unequivocal as it might need to be to effectively confront and erode the culture of fatigue.

In addition, there is increasingly solid evidence to suggest that the effects of fatigue on performance differ dramatically and consistently across individuals. For example, Czeisler (2009, 259–60), the sleep scientist quoted in the introduction who likened working while fatigued to working while drunk, described one of his studies as showing that "approximately one-quarter of the participants account for roughly two-thirds of the attentional failures during ~30 hours of wakefulness" and that "stable individual trait differences accounted for 67% to 92% of the variance in the cognitive performance decrement induced by sleep loss." In their recent review of inter-individual variability in responses to sleep loss, Tkachenko and Dinges (2018, 29) argue that it is indeed sizable and ubiquitous, and that the mechanisms behind what appears to be phenotypic vulnerability to sleep loss remain unexplained. Evidence of this sort provides ready ammunition for those who wish to argue or imagine that their surgical capabilities are largely unaffected by fatigue.

A second step involves an effort to provide more direct, personalized, and objective assessments of fatigue. Currently, clinicians know their recent sleep patterns, extent of wakefulness, and their subjective sense of sleepiness, none of which provide particularly good information about fatigue-related impairment or whether an individual is likely to suffer considerably or only slightly from sleep loss. What would help is to have clinicians receive, perhaps as they enter or consider training, tests akin to those conducted in sleep laboratories. In that way, everyone would receive objective baseline evidence about their general sensitivity to sleep loss, and for some that evidence should help them to realize its substantial adverse consequences.

What would also help is a quick and easily administered assessment of fatigue impairment, much akin to a field sobriety test. Several technologies are in various stages of development. For example, in a recent landmark experimental study of internal medicine residents, investigators deployed a three-minute, smartphone-based application of the Psychomotor Vigilance Test (PVT-B) to measure alertness and performance lapses (Basner et al. 2019). Similarly, Reifman et al. (2019, 1) describe their 2B-AlertApp as a smartphone application "that progressively learns an individual's trait-like response to sleep deprivation in real time, to generate increasingly more accurate individualized predictions of alertness." We are unaware of any individual or programmatic implementation of these technologies, but we suspect both are on the horizon. Our sense is that credible and readily available information about fatigue-related vulnerabilities and impairments might upend the culture of fatigue.

A third step is the most important, but also the most difficult. Any effort to confront and erode fatigue culture would need to address practice. A safety culture requires that beliefs be paired with "meaningful practices" that "enact a safety culture" (Vogus, Sutcliffe, and Weick 2010, 65) by ensuring that surgeons need not operate or provide patient care while fatigued. Although surgeons will need to play a key role in enacting practices supportive of a safety culture, dramatic behavioral and cultural change will also be required of patients, referring physicians, surgery departments, other hospital departments and staff, and the health care system as a whole (Nurok, Czeisler, and Lehmann 2010). All of those forces encourage surgeons to work while fatigued, and that would need to stop. These steps would neutralize the formidable "real world" argument, which we see as the most important buttress of fatigue culture, by reformulating culture along with professional and organizational practices. Admittedly, this is no small task.

In our view, it would be a mistake to conclude that medicine is a uniquely recalcitrant institution when it comes to issues related to sleep and fatigue. Culture and social organization perpetuate fatigue-related practices in many other realms of modern life, where notions such as "I'll sleep when I'm dead" flood popular consciousness (Huffington 2016). One good example involves school starting times. Research on children documents how important sleep is for learning, physical and mental health, behavioral issues, and vehicular safety among teenagers, as well as academic performance; it has also demonstrated links between delayed school starting times and improvements in those outcomes (Walker 2017, 308–16; Lo et al. 2018; Bauducco et al. 2020). Prominent organizations like the American Academy of Pediatrics, the American Medical Association, and the American Academy of Sleep Medicine recommend a school starting time no earlier than 8:30 a.m. However, evidence shows that fewer than 15 percent of public high schools, and 19 percent of public middle schools, start at that recommended time or later, and that fewer than 25 percent of children aged eleven to eighteen get sufficient sleep (Wheaton, Ferro, and Croft 2015; Walker 2017, 316). The sleep scientist Walker (2017, 314) characterizes this situation in rather stark terms: "we are failing our children in the most spectacular manner with the current model of early school start times." Surely, we love our children, but with surprisingly few exceptions, we also ignore these issues. No doubt the practical challenges of reorganizing the temporal flow of how days begin—which would affect parents, bus drivers, teachers, and children alike—are indeed substantial.

As we see it, this predicament has much in common with the work-hour reforms and prompts similar groans and exasperation when it comes to the myriad of cultural and structural changes required to accomplish what would seem to be a simple and sensible change supported by leading medical organizations and sleep science. The prospects for realizing policy changes in medicine, schooling, and other settings are curtailed by entrenched aspects of culture and social organization that amount to what Williams (2011, xiii, emphasis in original) conceptualized as "*sleep-negating* or *sleep-neglecting* ideas and ideologies, discourses and debates, policies and practices." In Williams's terms, our analysis explored and explained how the occupational culture and social organization of surgical training and practice interlock to perpetuate sleep neglect and impede the reforms.

TRAINING AND WORKING FOR EFFICIENCY

Bosk and his colleagues were the first to explore the culture of efficiency and how it squared with work-hour reforms. Recall that it means conciseness, where only the most germane information is provided in a patient presentation, note, or hallway conversation. It also implies the expeditious processing of patients and minimizing things like length of stay, re-admissions within thirty days, and rates of hospital-acquired infections. Szymczak and Bosk (2012, 350–351, 355) called efficiency "the predominant value organizing the professional and occupational culture of residency" and saw it as a group norm, wherein residents cooperate to manage their demanding workloads. Efficient residents strategically prioritize work tasks, take appropriate and timely action, anticipate problems, and dispatch those that arise.

As Bosk and his colleagues described it, the substantial workloads residents face demand efficiency. Efficiency has become something residents and their attendings look for as evidence of skill and professional development. In part, a surgeon's efficiency is based on acquired medical knowledge, as that increases his or her capacity to anticipate, identify, and then address emergent medical problems. But in the face of complex patients, high workloads, and oftentimes sparse staffing, even the most efficient residents are unable to *always* complete their work. As shown by Bosk and his colleagues and corroborated by our analysis, residents quietly stay late to complete their work and under-report their hours because they fear drawing attention and being labelled inefficient (Szymczak et al. 2010, 373).

Our analysis extends and elaborates what was developed by Bosk and his colleagues by identifying additional ways the culture of efficiency bears on the prospects of work-hour reforms. In our analysis of stay-or-go decisions, we found that residents often felt it was inefficient to pass off work to a night resident or team, and such reasoning prompted them to stay to complete the work themselves. Some described how they would have to spend time searching for an available night resident, invest additional time to explain what needed to be done, and in many cases further describe special circumstances or rationales for the care. In cases like this, residents did a quick calculation: what is more efficient, me staying and doing the work, or handing it off? These calculations often invoked professionalism too, as residents would say that asking an incoming night-float resident to do something like meet with a family was "horribly inefficient and unprofessional." It was inefficient because it would take too long for the night-float resident to come up to speed on the patient and family circumstances; it was unprofessional because the night resident would be a new face who lacked rapport and trust. Also, staying to complete some aspect of patient care means that a resident could go home knowing it was done rather than hoping it would be done, thus tying into notions of patients coming first.

Efficiency also plays a leading role in shaping practices regarding medical records, operative notes, and patient handoffs. All three forms of communication are flawed in ways that mean pertinent information is not readily accessible to those who have not been directly involved in a patient's care. Medical records tend to be the product of interns, the least experienced members of the surgical team, and are not always kept up to date as patient conditions and care plans change. Similarly, operative notes often fail to convey the nuances of the procedure or highlight postoperative problems that might arise. As we probed why residents and attendings did not do a better, more complete job with these documents, we found that it was driven in large part by the culture of efficiency, as there is a lot of work to be done and their sense is that thorough charting and operative notes are simply not possible. As one resident put it, "in order to get anything done, you have to make choices, and one choice most of us make is to be less compulsive about recording everything" (PGY4-M). Likewise, handoffs were often hasty events that conveyed few details and even fewer opportunities to jointly round on patients, things that would enrich the information transferred and hence the capabilities and confidence of incoming residents. Again, the perception of time constraints and the need to convey "just the meat" drove resident behavior. The inadequacy of medical records, operative notes, and patient handoffs means that shift changes represent a real risk to patients, a risk that surgeons recognize but have yet to rectify. The speed-up ushered in by prospective payment in the 1980s spawned a culture of efficiency that now undermines the reforms.

A Parting Thought

In closing, we express an ambivalence that echoes, amplifies, and updates that voiced nearly forty years ago by Zerubavel (1981, 165), a luminary in the study of work and time. As he observed work practices in a hospital, he noted that the behavior of nurses, compared with physicians, seemed much more constrained by time. In short, when nurses were "on" and "off" duty seemed to be more dictated by the clock than the ebb and flow of patient care needs. He characterized clock-driven professional involvements of that sort as "bureaucratized," and went on to make the following observations:

> The bureaucratization of professional commitments is particularly impressive in the case of a profession like nursing, since it implies its having already penetrated one of the most sacred domains of our life, namely health care. If commitments, concern, and motivation can be bureaucratized in a domain where literally vital problems are a daily matter, is there any domain of social life where they cannot be?

Zerubavel might have misunderstood the behavior of nurses, and it is emphatically not our intent to cast aspersions on nurses, who we greatly value and have witnessed to behave in nonbureaucratized ways routinely. Rather, we believe that the evidence we have presented points to the conclusion that this highly important domain of life has been nudged in the direction of bureaucratizing the professional commitments of residents for now, and perhaps attending physicians in the not-to-distant future. In at least the short run, these changes have sparked on-going struggles and resistance, but how they will play out over the long run is unclear to us. But as in much of life, a loss can be accompanied by an offsetting gain, as the reforms curb somewhat the extraordinary temporal appetite of one of the most time demanding or "greedy" institutions (Coser 1974). Temporal rigidities permit social inaccessibility and private time, and thus become "among the foremost liberators of the modern individual" (Zerubavel 1981, 166).

As we see it, a primary challenge for students of professions and organizations—and for those in the workaday world of medicine—is to find some way to nurture the ethic of nonbureaucratized professional commitments in temporally constrained institutions. While there is much to applaud about the ideal and practice of "putting patients first," it unfortunately implies hardship if not suffering among those who strive to embrace it. In addition, sleep science suggests that putting patients first might also put patients in harm's way, at least occasionally. In an earlier, profound, and still highly relevant consideration of surgeons, Cassell (1991) noted that the increasing prominence of litigation in healthcare came with risks, some known, others not. When physicians, she mused, come to be seen as potential antagonists, does the patient become a potential enemy? Does it change how physicians care for patients? In describing the behavior of what she considered the best surgeons in her fieldwork, she made the following observation:

Such caring, such conscientiousness, such concentration of effort and attention involves something close to love. This gift cannot be purchased, demanded, extorted. It is bestowed freely, or not at all. (Cassell 1991, 208–9)

Here, we move past legal concerns to consider time: how can we devote ourselves to others professionally while also keeping time in mind if not an eye on the clock?

References

Abernathy, Charles, and Robert M. Hamm. 1995. *Surgical Intuition: What It Is and How to Get It.* Philadelphia, PA: Hanley and Belfus.

ACGME (Accreditation Council for Graduate Medical Education). 2004. "The ACGME's Approach to Limit Resident Duty Hours 12 Months after Implementation: A Summary of Achievements." ACGME, April 2004. www.acgme.org/Portals/0/PFAssets/ PublicationsPapers/dh_dutyhoursummary2003-04.pdf.

_____. 2010. "Common Program Requirements." ACGME, July 1, 2011. www.acgme.org/ Portals/0/PFAssets/ProgramResources/Common_Program_Requirements_07012011.pdf.

_____. 2017. "Common Program Requirements." ACGME, July 1, 2017. www.acgme.org/ Portals/0/PFAssets/ProgramRequirements/CPRs_2017-07-01.pdf.

Acker, Joan. 1992. "From Sex Roles to Gendered Institutions." *Contemporary Sociology* 21 (5): 565–69.

Ahmed, Najma, Katherine S. Devitt, Itay Keshet, Jonathan Spicer, Kevin Imrie, Liane Feldman, Jonathan Cools-Lartigue, Ahmed Kayssi, Nir Lipsman, Maryam Elmi, Abhaya V. Kulkarni, Chris Parshuram, Todd Mainprize, Richard J. Warren, Paola Fata, M. Sean Gorman, Stan Feinberg, and James Rutka. 2014. "A Systematic Review of the Effects of Resident Duty Hour Restrictions in Surgery: Impact on Resident Wellness, Training, and Patient Outcomes. *Annals of Surgery* 259 (6): 1041–53.

American Board of Surgery. 2016. "ABS Position Statement on the ACGME Duty Hour Restrictions." Commentary invited by the ACGME. www.acgme.org/What-We-Do/ Accreditation/Clinical-Experience-and-Education-formerly-Duty-Hours/2016- Position-Statements-on-Duty-Hours-and-the-Learning-and-Working-Environment.

American College of Surgeons. 2016. "ACS Position Statement on the ACGME Duty Hour Restrictions." Commentary invited by the ACGME. www.acgme.org/What-We-Do/ Accreditation/Clinical-Experience-and-Education-formerly-Duty-Hours/2016- Position-Statements-on-Duty-Hours-and-the-Learning-and-Working-Environment.

Arora, Vineet M., Jeanne M. Farnan, and Holly J. Humphrey. 2012. "Professionalism in the Era of Duty Hours: Time for a Shift Change?" *JAMA* 308 (21): 2195–96.

Arora, Vineet M., Emily Georgitis, Juned Siddique, Ben Vekhter, James N. Woodruff, Holly J. Humphrey, and David O. Meltzer. 2008. "Association of Workload of On-Call Medical Interns with On-Call Sleep Duration, Shift Duration, and Participation in Educational Activities." *JAMA* 300 (10): 1146–53.

Asch, David A., and Ruth M. Parker. 1988. "The Libby Zion Case: One Step Forward or Two Steps Back?" *New England Journal of Medicine* 318 (12): 771–75.

Association of Program Directors in Surgery. 2016. "APDS Position Statement on the ACGME Duty Hour Restrictions." Commentary invited by the ACGME. www.acgme.org/What-We-Do/Accreditation/Clinical-Experience-and-Education-formerly-Duty-Hours/2016-Position-Statements-on-Duty-Hours-and-the-Learning-and-Working-Environment.

Bahouth, Mona, Mary Beth Esposito-Herr, and Timothy J. Babineau. 2007. "The Expanding Role of the Nurse Practitioner in an Academic Medical Center and Its Impact on Graduate Medical Education." *Journal of Surgical Education* 64 (5): 282–88.

Baldwin, DeWitt C., Jr., Steven R. Daugherty, Ray Tsai, and Michael J. Scott Jr. 2003. "A National Survey of Residents' Self-Reported Work Hours: Thinking beyond Specialty." *Academic Medicine* 78 (11): 1154–63.

Baldwin, DeWitt C., Jr., Steven R. Daugherty, P. Ryan, and N. A. Yaghmour. 2010. "Changes in Resident Work and Sleep Hours 1999 to 2009: Results from a Survey of 4 Specialties." *Journal of Graduate Medical Education* 2 (4): 656–58.

Barger, Laura K., Brian E. Cade, Najib T. Ayas, John W. Cronin, Bernard Rosner, Frank E. Speizer, and Charles A. Czeisler. 2005. "Extended Work Shifts and the Risk of Motor Vehicle Crashes among Interns." *New England Journal of Medicine* 352 (2): 125–34.

Barley, Stephen R. 1988. "On Technology, Time, and Social Order: Technically Induced Change in the Temporal Organization of Radiological Work." In *Making Time: Ethnographies of High Technology Organizations*, edited by Frank A. Dubinskas, 123–69. Philadelphia, PA: Temple University Press.

Barone, James E., and Michael E. Ivy. 2004. "Resident Work Hours: The Five Stages of Grief." *Academic Medicine* 79 (5): 379–80.

Basner, Mathias, David F. Dinges, Judy A. Shea, Dylan S. Small, Jingsan Zhu, Laurie Norton, Adrian J. Ecker, Cristina Novak, Lisa M. Bellini, and Kevin G. Volpp. 2017. "Sleep and Alertness in Medical Interns and Residents: An Observational Study on the Role of Extended Shifts." *Sleep* 40 (4): 1–8.

Basner, Mathias, Hengyi Rao, Namni Goel, and David F. Dinges. 2013. "Sleep Deprivation and Neurobehavioral Dynamics." *Current Opinion Neurobiology* 23 (5): 854–53.

Basner, Mathias, David A. Asch, Judy A. Shea, Lisa M. Bellini, Michele Carlin, Adrian J. Ecker, Susan K. Malone, Sanjay V. Desai, Alice L. Sternberg, James Tonascia, David M. Shade, Joel T. Katz, David W. Bates, Orit Even-Shoshan, Jeffrey H. Silber, Dylan S. Small, Kevin G. Volpp, Christopher G. Mott, Sara Coats, Daniel J. Mollicone, and David F. Dinges. 2019. "Sleep and Alertness in a Duty-Hour Flexibility Trial in Internal Medicine." *New England Journal of Medicine* 380 (10): 915–23.

Bauducco, Serena Valeria, Ida K. Flink, Katja Boersma, and Steven J. Linton. 2020. "Preventing Sleep Deficit in Adolescents: Long-Term Effects of a Quasi-Experimental School-Based Intervention Study." *Journal of Sleep Research* 29 (1): e12940.

Becker, Howard S., Blanche Geer, Everett C. Hughes, and Anselm L. Strauss. 1961. *Boys in White: Student Culture in Medical School.* New Brunswick, NJ: Transaction Publishers.

Bennett, Christopher L., David A. McDonald, Stephen C. Dorner, and Eric S. Nadel. 2017. "Association of the 2003 and 2011 ACGME Resident Duty Hour Reforms with Internal Medicine Initial Certification Examination Performance." *Journal of Graduate Medical Education* 9 (6): 79–90.

Berger, Jonathan, and Jonathan D'Cunha. 2012. "Measuring What We Value: Quantifying the Impact of the Physician Extender in Surgical Care." *Seminars in Thoracic and Cardiovascular Surgery* 24 (4): 85–86.

Bilimoria, Karl Y., Jeanette W. Chung, Larry V. Hedges, Allison R. Dahlke, Remi Love, Mark E. Cohen, David B. Hoyt, Anthony D. Yang, John L. Tarpley, John D. Mellinger, David M. Mahvi, Rachel R. Kelz, et al. 2016. "National Cluster-Randomized Trial of Duty-Hour Flexibility in Surgical Training." *New England Journal of Medicine* 374 (8): 713–27.

Blitz, Jason B., Amy E. Rogers, Michael M. Polmear, and Alfred J. Owings. 2017. "Duty Hour Compliance: A Survey of U.S. Military Medical Interns and Residents." *Military Medicine* 182 (11/12): 1997–2004.

Blum, Alexander B., Farbod Raiszadeh, Sandra Shea, David Mermin, Peter Lurie, Christopher P. Landrigan, and Charles A. Czeisler. 2010. "U.S. Public Opinion Regarding Proposed Limits on Resident Physician Work Hours." *BMC Medicine* 8: article # 33. doi.org/10.1186/1741-7015-8-33.

Boex, James R., and Peter J. Leahy. 2003. "Understanding Residents' Work: Moving Beyond Counting Hours to Assessing Educational Value." *Academic Medicine* 78 (9): 939–44.

Bolster, Lauren, and Liam Rourke. 2015. "The Effect of Restricting Residents' Duty Hours on Patient Safety, Resident Well-Being, and Resident Education: An Updated Systematic Review." *Journal of Graduate Medical Education* 7 (3): 349–63.

Bosk, Charles L. 1979. *Forgive and Remember: Managing Medical Failure.* Chicago: University of Chicago Press.

Bronwyn, Fryer. 2006. "Sleep Deficit: The Performance Killer. A Conversation with Harvard Medical School Professor Charles A. Czeisler." *Harvard Business Review* 84 (10): 53–59.

Brooks, Joanna Veazey, and Charles L. Bosk. 2012. "Remaking Surgical Socialization: Work Hour Restrictions, Rites of Passage, and Occupational Identity." *Social Science & Medicine* 75 (9): 1625–32.

Bryne, John M., Lawrence K. Loo, and Dan W. Giang. 2015. "Duty Hour Reporting: Conflicting Values in Professionalism." *Journal of Graduate Medical Education* 7 (3): 395–400.

Buch, Kerri E., Mia Y. Genovese, Jennifer L. Conigliaro, Scott Q. Nguyen, John C. Byrn, Carmine L. Novembre, and Celia M. Divino. 2008. "Non-Physician Practitioners' Overall Enhancement to a Surgical Resident's Experience." *Journal of Surgical Education* 65 (1): 50–53.

Burchiel, Kim J., Rowen K. Zetterman, Kenneth M. Ludmerer, Ingrid Philibert, Timothy P. Brigham, Kathy Malloy, James A. Arrighi, Stanley W. Ashley, Jessica L. Bienstock, Peter J. Carek, Ricardo Correa, David A. Forstein, Robert R. Gaiser, Jeffrey P. Gold, George A. Keepers, Benjamin C. Kennedy, Lynne M. Kirk, Anai Kothari, Lorrie A. Langdale, Philip H. Shayne, Steven C. Stain, Suzanne K. Woods, Claudia Wyatt-Johnson, and Thomas J. Nasca. 2017. "The 2017 ACGME Common Work Hour Standards: Promoting Physician Learning and Professional Development in a Safe, Humane Environment." *Journal of Graduate Medical Education* 9 (6): 692–96.

Caniano, Donna A., and Stanley J. Hamstra. 2016. "Program Strengths and Opportunities for Improvement Identified by Residents during ACGME Site Visits in 5 Surgical Specialties." *Journal of Graduate Medical Education* 8 (2): 208–13.

Carpenter, Robert O., Mary T. Austin, John L. Tarpley, Marie R. Griffin, and Kimberly D. Lomis. 2006. "Work-Hour Restrictions as an Ethical Dilemma for Residents." *American Journal of Surgery* 191 (4): 527–32.

Cassell, Joan. 1991. *Expected Miracles: Surgeons at Work*. Philadelphia, PA: Temple University Press.
_____. 1998. *The Woman in the Surgeon's Body*. Cambridge, MA: Harvard University Press.
Chikwe, Joanna, Anthony C. de Suoza, and John R. Pepper. 2004. "No Time to Train the Surgeons." *British Medical Journal* 328 (7437): 418–19.
Christmas, A. Britton, Jennifer Reynolds, Samantha Hodges, Glen A. Franklin, Frank B. Miller, J. David Richardson, and Jorge L. Rodriguez. 2005. "Physician Extenders Impact Trauma Systems." *Journal of Trauma Injury, Infection, and Critical Care* 58 (5): 917–20.
Colten, Harvey R., and Bruce M. Altevogt, eds. 2005. *Sleep Disorders and Sleep Deprivation: An Unmet Public Health Problem*. Washington, DC: National Academies Press.
Cooke, Molly, David M. Irby, and Bridget C. O'Brien. 2010. *Educating Physicians: A Call for Reform of Medical School and Residency*. San Francisco, CA: Jossey-Bass.
Coser, Lewis A. 1974. *Greedy Institutions: Patterns of Undivided Commitment*. New York: Free Press.
Czeisler, Charles A. 2009. "Medical and Genetic Differences in the Adverse Impact of Sleep Loss on Performance: Ethical Considerations for the Medical Profession." *Transactions of the American Clinical and Climatological Association* 120: 249–85.
Czeisler, Charles A., Carlos A. Pellegrini, and Robert M. Sade. 2013. "Should Sleep-Deprived Surgeons Be Prohibited from Operating without Patients' Consent?" *Annals of Thoracic Surgery* 95: 757–66.
de Costa, Josephine, José Chen-Xu, Zineb Bentounsi, and Dominique Vervoort. 2018. "Women in Surgery: Challenges and Opportunities." *International Journal of Surgery: Global Health* 1: e02.
Derickson, Alan. 2014. *Dangerously Sleepy: Overworked Americans and the Cult of Manly Weakness*. Philadelphia: University of Pennsylvania Press.
Desai, Sanjay V., Leonard Feldman, Lorrel Brown, Rebecca Dezube, Hsin-Chieh Yeh, Naresh Punjabi, Kia Afshar, Michael R. Grunwald, Colleen Harrington, Rakhi Naik, and Joseph Cofrancesco Jr. 2013. "Effect of the 2011 vs. 2003 Duty Hour Regulation-Compliant Models on Sleep Duration, Trainee Education, and Continuity of Patient Care among Internal Medicine House Staff: A Randomized Trial." *JAMA Internal Medicine* 173 (8): 649–55.
Desai, Sanjay V., David A. Asch, Lisa M. Bellini, Krisda H. Chaiyachati, Manqing Liu, Alice L. Sternberg, James Tonascia, Alyssa M. Yeager, Jeremy M. Asch, Joel T. Katz, Mathias Basner, David W. Bates, et al., for the iCOMPARE Research Group. 2018. "Education Outcomes in a Duty-Hour Flexibility Trial in Internal Medicine." *New England Journal of Medicine* 378: 1494–508.
Doyle, Terry, and Todd Zakrajsek. 2013. *The New Science of Learning: How to Learn in Harmony with your Brain*. Sterling, VA: Stylus Publishing.
Drolet, Brian C., Matthew Schwede, Kenneth D. Bishop, and Staci A. Fischer. 2013. "Compliance and Falsification of Duty Hours: Reports from Residents and Program Directors." *Journal of Graduate Medical Education* 4 (3): 368–73.
Durkin, Emily Tompkins, Robert McDonald, Alejandro Munoz, and David Mahvi. 2008. "The Impact of Work Hour Restrictions on Surgical Resident Education." *Journal of Surgical Education* 65: 54–60.
Eddy, David. 1988. "Variations in Physician Practice: The Role of Uncertainty." In *Professional Judgment: A Reader in Clinical Decision Making*, edited by Jack Dowie and Arthur Elstein, 45–59. New York: Cambridge University Press.

Epstein, Nancy E. 2017. "Discrimination against Female Surgeons Is Still Alive: Where Are the Full Professorships and Chairs of Departments?" *Surgical Neurology International* 8: 93.

Fessler, Henry E. 2005. "To the Editor." *New England Journal of Medicine* 352 (7): 726.

Fischer, Josef E., Gerald B. Healy, and L. D. Britt. 2009. "Surgery Is Different: A Response to the IOM Report." *American Journal of Surgery* 197 (2): 135–36.

Fletcher, Kathlyn E., Willie Underwood III, Steven Q. Davis, Rajesh S. Mangrulkar, Laurence F. McMahon, and Sanjay Saint. 2005. "Effects of Work Hour Reduction on Residents' Lives: A Systematic Review." *JAMA* 294: 1088–100.

Foley, P. J., R. E. Roses, R. R. Kelz, A. S. Resnick, N. N. Williams, J. L. Mullen, L. R. Kaiser, and Jon B. Morris. 2008. "The State of General Surgery Training: A Different Perspective." *Journal of Surgical Education* 65 (6): 494–98.

Freidson, Eliot. 1988. *Profession of Medicine: A Study of the Sociology of Applied Knowledge.* Chicago: University of Chicago Press.

_____. 2001. *Professionalism: The Third Logic.* Chicago: University of Chicago Press.

Gaba, David M., and Steven K. Howard. 2002. "Fatigue among Clinicians and the Safety of Patients." *New England Journal of Medicine* 347 (16): 1249–55.

Gadacz, Thomas R., and James J. Bason. 2005. "A Survey of the Work Effort of Full-Time Surgeons of the Southeastern Surgical Congress." *American Surgeon* 71 (8): 674–81.

Gallicchio, Lisa, and Bindu Kalesan. 2009. "Sleep Duration and Mortality: A Systematic Review and Meta-Analysis. *Journal of Sleep Research* 18 (2): 148–58.

Groopman, Jerome. 2007. *How Doctors Think.* Boston, MA: Houghton Mifflin Company.

Gurjala, Anandev, Peter Lurie, Ladi Haroona, Joshua P. Rising, Bertrand Bell, Kingman P. Strohl, and Sidney M. Wolfe. 2001. "Petition Requesting Medical Residents Work Hour Limits." Petition to the Occupational Safety and Health Administration, Public Citizen, April 30, 2001. www.citizen.org/our-work/health-and-safety/petition-requesting-medical-residents-work-hour-limits.

Hafferty, Frederic W., and John B. McKinlay. 1993. *The Changing Medical Profession: An International Perspective.* New York: Oxford University Press.

Hafferty, Frederic W., and Brian Castellani. 2010. "The Increasing Complexities of Professionalism." *Academic Medicine* 85 (2): 288–301.

Hafferty, Frederic W., and Jon C. Tilburt. 2015. "Fear, Regulations, and the Fragile Exoskeleton of Medical Professionalism." *Journal of Graduate Medical Education* 7 (3): 344–48.

Harnik, Ian G. 2005. "To the Editor." *New England Journal of Medicine* 352 (7): 726.

Harper, Douglas. 1987. *Working Knowledge: Skill and Community in a Small Shop.* Chicago: University of Chicago Press.

Haskins, Julia. 2019. "Where Are All the Women in Surgery?" Association of American Medical Colleges, July 15, 2009. www.aamc.org/news-insights/where-are-all-women-surgery.

Hayman, Amanda V., John L. Tarpley, David H. Berger, Mark A. Wilson, Edward H. Livingston, and Melina R. Kibbe. 2012. "How Is the Department of Veterans Affairs Addressing the New Accreditation Council for Graduate Medical Education Intern Work Hour Limitations? Solutions from the Association of Veterans Affairs Surgeons." *American Journal of Surgery* 204 (5): 655–62.

Huffington, Arianna. 2016. *The Sleep Revolution: Transforming Your Life, One Night at a Time.* New York: Harmony.

Hughes, Everett C. 1984. *The Sociological Eye.* New Brunswick, NJ: Transaction.

Hunter, Kathryn Montgomery. 1991. *Doctors' Stories: The Narrative Structure of Medical Knowledge*. Princeton, NJ: Princeton University Press.

Jagannathan, Jay, G. Edward Vates, Nader Pouratian, Jason P. Sheehan, James Patrie, M. Sean Grady, and John A. Jane Sr. 2009. "Impact of the Accreditation Council for Graduate Medical Education Work-Hour Regulations on Neurosurgical Resident Education and Productivity." *Journal of Neurosurgery* 110 (5): 820–27.

Jagsi, Reshma, and Rebecca Surender. 2004. "Regulation of Junior Doctors' Work Hours: An Analysis of British and American Doctors' Experiences and Attitudes." *Social Science and Medicine* 58 (11): 2181–91.

Jones, P. Eugene, and James F. Cawley. 2009. "Workweek Restrictions and Specialty-Trained Physician Assistants: Potential Opportunities." *Journal of Surgical Education* 66 (3): 152–57.

Kahn, Steven A., Sarah A. Davis, Caroline T. Banes, Bradley M. Dennis, Addison K. May, and Oliver D. Gunter. 2015. "Impact of Advanced Practice Providers (Nurse Practitioners and Physician Assistants) on Surgical Residents' Critical Care Experience." *Journal of Surgical Research* 199 (1): 7–12.

Kairys, John C., Kandace McGuire, Albert G. Crawford, and Charles J. Yeo. 2008. "Cumulative Operative Experience Is Decreasing during General Surgery Residency: A Worrisome Trend for Surgical Trainees?" *Journal of the American College of Surgeons* 206 (5): 804–12.

Kaiser Family Foundation. 2004. "Five Years after IOM Report on Medical Errors, Nearly Half of All Consumers Worry about the Safety of Their Health Care." Kaiser Family Foundation, November 15, 2004. www.kff.org/other/poll-finding/five-years-after-iom-report-on-medical.

Katlic, Mark R., and JoAnn Coleman. 2018. "Surgical Intuition." *Annals of Surgery* 268 (6): 935–37.

Kellogg, Katherine C. 2011. *Challenging Operations: Medical Reform and Resistance in Surgery*. Chicago: University of Chicago Press.

Kennedy, Tara J. T., Glen Regehr, G. Ross Baker, and Lorelei Lingard. 2009. "Preserving Professional Credibility: Grounded Theory Study of Medical Trainees' Requests for Clinical Support." *BMJ* 338: b128.

Kohn, Linda T., Janet M. Corrigan, and Molla S. Donaldson, eds. 2000. *To Err Is Human: Building a Safer Health System*. Washington, DC: National Academy Press.

Kreutzer, Lindsey, Allison R. Dahlke, Remi Love, Kristen A. Ban, Anthony D. Yang, Karl Y. Bilimoria, and Julie K. Johnson. 2017. "Exploring Qualitative Perspectives on Surgical Resident Training, Well-Being, and Patient Care." *Journal of the American College of Surgeons* 224 (2): 149–59.

Krueger, Kristine J., and Edward C. Halperin. 2010. "Paying Physicians to Be on Call: A Challenge for Academic Medicine." *Academic Medicine* 85: 1840–44.

Landrigan, Christopher P., Jeffrey M. Rothschild, John W. Cronin, Rainu Kaushal, Elisabeth Burdick, Joel T. Katz, Craig M. Lilly, Peter H. Stone, Steven W. Lockley, David W. Bates, and Charles A. Czeisler. 2004. "Effects of Reducing Interns' Work Hours on Serious Medical Errors in Intensive Care Units." *New England Journal of Medicine* 351 (18): 1838–48.

Landrigan, Christopher P., Laura K. Barger, Brian E. Cade, Najib T. Ayas, and Charles A. Czeisler. 2006. "Interns' Compliance with Accreditation Council for Graduate Medical Education Work-Hour Limits." *JAMA* 296 (9): 1063–70.

Leape, Lucian L. 1997. "A Systems Analysis Approach to Medical Error." *Journal of Evaluation in Clinical Practice* 3 (3): 213–22.

Lo, June C., Su Mei Lee, Xuan Kai Lee, Karen Sasmita, Nicholas I. Y. N. Chee, Jesisca Tandi, Wei Shan Cher, Joshua J. Gooley, and Michael W. L. Chee. 2018. "Sustained Benefits of Delaying School Start Time on Adolescent Sleep and Well-Being." *Sleep* 41 (6): 1–8.

Lockley, Steven W., John W. Cronin, Erin E. Evans, Brian E. Cade, Clark J. Lee, Christopher P. Landrigan, Jeffrey M. Rothschild, Joel T. Katz, Craig M. Lilly, Peter H. Stone, Daniel Aeschbach, and Charles A. Czeisler. 2004. "Effect of Reducing Interns' Weekly Work Hours on Sleep and Attentional Failures." *New England Journal of Medicine* 351 (18): 1829–37.

Ludmerer, Kenneth M. 2015. *Let Me Heal: The Opportunity to Preserve Excellence in American Medicine*. New York: Oxford University Press.

MacKenzie, Donald, and Graham Spinardi. 1995. "Tacit Knowledge, Weapons Design, and the Uninvention of Nuclear Weapons." *American Journal of Sociology* 101 (1): 44–99.

Melbin, Murray. 1987. *Night as Frontier: Colonizing the World after Dark*. New York: Free Press.

Mendelson, Wallace B. 2017. *The Science of Sleep: What It Is, How It Works, and Why It Matters*. Chicago: University of Chicago Press.

Merton, Robert K., George G. Reader, and Patricia Kendall, eds. 1957. *The Student Physician: Introductory Studies in the Sociology of Medical Education*. Cambridge, MA: Harvard University Press.

Michalec, Barret, and Frederic W. Hafferty. 2013. "Stunting Professionalism: The Potency and Durability of the Hidden Curriculum within Medical Education." *Social Theory & Health* 11 (4): 388–406.

Mickleborough, Tim. 2015. "Intuition in Medical Practice: A Reflection on Donald Schön's Reflective Practitioner." *Medical Teacher* 37 (10): 889–91.

Miller, Craig A. 2008. *The Making of a Surgeon in the 21st Century*. Grass Valley, CA: Blue Dolphin Publishing.

Mizrahi, Teri. 1986. *Getting Rid of Patients: Contradictions in the Socialization of Physicians*. New Brunswick, NJ: Rutgers University Press.

Moeller, Andrew, Jordan Webber, and Ian Epstein. 2016. "Resident Duty Hour Modification Affects Perceptions in Medical Education, General Wellness, and Ability to Provide Patient Care." *BMC Medical Education* 16: 1–7.

Moote, Marc, Cathleen Krsek, Ruth Kleinpell, and Barbara Todd. 2011. "Physician Assistant and Nurse Utilization in Academic Medical Centers." *American Journal of Medical Quality* 26 (6): 452–60.

Moulton, Carol-anne E., Glenn Regehr, Maria Mylopoulos, and Helen M MacRae. 2007. "Slowing Down When You Should: A New Model of Expert Judgment." *Academic Medicine* 82 (10 Suppl.): S109–16.

New York State Committee on Emergency Services. 1987. *Final Report of the New York State Ad Hoc Advisory Committee on Emergency Services*. Albany, NY: New York State Health Department.

Nitkin, Karen. 2019. "The Rise of Female Surgeons at Johns Hopkins." Johns Hopkins Medicine, August 28, 2017. www.hopkinsmedicine.org/news/articles/the-rise-of-female-surgeons-at-johns-hopkins.

Nurok, Michael, Charles A. Czeisler, and Lisa Soleymani Lehmann. 2010. "Sleep Deprivation, Elective Surgical Procedures, and Informed Consent." *New England Journal of Medicine* 363: 2577–79.

Oliveira, A. C., C. S. Gama, and A. O. Paula. 2017. "Multimodal Strategy to Improve the Adherence to Hand Hygiene and Self-Assessment of the Institution for the Promotion and Practice of Hand Hygiene." *Journal of Public Health* 40 (1): 163–68.

Orlikowski, Wanda J., and JoAnne Yates. 2002. "It's about Time: Temporal Structuring in Organizations." *Organization Science* 13 (6): 684–700.

Osler, William. 1906. *Aequanimitas, with Other Addresses to Medical Students, Nurses and Practitioners of Medicine*, 2nd ed. Philadelphia, PA: P. Blakiston's Son and Company.

Parshuram, Christopher S., Andre C. K. B. Amaral, Niall D. Ferguson, G. Ross Baker, Edward E. Etchells, Virginia Flintoft, John Granton, Lorelei Lingard, Haresh Kirpalani, Sangeeta Mehta, Harvey Moldofsky, Damon C. Scales, Thomas E. Stewart, Andrew R. Willan, and Jan O. Friedrich. 2015. "Patient Safety, Resident Well-Being and Continuity of Care with Different Resident Duty Schedules in the Intensive Care Unit: A Randomized Trial." *Canadian Medical Association Journal* 187 (5): 321–29.

Patel, Mitesh S., Kevin G. Volpp, Dylan S. Small, Alexander S. Hill, Orit Even-Shoshan, Lisa Rosenbaum, Richard N. Ross, Lisa Bellini, Jingsan Zhu, and Jeffrey H. Silber. 2014. "Association of the 2011 ACGME Resident Duty Hour Reforms with Mortality and Readmissions among Hospitalized Medicare Patients." *JAMA* 312 (22): 2354–73.

Patient and Physician Safety and Protection Act of 2005. HR 1228 / S 1297. 109th Cong. www.congress.gov/bill/109th-congress/house-bill/1228/text.

Pennell, Nathan A., Joyce F. Liu, and Michael J. Mazzini. 2005. "To the Editor." *New England Journal of Medicine* 352 (7): 726.

Perry, Henry B., Don E. Detmer, and Elinor L. Redmond. 1981. "The Current and Future Role of Surgical Physician Assistants." *Annals of Surgery* 193 (2): 132–37.

Petersdorf, Robert G., and James Bentley. 1989. "Residents' Work Hours and Supervision." *Academic Medicine* 64 (4): 175–81.

Pezzi, Christopher, Thomas Leibrandt, Sree Suryadevara, Janice K. Heller, Donna Hurley-Martonik, and John S. Kukora. 2009. "The Present and Future Use of Physician Extenders in General Surgery Training Programs: One Response to the 80-Hour Work Week." *Journal of the American College of Surgeons* 2008 (4): 587–91.

Philibert, Ingrid. 2005. "Sleep Loss and Performance in Residents and Non-Physicians: A Meta-Analytic Examination." *Sleep* 28 (11): 1392–402.

————. 2016. "What Is Known: Examining the Empirical Literature in Resident Work Hours Using 30 Influential Articles." *Journal of Graduate Medical Education* 8 (5): 795–805.

Philibert, Ingrid, and Cynthia Taradejna. 2011. "A Brief History of Duty Hours and Resident Education." In *The ACGME 2011 Duty Hours Standards: Enhancing Quality of Care, Supervision, and Resident Professional Development*, edited by Ingrid Philibert and Steven Amis, 5–11. Chicago: Accreditation Council for Graduate Medical Education. www.acgme.org/Portals/0/PDFs/jgme-monograph[1].pdf.

Philibert, Ingrid, Thomas Nasca, Timothy Brigham, and Jane Shapiro. 2013. "Duty-Hour Limits and Patient Care and Resident Outcomes: Can High-Quality Studies Offer Insight into Complex Relationships?" *Annual Review of Medicine* 64: 467–83.

Poirier, Suzanne. 2009. *Doctors in the Making: Memoirs and Medical Education*. Iowa City: University of Iowa Press.

Polanyi, Michael. 1962. "Tacit Knowing: Its Bearing on Some Problems of Philosophy." *Reviews of Modern Physics* 34 (4): 601–16.

Preston, Charles M., Sidney M. Wolfe, Charles A. Czeisler, Christopher P. Landrigan, Farbod Raiszadeh, and Bertrand Bell. 2010. "Petition to the Occupational Safety and Health Administration." Public Citizen, September 2, 2010. www.citizen.org/sites/default/files/1917.pdf.

Rajaram, Ravi, Jeanette W. Chung, Mark E. Cohen, Allison R. Dahlke, Anthony D. Yang, Joshua J. Meeks, Clifford Y. Ko, John L. Tarpley, David B. Hoyt, and Karl Y. Bilimoria. 2015. "Association of the 2011 ACGME Resident Duty Hour Reform with Postoperative Patient Outcomes in Surgical Specialties." *Journal of the American College of Surgeons* 221 (3): 748–57.

Reifman, Jaques, Sridhar Ramakrishnan, Jianbo Liu, Adam Kapela, Tracy J. Doty, Thomas J. Balkin, Kamal Kumar, and Maxim Y. Khitrov. 2019. "2B-Alert App: A Mobile Application for Real-Time Individualized Prediction of Alertness." *Journal of Sleep Research* 28 (2): 1–8.

Reines, H. David, Linda Robinson, Stephanie Nitzchke, and Anne Rizzo. 2007. "Defining Service and Education: The First Step to Developing the Correct Balance." *Surgery* 142 (2): 303–10.

Rejtar, Marketa, Lee Ranstrom, and Christina Allcox. 2017. "Development of the 24/7 Nurse Practitioner Model on the Inpatient Pediatric General Surgery Service at a Large Tertiary Care Children's Hospital and Associated Outcomes." *Journal of Pediatric Health Care* 31 (1): 131–40.

Relman, Arnold S. 1988. "Assessment and Accountability: The Third Revolution in Medical Care." *New England Journal of Medicine* 319 (18): 1220–22.

Resnick, Andrew S., Barbara A. Todd, James L. Mullen, and Jon B. Morris. 2006. "How Do Surgical Residents and Non-Physician Practitioners Play Together in the Sandbox?" *Current Surgery* 63 (2): 155–64.

Riebschleger, Meredith, and Thomas J. Nasca. 2011. "New Duty Hour Limits: Discussion and Justification." In *The ACGME 2011 Duty Hour Standards: Enhancing Quality of Care, Supervision, and Resident Professional Development*, edited by Ingrid Philibert and Steve Amis, 29–38. Chicago: Accreditation Council for Graduate Medical Education. www.acgme.org/Portals/0/PDFs/jgme-monograph[1].pdf.

Robles, Lourdes, Michele Slogoff, Eva Ladwig-Scott, Dan Zank, Mary Kay Larson, Gerard Aranha, and Maro Shoup. 2011. "The Addition of a Nurse Practitioner to an Inpatient Surgical Team Results in Improved Use of Resources." *Surgery* 150 (4): 711–17.

Romanchuk, Ken. 2004. "The Effect of Limiting Residents' Work Hours on Their Surgical Training: A Canadian Perspective." *Academic Medicine* 79 (5): 384–85.

Rosen, Ilene M., Phyllis A. Gimotty, Judy A. Shea, and Lisa M. Bellini. 2006. "Evolution of Sleep Quantity, Sleep Deprivation, Mood Disturbances, Empathy, and Burnout among Interns." *Academic Medicine* 81 (1): 82–85.

Rosenbaum, Julie R. 2004. "Can Residents Be Professional in 80 or Fewer Hours a Week?" *American Journal of Medicine* 117 (11): 846–50.

Rosenbaum, Lisa, and Daniela Lamas. 2019. "Eyes Wide Open—Examining the Data on Duty-Hour Reform. *New England Journal of Medicine* 380 (10): 969–70.

Sanfey, Hilary, Joe Cofer, Jonathan R. Hiatt, Matthew Hyser, Colleen Jakey, Stephen Markwell, John Mellinger, Richard Sidwell, Douglas Smink, Stephen Wise, Chris Wohltman, and Gary Dunnington. 2011. "Service or Education: In the Eye of the Beholder." *Archives of Surgery* 145 (12): 1389–95.

Scally, Christopher P., Andrew M. Ryan, Jyothi R. Thumma, Paul G. Gauger, and Justin B. Dimick. 2015. "Early Impact of the 2011 ACGME Duty Hour Regulations on Surgical Outcomes." *Surgery* 158 (6): 1453–61.

Schein, Edgar H. 2004. *Organizational Culture and Leadership*, 3rd ed. San Francisco: Jossey-Bass.

Schwartz, Alan, Cleo Pappas, Philip Bashook, Georges Bordage, Marcia Edison, Bharati Prasad, and Valerie Swiatkowski. 2009. *Conceptual Frameworks in the Study of Duty Hour Changes in Graduate Medical Education: An Integrative Review*. Chicago: ACGME. www.acgme.org/portals/0/PDFs/UofI_-_Conceptual_frameworks_in_the_study_of_duty_hour_changes_in_GME.pdf.

Sekimoto, Miho, Yuichi Imanaka, Nobuko Kitano, Tatsuro Ishizaki, and Osamu Takahashi. 2006. "Why Are Physicians Not Persuaded by Scientific Evidence? A Grounded Theory Interview Study." *BMC Health Services Research* 6: 92.

Silber, Jeffrey H., Lisa M. Bellini, Judy A. Shea, Sanjay V. Desai, David F. Dinges, Mathias Basner, Orit Even-Shoshan, Alexander S. Hill, Lauren L. Hochman, Joel T. Katz, Richard N.

Ross, David M. Shade, Dylan S. Small, Alice L. Sternberg, James Tonascia, Kevin G. Volpp, and David A. Asch. 2019. "Patient Safety Outcomes under Flexible and Standard Resident Duty-Hour Rules." *New England Journal of Medicine* 380 (10): 915–23.

Stahlfeld, Kurt R., John M. Robinson, and Élan C. Burton. 2008. "What Do Physician Extenders in a General Surgery Residency Really Do?" *Journal of Surgical Education* 65 (5): 354–58.

Szymczak, Julia E., Joanna Veazey Brooks, Kevin G. Volpp, and Charles L. Bosk. 2010. "To Leave or to Lie? Are Concerns about a Shift-Work Mentality and Eroding Professionalism as a Result of Duty-Hour Rules Justified?" *Milbank Quarterly* 88 (3): 350–81.

Szymczak, Julia E., and Charles L. Bosk. 2012. "Training for Efficiency: Work, Time, and Systems-Based Practice in Medical Residency." *Journal of Health and Social Behavior* 53 (3): 344–58.

Tabrizian, Parissa, Uma Rajhbeharrysingh, Sergey Khaitov, and Celia M. Divino. 2011. "Persistent Noncompliance with the Work-Hour Regulation." *Archives of Surgery* 146 (2): 175–78.

Temple, John. 2014. "Resident Duty Hours around the Globe: Where Are We Now?" *BMC Medical Education* 14 (Suppl. 1): S8.

Thourani, Vinod H., and Joseph I. Miller Jr. 2006. "Physician Assistants in Cardiothoracic Surgery: A 30-Year Experience in a University Center." *Annals of Thoracic Surgery* 81 (1): 195–200.

Tkachenko, Olga, and David F. Dinges. 2018. "Interindividual Variability in Neurobehavioral Response to Sleep Loss: A Comprehensive Review." *Neuroscience and Biobehavioral Reviews* 89: 29–48.

Timmermans, Stefan, and Marc Berg. 2003. *The Gold Standard: The Challenge of Evidence-Based Medicine and Standardization in Health Care.* Philadelphia, PA: Temple University Press.

Todd, Barbara A., Andrew Resnick, Rebecca Stuhlemmer, Jon B. Morris, and James Mullen. 2004. "Challenges of the 80-Hour Resident Work Rules: Collaboration between Surgeons and Nonphysician Practitioners." *Surgical Clinics of North America* 84 (6): 1573–86.

Ulmer, Cheryl, Dianne Miller Wolman, and Michael M. E. Johns, eds. Committee on Optimizing Graduate Medical Trainee (Resident) Hours and Work Schedules to Improve Patient Safety. Institute of Medicine. 2008. *Resident Duty Hours: Enhancing Sleep, Supervision, and Safety.* Washington, DC: National Academies Press.

Van Dijk, Manon D., Sanne A. Mulder, Vicki Erasmus, A. H. Elise van Beeck, Joke M. J. J. Vermeeen, Xiaona Liu, Ed F. van Beeck, and Margreet C. Vos. 2019. "A Multimodal Regional Intervention Strategy Framed as Friendly Competition to Improve Hand Hygiene Compliance." *Infection Control and Hospital Epidemiology* 40 (2): 187–93.

Van Dongen, Hans P. A., Greg Maislin, Janet M. Mullington, and David F. Dinges. 2003. "The Cumulative Cost of Additional Wakefulness: Dose-Response Effects on Neurobehavioral Functions and Sleep Physiology from Chronic Sleep Restriction and Total Sleep Deprivation." *Sleep* 26 (2): 117–26.

Van Eaton, Erik G., Karen D. Horvath, and Carlos A. Pellegrini. 2005. "Professionalism and the Shift Mentality: How to Reconcile Patient Ownership with Limited Work Hours." *Archives of Surgery* 140 (3): 230–35.

Vaughn, Danny M., Christopher L. Stout, Beth L. McCampbell, Joshua R. Groves, Albert L. Richardson, William K. Thompson, Martin L. Dalton, and Don K. Nakayama. 2008. "Three-Year Results of Mandated Work Hour Restrictions: Attending and Resident Perspectives and Effects in a Community Hospital." *American Surgeon* 74 (6): 542–46.

Veasey, Sigrid, Raymond Rosen, Barbara Barzansky, Ilene Rosen, and Judith Owens. 2002. "Sleep Loss and Fatigue in Residency Training." *JAMA* 288 (9): 1116–24.

Vogus, Timothy J., Kathleen M. Sutcliffe, and Karl E. Weick. 2010. "Doing No Harm: Enabling, Enacting, and Elaborating a Culture of Safety in Health Care." *Academy of Management Perspectives* 24 (4): 60–77.

Walker, Matthew. 2017. *Why We Sleep: Unlocking the Power of Sleep and Dreams.* New York: Scribner.

Watson, Nathaniel F., M. Safwan Badr, Gregory Belenky, Donald L. Bliwise, Orfeu M. Buxton, Daniel Buysse, David F. Dinges, James Gangwisch, Michael A. Grandner, Clete Kushida, Raman K. Malhotra, Jennifer L. Martin, Sanjay R. Patel, Stuart Quan, and Esra Tasali. 2015a. "Recommended Amount of Sleep for a Healthy Adult: A Joint Consensus Statement of the American Academy of Sleep Medicine and Sleep Research Society." *Sleep* 38 (6): 843–44.

Watson, Nathaniel F., M. Safwan Badr, Gregory Belenky, Donald L. Bliwise, Orfeu M. Buxton, Daniel Buysse, David F. Dinges, James Gangwisch, Michael A. Grandner, Clete Kushida, Raman K. Malhotra, Jennifer L. Martin, Sanjay R. Patel, Stuart Quan, and Esra Tasali. 2015b. "Joint Consensus Statement of the American Academy of Sleep Medicine and Sleep Research Society on the Recommended Amount of Sleep for a Healthy Adult: Methodology and Discussion." *Journal of Clinical Sleep Medicine* 11 (8): 931–52.

Weinger, Matthew B., and Sonia Ancoli-Israel. 2002. "Sleep Deprivation and Clinical Performance." *JAMA* 287 (8): 955–57.

Weinstein, Neil D. 1989. "Optimistic Biases about Personal Risks." *Science* 246 (4935): 1232–33.

Wendland, Claire L. 2010. *A Heart for the Work: Journeys through an African Medical School.* Chicago: University of Chicago Press.

West, Michaela A., Shelley Hwang, Ronald V. Maier, Nita Ahuja, Peter Angelos, Barbara L. Bass, Karen J. Brasel, Herbert Chen, Kimberly A. Davis, Timothy J. Eberlein, Yuman Fong, Caprice C. Greenberg, Keith D. Lillemoe, Mary C. McCarthy, Fabrizio Michelassi, Patricia J. Numann, Sareh Parangi, Jorge D. Reyes, Hilary A. Sanfey, Steven C. Stain, Ronald J. Weigel, and Sherry M. Wren. 2018. "Ensuring Equity, Diversity, and Inclusion in Academic Surgery: An American Surgical Association White Paper." *Annals of Surgery* 268 (3): 403–7.

Wheaton, Anne G., Gabrielle A. Ferro, and Janet B. Croft. 2015. "School Start Times for Middle School and High School Students—United States, 2011–12 School Year." *Morbidity and Mortality Weekly Report (MMWR)* 64 (30): 809–13. www.cdc.gov/mmwr/preview/mmwrhtml/mm6430a1.htm.

Wilensky, Harold. 1964. "The Professionalization of Everyone?" *American Journal of Sociology* 70: 137–58.

Williams, Simon J. 2011. *The Politics of Sleep: Governing (Un)consciousness in the Late Modern Age.* London, England: Palgrave Macmillan.

Williamson, A. M., and Anne-Marie Feyer. 2000. "Moderate Sleep Deprivation Produces Impairments in Cognitive and Motor Performance Equivalent to Legally Prescribed Levels of Alcohol Intoxication." *Occupational and Environmental Medicine* 57: 649–55.

Willis, Ross E., James E. Coverdill, John D. Mellinger, J. Craig Collins, John R. Potts III, and Daniel L. Dent. 2009. "Views of Surgery Program Directors on the Current ACGME and Proposed IOM Duty-Hour Standards." *Journal of Surgical Education* 66 (4): 216–21.

Winslow, E. R., M. C. Bowman, and M. E. Klingensmith. 2004. "Surgeon Workhours in the Era of Limited Resident Workhours." *Journal of the American College of Surgeons* 198: 111–17.

Winslow, E. R., L. Berger, and M. E. Klingensmith. 2004. "Has the 80-Hour Workweek Increased Faculty Hours?" *Current Surgery* 61: 602–8.

Woodrow, Sarah I., Jason Park, Brian J. Murray, Calvin Wang, Mark Bernstein, Richard K. Reznick, and Stanley J. Hamstra. 2008. "Differences in the Perceived Impact of Sleep Deprivation among Surgical and Non-surgical Residents." *Medical Education* 42 (5): 459–67.

Wynia, Matthew K., Maxine A. Papadakis, William M. Sullivan, and Frederic W. Hafferty. 2014. "More Than a List of Values and Desired Behaviors: A Foundational Understanding of Medical Professionalism." *Academic Medicine* 89 (5): 712–14.

Yaghoubian, Arezou, Joseph Galante, Amy Kaji, Mark Reeves, Marc Melcher, Ali Salim, Matthew Dolich, and Christian de Virgilio. 2012. "General Surgery Resident Remediation and Attrition." *Archives of Surgery* 147 (9): 829–33.

Yoo, Seung-Schik, Peter T. Hu, Ninad Gujar, Ferenc A. Jolesz, and Matthew P. Walker. 2007. "A Deficit in the Ability to Form New Human Memories without Sleep." *Nature Neuroscience* 10 (3): 385–92.

Zerubavel, Eviatar. 1979. *Patterns of Time in Hospital Life*. Chicago: University of Chicago Press.

_____. 1981. *Hidden Rhythms: Schedules and Calendars in Social Life*. Chicago: University of Chicago Press.

Zhou, Xuan, Sally A. Ferguson, Raymond W. Matthews, Charli Sargent, David Darwent, David J. Kennaway, and Gregory D. Roach. 2012. "Mismatch between Subjective Alertness and Objective Performance under Sleep Restriction Is Greatest during the Biological Night." *Journal of Sleep Research* 21 (1): 40–49.

Zion, Sidney. 1989. "Doctors Know Best?" *New York Times*, May 13, 1989, 25.

Index

Italicized page numbers refer to tables

Abernathy, Charles, 16
academic programs
  appeal of, *127*, 128, 133–38
  and APPs, 124, *139*, 140–41
  and duty-hour restrictions, 33, 55, *79*, 80,
    118
  See also program type
ACGME (Accreditation Council for Graduate
  Medical Education)
  APPs and duty hour compliance, 124–26
  and fatigue, 27, 31, 33, 42–43, 184
  and non-surgical specialties, 21
  program accreditation and compliance, 2,
    94–98
  rules revisions, 150–53, 168–69
  work hour and schedule reforms, 2, 9–11,
    180
advanced practice nurses (APN), 142–43. *See*
  also APPs (advanced practice providers)
advanced practice providers. *See* APPs
  (advanced practice providers)
age, 7, *127*, 128
Altevogt, Bruce M., 7
American Academy of Pediatrics, 186
American Academy of Sleep Medicine, 186

American Board of Surgery (ABS), 169
American College of Surgeons (ACS), 169
American Medical Association, 10, 186
Ancoli-Israel, Sonia, 8
APPs (advanced practice providers)
  and communication, 124–25, 130–32, *139*,
    140, 142, 144–47
  and community-based programs, 134–36,
    138–40, *139*
  faculty assessment of impact, 137–40, *139*
  and resident education, 125–26, 140–47,
    181–82
  and work hours reduction, 49, *79*, 99, 123–
    26, 141–43
Association of American Medical Colleges, 10
Association of Program Directors in Surgery
  (APDS), 3, 169
attendings. *See* faculty
attention span, 7–8, 30, *30*, *32*, 38–41. *See*
  also fatigue
author roles, 26
autobiography, 2

Baldwin, DeWitt C., 2
Barone, James E., 3

Bell, Bertrand M., 9–10
Bell Regulations (New York State Health Code, 1989), 10
Berg, Marc, 176
board certification, 1, 100, 142
Bosk, Charles L.
  occupational culture, 11, 20, 100, 187
  research limitations, 25
  resident errors and work-hour reforms, 101–4, 110–11, 174, 180, 182–83
  workload patterns, 126, 129, 134
Boys in White (Beck et al.), 18
breast surgeons, 35, 175. *See also* medical specialties
Brooks, Joanna Veazey, 11, 174
bureaucracy and bureaucratization, 15, 189
Burton, Élan C., 123

Canada, 22
caregiver care, 3, 49, 99, *114*, 119, 121–22, 168. *See also* work-life balance
Cassell, Joan, 12, 28, 46, 189–90
Castellani, Brian, 180
Challenging Operations: Medical Reform and Resistance (Kellogg), 13, 173–74
check-out, 17, 51. *See also* handoffs
chief residents
  clinical supervision, 59, 73–74, 93–94
  communication, 132–33, 136, 145
  fatigue management, 1, 161, 170–71
  teaching role, 96–97, 110–13, 161
children and childbearing, 12, 119, 175, 186. *See also* work-life balance
clinical skills, 123, *155–57*, 167–68, 184–85
closed loop or "say back" strategies, 72
cognitive performance, 8–9, 14, 29, 38–39, 53, 57, 164–65, 185. *See also* fatigue
Colten, Harvey R., 7
communication
  and APPs, 124–25, 130–32, *139*, 140, 142, 144–47
  and chief resident role, 132–33, 136, 145
  and continuity of care, 53–55, *54, 56*, 60–64
  handoffs and end-of-shift delays, 72–73, *77–78*, 132
  and medical records, 15–17, 51–53, 58, 61–64, 66–67, 182–83, 188

communication (*continued*)
  and new professionalism and team-based care, 74–76, 144–47
  and reform impact assessment, *154–57*, 188
community-based programs
  and APPs, 134–36, 138–40, *139*
  and fatigue culture, 33
  in research sample, 24–25, 31, 175
  See also program type
consumer movement, 9
continuity of care
  and APPs, 137, *139*, 181
  and family conferences, 63, 82–84, 188
  and professionalism, *114*, 115–18, 183
  shift limits faculty assessment, 28–29, 51–58, *54, 56*, 106, 136–37, 168–70
  and sixteen-hour intern cap, 150, 159–60
  See also handoffs; patient familiarity
Conyers, John, 10
coordination of care, 70–72, 119. *See also* team-based care
Corzine, Jon, 10
Coverdill, James E., 23–26
cross coverage. *See* night float and cross coverage
Czeisler, Charles A., 6, 185

Dangerously Sleepy: Overworked Americans and the Cult of Manly Wakefulness (Derickson), 12
defensive medicine, 98
delayed departures, 74–80, *77–79*, 84–88, 180. *See also* work hours
Denmark, 22
Dinges, David F., 185
doctor-patient relationship, 52–56, *54, 56*, 103
dumping, 19–21, 76–78, *77–78*, 84–88, 107–8, 179. *See also* handoffs
duty-hour compliance, 2–3, 10, 21, 94–99, *139*, 139–40. *See also* work hours

efficiency
  culture of, 19–22
  and handoffs, 81–82, 92, 179
  and surgical culture, 18, 36, 38–39, 84–90, 182, 187–88
  and workload, 87–88
Eliot, T. S., 73

emotions, 6, 29–30, *30*, *32*, 38, 149
empathy, *30*, 38, 49, 121
ethics, 18–21, 73, 100, 103–4, 171–72
experience level
  and fatigue assessment, 31–33, *32*
  and intern cap assessment, 154–56, *155*
  and professionalism assessment, *114*,
    116–19
  as research variable, 25
  and work hours assessment, 52–56, *54*, *56*,
    79, *127*, 128
experiential learning, 4–5, 42–43, 161–62

faculty
  APP role assessment, 137–40, *139*, 144–47
  and clinical care involvement, 129–30, 133,
    136–37, 147–49
  fatigue impact assessment, *30*, *32*, 33–36,
    39–41
  and handoffs, 66–67
  intern cap assessment, 152, *154–55*, 156,
    157
  and professionalism and work-hour
    reforms, 96–98, 101, 113
  quality and continuity of care assessment,
    52–56, *54*, *56*
  teaching time, 134–38
  workload of, 118, 123–24, 126–37,
    127, 149
  and work rule revisions, 168–69
family conferences, 63, 82–84, 188
fatigue
  and attention span, 7–8, 30, *30*, *32*
  and belief assessment, 29–33, *30*, *32*
  and cognitive performance, 8–9, 14, 29–30,
    38–39, 53, 57, 164–65, 185
  culture of, 12–13, 28–33, *32*, 36–37, 41–47,
    169–71, 184–86
  mitigation strategies, 27–33, *30*, *32*, 40,
    42–45, 49, 161–62
  need for experience working with, *30*, *32*,
    33–37, 41–49
  patient care assessment of, 38–41
  and patient familiarity and continuity,
    51–56, *54*, *56*
  and political pressure for reform, 9–11
  and reaction time, 38–39
  and safety culture, 184–86

fatigue (*continued*)
  and sixteen-hour intern cap assessment,
    155–57, 161–63
  and sleep deprivation, 2, 6–9, 185
  and sleep science, 9–11, 27, 184, 186, 189
  and smartphone-based applications, 185
  and staffing levels, 177
federal legislation and oversight, 10
Flexner Report (1910), 3
Forgive and Remember (Bosk), 126
Freidson, Eliot, 176
fresh-eyes perspective, 68–70. *See also*
    handoffs
functional interchangeability, 15–18, 51,
    182–83, 188–89

Gaba, David M., 8
gender
  and choice of specialty, 12–15, 173–76
  and delayed departures, *77–78*, 78–80, *79*
  and faculty workload, *127*, 128
  and fatigue, 12–15, 31–32, *32*
  and intern shift limits, 156, *157*
  and professionalism, *114*, 115–16
  and quality and continuity of care assess-
    ment, 55, *56*
*Getting Rid of Patients: Contradictions in the
    Socialization of Physicians* (Mizrahi), 18
graduate medical education community
    (GME), 168–69

Hafferty, Frederic W., 3, 179–80
Halperin, Edward C., 184
Hamm, Robert M., 16
handoffs
  and continuity of care, 15, 17, 50–53,
    58–64, 68–73, 132, 188
  and dumping, 19–21, 76–78, *77–78*, 84–88,
    106–8, 179
  and new professionalism, 178–79
  and social organization, 64–68
  supervision and oversight of, 65–68
  See also functional interchangeability;
    medical records; night float and cross
    coverage
healthcare costs, 18, 98
healthcare system, 48, 98–99, 186
high throughput healthcare, 5, 18

Horvath, Karen D., 74–76, 178
Howard, Steven K., 8
Hughes, Everett C., 176
Hunter, Kathryn Montgomery, 183

information transfer, 16–17, 53, *54, 56,* 58–61,
    72–75, 84, 106, *154–55, 157*
Institute of Medicine (IOM), 2, 10, 27, 68,
    100, 150, 179
institutional review boards (IRB), 23, 25–26
intensive care, 71, 124–25, 151
interns
    and shift limit assessment, *154–55, 157,*
        166–69
    supervision of, 9–10, 93
    transition to residency, 47–49, 160–68
    and work hours and limits, 7–10, 27–29,
        66–67, 82–83, 135, 144–45, 150–60
intuition and tacit knowledge, 15–18, 60–61,
    182–83
Iron Man culture, 13–14
Ivy, Michael E., 3

job sharing, 49
Johns Hopkins Hospital, 4–5, 12–13

Kaiser Family Foundation, 28
Kaiser Permanente, 118
Kellogg, Katherine C., 13–14, 25, 46, 125,
    173–74
knowing-in-action, 16
Koop, C. Everett, 98
Krueger, Kristine J., 184

Landrigan, Christopher P., 8
Leape, Lucian L., 179
legal concerns and litigation, 9–10, 17, 63–64,
    189–90
legitimating accounts, 13–14, 177
Libby Zion case, 9–10
long-call shifts, 161, 163, 178
long-hour culture, 3–10, 13–14, 28, 41–42, 44,
    92, 95–96
Ludmerer, Kenneth M., 3, 5, 182

machismo, 46, 174. *See also* gender
medical errors
    and fatigue, 7–10, 28–29, 40–41, 55–58,
        150–51, 165

medical errors (*continued*)
    and handoffs, 50, 53–55, *54, 56,* 170
    normative errors, 102–3, 110–13, 182–84
    technical and judgmental errors, 101–4, 169
    and training, 40–41
medical records, 15–17, 51–53, 58, 61–64,
    66–67, 124, 142, 182–83, 188
medical school, 18, 158–59, 165–66
medical specialties
    and board certification, 1, 100, 142
    and gender, 12–15, 173–76
    and surgical sub-specialties, 35, 141, 144,
        146, 175
    and work hours, 2–3, 10–12, 21–25, 28, 35,
        72, 152
Melbin, Murray, 179
Mellinger, John D., 24–26, 177
memoirs, 1–2
memory, 7, 30, *30,* 40–41
men, 12–15, 119, 174–76. *See also* gender
micro-institutional approach, 13–14
mid-level providers. *See* APPs (advanced
    practice providers)
Miller, Craig A., 1–2
morbidity and mortality conferences, 23–24,
    112–13, 149

naps, *30,* 31–33, *32,* 40, 45. *See also* fatigue
"New Duty Hour Limits: Discussion and
    Justification" (ACGME), 151
New England Journal of Medicine, 7, 9
new professionalism, 74–76, 85–88, 178–80.
    See also professionalism
New York State, 124
New York State Committee on Emergency
    Services (1987), 10
New York State Department of Health, 9–10
New York State Health Code, 10
New Zealand, 22
night float and cross coverage
    delayed departures, 74–79, *77–78,* 84–88, 180
    patient care and work-hour reforms, 17,
        52–57, *54, 56,* 72, 80–84, 86
    and surgical culture, 107, 177–79
    and workload, 65–66, 69–70, 130–31
    See also handoffs; staffing levels
non-physician providers. *See* APPs (advanced
    practice providers)
normative belief system, 19

normative errors, 102–3, 110–13, 182–83
nurse practitioners (NPs), 124, 143–44. *See also* APPs (advanced practice providers)
nurses, 120, 125, 132, 148, 189

occupational culture, 11–15, 17–18, 20–21, 42–43, 174–75, 182–88. *See also* surgical culture
Occupational Safety and Health Administration (OSHA), 10
on call schedules
 faculty workload assessment, 126–28, *127*, 130–31
 and work-hour reforms, 34–35, 42, 59, 65, 92–93, 138, 184
operative notes, 17, 61–64, 66–67, 182–83, 188. *See also* medical records
Osler, William, 5

paperwork, 40, 47, 125, 129
Patient and Physician Safety and Protection Act of 2005, 10
patient commitment, 19–20, 94–95, *114*, 115–17, 119–22, *155–57*, 182–83, 188–89. *See also* professionalism; surgical culture
patient expectations, 34–36
patient familiarity
 and APPs, 137, *139*, 144–46, 181
 and fresh eyes, 68–70
 and night coverage, 82–84, 130, 177–78
 and professionalism, 56–58, 107, 110–13, *114*, 115, 182–83
 and work hours rules, 17–20, 51–58, *54*, *56*, 110–12
patient ownership
 and new professionalism and teamwork, 74–75, 85–86, 178–79
 and professionalism, 72–73, 110–13, *114*, 116–21, 183
 and shift mentality, 104–10
patient safety, 41, 46–47, *54*, 153–56, *154–55*, *157*, 161–62
patient trust, 69–71
patient volume and turnover, 5–6, 18, 22, 59–60, 72, 123
pattern recognition and judgment, 43–44, 159–60, 169–70
Patterns of Time in Hospital Life (Zerubavel), 51
Pellegrini, Carlos A., 74–76, 178

PGY level. *See* experience level
pharmacologic agents and technologies, 98
Philibert, Ingrid, 11
physician assistants (PAs), 143. *See also* APPs (advanced practice providers)
physician extenders. *See* APPs (advanced practice providers)
Poirier, Suzanne, 1
Polanyi, Michael, 16, 183
post-residency fellowship programs, 12, 97, 137, 175
practice extenders. *See* APPs (advanced practice providers)
preoperative and postoperative care, 22, 102, 136–37, *139*, 139–43, 160, 181. *See also* continuity of care
professional development
 of interns, 152–53, *154–57*
 of residents, 3, 137, *139*, 169, 181, 187
professional identity formation, 120–22
professionalism
 and commitment to patient, 94–96, 120–22, 147–49, *155–57*, 182–83, 188–90
 and ethics and work-hour reforms, 18–21, 169–71, 179–80
 and medical specialties, 21–22
 new professionalism, 74–76, 85–88, 178–80
 and normative errors, 110–13, 182–183
 and patient ownership, 72–73, 104–13, *114*, 116–22, 178, 183
 and reform conflict assessment, 113–17, *114*
 and surgical culture, 100–104, 182–83, 188
program size, 23, *79*
program type
 and APPs, 124, 138–41, *139*
 and duty-hour restrictions, 52–56, *54*, *56*, *79*, 80, 118
 and fatigue-related effects, 31–33, *32*
 in research sample, 24–25, 31, 175
 See also academic programs; community-based programs
Psychomotor Vigilance Test (PVT-B), 185

Reifman, Jaques, 185
relational spaces, 14
research methods
 fieldwork sites, 23–24

research methods (*continued*)
 sample characteristics and breadth,
  22–25, 175
 scope and techniques of, 23–25
 statistical and qualitative analyses, 26
 survey questions, 29–31
residency programs
 accreditation, 2, 98
 as gendered institution, 12–13
 history of, 3–4
 structure and culture of, 3–5
 See also academic programs; ACGME
  (Accreditation Council for Graduate
  Medical Education); community-based
  programs
Residency Review Committees (RRC), 10
residents
 and APPs, 124–26, 140–47
 attrition and burnout, 121–22, 170–71
 board certification, 1, 100, 142
 and efficiency, 87–88
 and experiential learning, 4–5, 42–43, 161–62
 and fatigue, *30, 32,* 33–37, 41–49, 170, 184
 and intern hours cap, 163–69
 professional development, 3, 137, *139,* 169,
  181, 187
 quality and continuity of care beliefs, 3–5,
  50–56, *54, 56*
 reform goals and resistance, 2–7, 151, 173–77
 status in program and intern performance
  assessment, 151–56, *154–55, 157*
 supervision of, 1, 4, 9–10, 72, 92–98, 123,
  129, 132, 151
 and transition from internship, 47–49,
  160–68
 work hour conflicts, 98–101, 134–38, 150,
  153, *155–57,* 156–60, 164
 work-hour reporting, 2, 21, 93–99
Robinson, John M., 123
rounding
 and APP roles, 124, 135, *139,* 140, 142,
  145, 181
 and normative errors, 110–12
 and patient familiarity, 57, 65–66, *77–78,*
  91, 93, 132, 188

safety culture, 184–86
Schein, Edgar H., 28, 179

Sekimoto, Miho, 176
shared care model, 73
shift changes. *See* handoffs
shift limits. *See* work hours
shift mentality, 104–10, *114,* 115, 118, 154,
 154–57
sign-out, 17, 51. *See also* handoffs
sixteen-hour intern cap, 150–69, *154–55, 157.*
 See also work hours
sleep deprivation, 6–9, 186. *See also* fatigue
sleep science, 9–11, 27, 184, 189. *See also*
 fatigue
smartphone-based applications, 185
social organization
 and response to reforms, 11, 14, 21–22,
  84–85, 89–95, 173, 177–82
 and transfer of care, 17–18, 55,
  64–68
Spencer, Rowena, 12
staffing levels, 19, 48–49, 69–70, 72, 80–84,
 98–99, 177, 181
Stahlfield, Kurt R., 123
standardized templates, 72
stay-or-go decisions, 19–20, 74–76, 80–88,
 130, 178, 187–88
Stewart, Potter, 87
stress, 28, 34, *127,* 128, 184
Student-Physician, The (Merton et al.), 18
supervision of residents, 1, 4, 9–10, 72, 92–98,
 123, 129, 132, 151
surgical culture
 and commitment to patients, 94–95, *114,* 115–
  17, 119–22, *155–57,* 171, 182–83, 188–89
 and fatigue, 184–88
 and patient ownership, 19–20, 64–68,
  86–92, 105–6, 117–22
 professionalism and reforms conflicts,
  100–101, 113–19, *114,* 115
 and resistance to reforms, 13–14, 17–18,
  28–29, 173–76, 179–83
 and team-based care, 64–68
 and trimming hours, 84–90, 92–95
Surgical Intuition (Abernathy et al.), 16
Surgical Research Service, 23
Szymczak, Julia E., 20, 187

team-based care
 and APPS, 141, 144–49

team-based care (*continued*)
  patient ownership and new professionalism, 116–19, 178–80
  and surgical culture and reforms, 51–52, 64–76, 81–88, 153, *155–57*
technical and judgment errors, 101–4, 169. *See also* medical errors
technical skills, 30, *30, 32*, 38–41, 120, 134
temporal flexibility, 16, 51, 182–83
temporal rigidity, 46, 51, 91, 189
temporal structure, 89–92, 180–81
Tilburt, Jon C., 3
Timmermans, Stefan, 176
Tkachenko, Olga, 185
To Err is Human (Kohn et al.), 10
trimming hours
  and attributions of laziness, 19, 89–90, 92, 102, 180
  and early departures, 91–92
  and late arrival, 91, 181
  and night staffing concerns, 80–84
  and social organization, 88–92
  See also work hours
twenty-four hour shift limits, 2, 150, 168–69
2B-AlertApp, 185

Van Eaton, Erik G., 74–76, 81, 88, 178
Veasey, Sigrid, 8–9
Veterans Health Administration (VHA), 48

Walker, Matthew, 186
Weinger, Matthew B., 8
Wilensky, Harold, 16, 183
Williams, Simon J., 187
Woman in the Surgeon's Body, The (Cassell), 12–13
women
  continuity of care and professionalism, *56, 114*, 115
  and faculty work experience, *127*, 128
  and fatigue, 31, *32*
  and support for reforms, 173–76
  in surgical specialty, 12–15, 173–76
  and work hours, *78–79, 78–80*, 156, *157*
  See also gender
work hours
  and APPs, 138–40, *139*

work hours (*continued*)
  arrival and departure times, 74–88, *77–78*, 91–92, 181
  duty hour rules, 2, 9–11, 150–53, 168–69, 180
  and education, 2–7
  and gender, 12, 156, *157*
  and patient trust, 170
  political pressure for reform, 9–11
  and rule compliance, 2–3, 10, 21, 92–99, *139*, 139–40
  and social organization, 88–92
  and surgical culture, 15–16, 19, 89–90, 92, 102, 121, 180
  See also ACGME (Accreditation Council for Graduate Medical Education)
work-life balance
  and family, *114*, 115–16, 118–19, 121, 170, 175
  and intern hour cap, 166–67
  professionalism and work hour conflicts, 49, *114*, 116–17
workloads
  and division of labor in residency programs, 123–26
  faculty clinical care, 129–38
  and faculty experience assessment, 126–28, *127, 129*
  and intern cap assessment, *154*
  and new professionalism, 179–80

Zerubavel, Eviatar, 15–17, 51, 61, 183, 188–89
Zion, Libby, 9–10
Zion, Sydney, 9

CPSIA information can be obtained
at www.ICGtesting.com
Printed in the USA
LVHW101404130622
721139LV00015B/112